Mestizo Spaces
Espaces Métissés

V. Y. Mudimbe
EDITOR

Bogumil Jewsiewicki
ASSOCIATE EDITOR

Mestizo Logics

Anthropology of Identity in Africa and Elsewhere

Jean-Loup Amselle

Translated by Claudia Royal

STANFORD UNIVERSITY PRESS
STANFORD, CALIFORNIA

Mestizo Logics: Anthropology of Identity in Africa and Elsewhere was originally published as *Logiques métisses: Anthropologie de l'identité en Afrique et ailleurs* © 1990, Editions Payot.

Assistance for the translation was provided by the French Ministry of Culture.

Stanford University Press
Stanford, California

CIP data appear at the end of the book

Contents

Preface to the English-Language Edition

The Anthropologist Faces the "Hardening" of Identities

It appears arbitrary to locate anthropology strictly on the side of culturalism, which comes out of German Romanticism, since universalism has also played a fundamental role in the discipline. In fact, these two tendencies are both present in the work of certain anthropologists, notably C. Lévi-Strauss and M. Sahlins. In *Islands of History* (1985), Sahlins insists on the historicity of each culture, that is, the universalism of history's shaping role in the culture. At the same time, he highlights the originality or specificity of each culture and in doing so introduces cultural relativism. Before Sahlins, Lévi-Strauss, in his study of "kinship atoms," "kinship structures," or "mythemes," took the side of universalism; by contrast, in *Race et histoire* (1961), he adopts a culturalist position.

These shifts in anthropology between an interest in small objects (cultures) and large objects (human beings, or the structures of the human mind) ensue, in fact, from the philosophical origin of the discipline. The genealogy of anthropological thinking can be traced to the *Völkerkunde* (study of the peoples) and to the political philosophy of human rights. It is also linked to the political thought of Leibniz and Kant, among others, who advocate both national particularism and universalism. This genealogy shines through some of the basic concepts of anthropology. The idea of segmentary societies, for example, probably emerged from trends in philosophical thinking concerning civil society. And the notions of culture and ethnic group are certainly linked to the idea of *Volksgeist* (spirit of the people).

The goal, then, is not to impute a single origin to anthropology—such as the study of a *Volksgeist*, the universalistic principle of Enlightenment thought, or the classificatory systems of eighteenth-century natural history—but rather to show that no matter what the genealogy of these entities may be, they have been thought of in isolation from historical context. In order to be integrated within comparative processes, whether inductive or deductive, the contents of anthropological categories must be abstracted from their historical contexts. Comparativism assumes diversity, and thereby guarantees that diversity will be found. However, cultures and societies should be approached in terms of their historicity, their history. Works by Dumézil and Lévi-Strauss attest to this necessity. Dumézil's *Mythe et épopée* appeals to a common European model, and Lévi-Strauss, notably in one recent book, *Histoire de Lynx* (1991), relocates the relationships between Indian myths and French tales within the framework of the ancient contacts between Asia and America—recognizing, in so doing, the fragility of such hypotheses.

Another tradition in anthropology has privileged effective relations between societies. I would prefer to see my work as emerging from such a tradition. This explains why in this book I have attempted to conceptualize identity in terms of originary syncretism. I believe, in fact, that mixture is originary. One of the most recent books of Paul Ricoeur substantiates this notion. In *Soi-même comme un autre* (1990), Ricoeur distinguishes between two aspects of identity, which are found at the level both of the individual and of collectivities. He highlights the necessity of contrasting the identity of "sameness" to the identity of "selfhood." "Sameness" manifests itself in stability of character and behavior, whereas "selfhood" is constructed in a permanent relation with alterity. This second category brings to the foreground notions of temporality and narrativity. For Ricoeur, personal and collective or communal identities are narratives composed of both history and fiction. In fact, individuals and groups have, besides durable traits of character, dispositions or acquired identifications through which the Other penetrates the formation of "sameness."

Looking at recent works by biologists, one recognizes the same notions of fluidity or flexibility of identity. These works leave aside morphological classifications–more specifically, the study of human races, which gave birth to physical anthropology. They have also left behind biochemical classification, which characterizes bacteria in terms of their capacity for decay or for generation. These two modes of classification now appear arbitrary to biologists. For many of them, the "order of nature" as described by Buffon and Linnaeus now seems obsolete. All types of classification, then, become arbitrary, and the sole element of stability is interfecundity, which clearly establishes borders between species. The same phenomenon is visible in immunology, where self and nonself are becoming less distinguishable. Thus, the fragility of identity emerges in biology: the relation of self to otherness is seen as on a par with the relationship between self and self. In negotiating these relations, a "learning process" transpires at the biological level, through which, according to some contemporary trends in biological thought, identity is constructed. A. M. Moulin's book on AIDS, *Le dernier langage de la médecine* (1991), exemplifies this trend.

To return to research topics more familiar to anthropologists, the analysis of the ethnographic material that I have collected during fifteen years of fieldwork in southern Mali, northern Guinea, and the northern Ivory Coast yields more or less similar conclusions. It appears that societies, cultures, or ethnic groups called Fulani, Bambara, Mandingo, Senufo, or Minyanka, far from constituting isolated identities, comprise systems or paradigms. Apropos of this set, I make the hypothesis of an initial totality that, by a process of declension, gave birth to various societies, various cultures. This initial totality encompasses elements of self-sustaining and market economies, of paganism and Islam, of oral and written traditions, or of "cold" and "hot," to appeal to Lévi-Strauss's famous distinction between "primitive" and developed societies.

To appropriate biological metaphors, the relationship between these elements must not be conceptualized in terms of oppositions and cleavages, but rather in terms of oscillation, of systole and diastole, of shrinkage and dilation, of multi-belongingness. Social life, in this area, appears surprisingly fluid; for instance, social actors may define themselves simultaneously as Moslems and pagans. In

fact, ancestor cults and saint cults are similar, if not identical. Therefore, in opposing paganism and Islam, anthropology produces difference from identity, and thus mirrors fundamentalism insofar as
it seeks pristine societies in order to delineate its own field and define the identity of the culture that produces anthropology.

Rather than opposing segmentary societies to state societies, the
small chiefdoms in which I have worked oscillate between segmentary and state structures. They do not constitute an intermediary
category between these two types of structures, as is claimed in
A. Southall's work on segmentary states, *Alur Society* (1953). The
oscillation of these small chiefdoms is historically defined by the
time of observation by the anthropologist and by the political environment in which they take place. In the same way, one must relativize the distinction between "cold" and "hot" societies–granted
that this distinction retains a certain validity. It appears problematic, however, to use this distinction heuristically with reference to
relations between Europe and the rest of the world. To characterize
certain societies as "cold" is equivalent to characterizing them as
"retarded." This denies their "coevalness," to borrow J. Fabian's expression from *Time and the Other* (1983). On the contrary, within a
well-delimited geographical space, such as Soudano-Sahelian West
Africa, there effectively exist "cold" and "hot" societies to the extent that some societies are denied historicity by societies that dominate them. I am thinking of Senufo and Minyanka societies, which
were subject to looting by surrounding states such as Segu and
Sikasso. This perspective has brought me to a center/periphery
mode of analysis, which highlights the role of the "frontier" as the
locus of historical dynamism. The approach is similar to ones
adopted by R. Cohen in "State Foundations" (1978) and I. Kopytoff
in *The African Frontier* (1987).

These hypotheses result not only from extended fieldwork–which
is in no way special–but also from research within numerous regions
of a well-circumscribed area. This has allowed me to observe systems of transformation. In fact, in contrast to anthropologists who,
after having studied an African village, move on to fieldwork in
Latin America or Asia, I have worked for fifteen years within societies that have been in contact for centuries. This has protected me
from being forced into large analytical leaps and from engaging in

abstract comparativism and the identification of structures. I have, on the contrary, been able to observe processes of identitary differences ensuing from one another.

Only with colonial conquest was this "chain of societies" (my term from "Ethnies et espaces," 1985) disarticulated so as to give birth to distinct ethnic groups (Fulani, Bambara, Mandingo, Senufo, Minyanka), to distinct political systems (state societies and stateless societies), and to distinct religious systems (paganism and Islam). Missionaries, district officers, and fieldworkers have also congealed identities that have subsequently been reappropriated by local social actors through a process of "working misunderstanding," to borrow D. C. Dorward's expression, which he uses in a historical discussion of the Tiv of Nigeria, "Ethnology and Administration" (1974). According to his work, based on a significant body of literature (administrative documents, works of social scientists), the populations of this region have asserted identity claims that are devoid of historical meaning prior to European conquest of the region. But in other cases, this interaction between literature and oral tradition predates European contact, as in Soudano-Sahelian West Africa, where Arabic literature has long coexisted with oral narratives.

Such notions can also be applied to other types of societies. E. Wilmsen, for instance, in *Land Filled with Flies* (1989), questions the representation of Kalahari Bushmen of Southern Africa as eternal hunter-gatherers. He shows instead that before colonization the Khoi, the San, the Tswana, and the Herero of this region were all engaged in a plurality of economic activities: foraging, hunting, rearing livestock, agriculture, trade, and handicraft production. They also maintained extensive ties with one another. Only with colonization were these networks of interconnectedness broken and replaced by circumscribed and reified societies and cultures as defined by the colonial administrators. Out of a situation of syncretism, colonization and the European gaze created societies, cultures, and ethnic groups. Ethnic confrontation and tribal conflict, which characterize contemporary African societies, have resulted, without a doubt, from the imposition of rigid systems of classification on otherwise flexible groups.

Interestingly, the same phenomenon is found in Eastern Europe.

The present situation in the former Soviet Union is comparable to the African context. Entire geographic areas encompassing disparate populations have been integrated into republics that are now claiming the status of independent nation-states. These republics resulted from Stalin's magical act of artificially carving them out. Specialists in Soviet studies have shown that an independent Ukraine has never existed within the borders of the ex-Soviet Union and that the states of Kirghiz, Turkmen, Uzbek, Tajik, and Kazakh are nation-states created ex nihilo within territories that have traditionally known only tribal, ethnic, and village organizations. After fifty years of fictive sovereignty, these republics have achieved autonomous existence. It is fascinating to note that Stalin, as commissary to the nationalities and as an innovator in his *Marxism and the National and Colonial Question* (1913), has played, for the Soviet Union, a role similar to the one played by the missionaries and district officers in Africa. In both cases, the political motto *divide et impera* and the practice of indirect rule have their roots in Jacobin politics and Marxist ideals. Like African ethnic groups, which were articulated by colonialism, the republics, carved out by Stalin, are becoming independent nation-states.

A number of conclusions emerge from these concrete examples. First, it is necessary to stress the dialogical character of identity. To be actualized, identity needs the Other, that is, it needs to circumscribe the Other as such. From this perspective, the growth of European nationalism in France, England, and Belgium during the nineteenth century appears closely related to the process of colonial expansion, to the labeling of the Other as primitive and the birth of primitivism in European art. The cohesion of those three European nations, as B. Jewsiewicki has demonstrated (1991), was supported by the belief in their superiority to conquered groups.

Conversely, the movements of decolonization in the 1950s and 1960s destabilized the unity of European nation-states. Without a counter-identification, European nation-states are facing implosions, fragmentation, and segmentation into a multiplicity of ethnic groups. Here, I return to the notion of an oscillation between state and segmentary structures. The emergence of regionalism and ethnicity in France (the Basques, Bretons, and Occitan), in Great Britain (the Irish), and in Belgium (the Walloons, the Flemish) could be explained by the disappearance of their colonial empires. Likewise, the assertion of independence by the Ukraine and Belarus, which are culturally close to Russia, could be explained by the collapse of the Russian and Soviet empire and by the end of the hegemony exercised by this state over its former colonies in the Caucasus and Central Asia, as well as its protectorate in Yugoslavia.

Are these claims for autonomy and independence justified? One must admit that African ethnic groups and the republics of the former Soviet Union were artificially created by external actions, but their nationals certainly have the right, if they wish, to gain a certain degree of autonomy from previous oppression and exaction by central powers. Recognizing their triviality, or artificiality, does not necessarily deny them the right to exist.

V. Y. Mudimbe, a Zairian writer and anthropologist and author of *The Invention of Africa* (1988), asks similar questions. He insists on the dynamism of the imposition of European knowledge on Africa, which he calls the "colonial library": writings by colonial administrators, missionaries, and ethnologists. He defends a position based upon the recognition of African systems of thought as intercultural fictions. As he shows, by drawing on works such as P. Tempels, *La philosophie bantoue* (1949), and M. Griaule, *Dieu d'eau* (1948), among others, African thinkers have invented an Africa that constitutes an indisputable tool of identitary definition.

In fact, identitary assertion depends upon the assimilation of the Other. And it is through the "cannibalization" of European works that African philosophers have rendered intelligible the mysteries of their cultures. From this perspective, Africa is the joint invention of Africans and Europeans, wherein each African enjoys the right to use this shared knowledge as the basis of his or her identity. This interpretation is akin to Ricoeur's and situates Mudimbe within what could be qualified as a "postmodern" trend. For the advocates of this trend, such as G.-E. Marcus and M. J. Fischer (1986), J. Clifford (Clifford and Marcus 1986, Clifford 1988), and C. Geertz (1988), anthropology is the product of a dialogical relation in which culture is an artifact or a "text" resulting from the joint effort of informants and anthropologists.

Postmodernism is defined by its opposition to the current discussion concerning the validity of certain anthropological works, no-

tably on the Kalahari Bushmen, as previously mentioned, and the
Dogon of Mali, which enjoy a high profile in journals such as *Current
Anthropology* (see, e.g., Wilmsen and Denbow, "Paradigmatic History of San-Speaking Peoples," 1990; Van Beek, "Dogon Restudied,"
1991). For postmodern anthropologists, the value of *Nuer* by Evans-
Pritchard or *Dieu d'eau* by Griaule is above all as an example of a certain discourse, and these works are accordingly analyzed in the same
manner as literary productions. Concerning identity, as seen in
Mudimbe's work, the postmodern standpoint, while recognizing
that ethnic, cultural, and national claims are arbitrary, considers
them fully legitimate nonetheless. It is fully legitimate for one to assert a Fulani identity, even if one's ancestors have never spoken Ful-
fulde, even if they have never practiced nomadic livestock rearing.
Moreover, it appears inappropriate for the anthropologist to demand
proof of authenticity from his informants (Amselle, "L'Ethnicité
comme volonté et comme représentation," 1987). The making of genealogies, the identification of possible ethnic conversions—in other
words, the constructivist approach to identity—is translated into an
act of anthropological censorship.

Anybody has the right to claim any identity, and it is illegitimate
for the anthropologist to erect himself or herself as the judge of the
legitimacy of proclaimed identities. I believe, however, that there
exists a limit to the expression of cultural, ethnic, or religious particularism: as a matter of fact, anybody can claim the identity of their
choice as long as it does not threaten the identity of others. It is at
this level that the question of human rights becomes relevant.

In the contemporary context of identity exacerbation, whether it
is actualized through ethnicity, nationalism, or religious fundamentalism, the object is not to eliminate differences in the name of
a secularism that would be a symmetric and reverse form of the phenomenon denounced. Consequently, in the face of universalistic
claims by particularism, social scientists and anthropologists here
simply have the right and the duty to lay bare the way in which specific identities, to borrow Boas's expression, have become what they
are. The unveiling of the processes of identitary construction would
in this case allow us to relativize the claims of social actors so as to
strike a compromise between the interests of the individual and the
interests of the collectivity. In this role as protector of human rights,

the anthropologist would be legitimized in deconstructing identities so as to protect what is universal in each of us.

My thanks to Alban Bensa and Dominique Colas for their intelligent advice.

J.-L. A.

Paris, July 1997

Translator's Note

      This book is a translation of *Logiques métisses: Anthropologie de l'identité en Afrique et ailleurs*, published by Bibliothèque scientifique Payot in 1990. The French word *métisse* comes from *métissage*, meaning "the crossing of two races." While the English corollary, *mestizo*, also means "a person of mixed blood," it more popularly suggests a person of mixed European and American Indian ancestry. For the translated title of this book, however, the term is meant to be understood in its broadest, most generic sense of "mixture" or "the result of a mixture."

Mestizo Logics

Introduction

This book does not bid farewell to anthropology; rather, it proposes a reversal of perspective. It is the fruit of fifteen years of fieldwork in and theoretical reflection on the Fulani, Bambara, and Mandingo chiefdoms of southwest Mali and northeast Guinea. My efforts here could be those of one more iconoclast who, like all the rest, will be forgotten. But criticism is not an end in itself. This epistemological and archeological study was prompted by a feeling that it was impossible to understand my chosen field using the theoretical instruments commonly employed by anthropologists.

This long field study and theoretical reflection culminated in a sort of disenchantment with the object, which led me to question the essence of what constitutes, in my mind, "ethnological reason." By ethnological thinking, I mean the continuity-breaking procedure that extracts, refines, and classifies with the intention of isolating types, whether they be in the realm of politics (state society versus stateless society), economics (self-sufficient versus market economy), religion (paganism versus Islam), ethnicity, or culture. This clearly unified theoretical perspective is one of the foundations of European domination over the rest of the planet, a sort of Ariadne's thread running through the history of Western thought. But to this ethnological thinking can be opposed "mestizo logics," that is, a continuist approach that would emphasize an originary syncretism or lack of distinctness.

The notion of mestizo logics could offer the interesting possibility of resolving a contemporary, confusing false dilemma: the dilemma that opposes the universalism of human rights to cultural relativism. My purpose here is to demonstrate that cultural relativism supposes both a close look and a distant look at social entities that in reality are shifting but which have been extracted from their context by the joint operations of travelers, missionaries, and officers. Before colonial expansion, there existed only a relatively unstable continuum of structures and cultural practices in those societies located on the axis connecting Europe to Africa. Is it not possible, though, to consider that the direct confrontation between the French and Toucouleur armies, for example, accentuated the coherence of each of the two cultures and at the same time intensified their differences?[1] Thus, the culturalist posture implies an abrupt, transitionless linkage and the dismantling of "chains of societies." In other words, it implies a relationship among distant societies through exploration or conquest, as well as the selection of decontextualized cultural traits, and the transcription of these discrete social unities composed by different cultures.[2] Every anthropologist with genuine field experience, however, knows that the culture he observes dissolves into a series or a reservoir of conflictual or peaceful practices used by its actors to continually renegotiate their identity. To set these practices in stone amounts to an essentialist vision of culture, which is ultimately a modern form of racism. In this sense, ethnology can lead to a legitimation of exclusion (as in apartheid).

Paradoxically, the universalism of natural law, which originated with the Enlightenment and which ethnological thinking rejects, has itself served to justify the European conquest of a good part of the planet in the name of the eradication of barbarous practices even if, in most cases, colonialist politics were actually founded on respect for indigenous customs and, consequently, on a diffuse culturalism. Natural law, which is the basis for the French ideology of assimilation, is supposed to be the best antidote to the ethnological or cultural thinking that wreaks havoc in both South Africa and the mind of Jean-Marie Le Pen.[3] Did not the Right in France just recently make demands concerning its own right to be different, which would quite naturally lead to a situation typical of apartheid?[4]

But in order to measure the effectiveness of this antidote, we must be able to determine precisely what we mean by "human rights." Not only is the meaning of the term extremely variable, but "human rights" are brandished as an emblem to determine what constitutes other cultures. The representation of the Other as a source of contrast is itself the result of a misrepresentation effected by ethnological reason. For the universalist-relativist debate is, in fact, the confrontation of two political systems: democracy and totalitarianism. We can read the facts of totalitarianism in the light of the facts of culture.

Faced with the idea of natural law, one can, of course, in the name of respect for indigenous customs or cultural relativism, claim the right of African cultures to practice excision or the right of Islamic nations to execute blasphemers. It still remains that these claims are the radical rejection of the idea, if not the practice, of democracy. It is possible that uses of "human rights" by the media and by political figures have inevitably produced a rejection of them in those on whom attempts were made to impose this emblem.

In order to contain the expansion of a Western model of democracy that they abhor and at the same time to define their own identity, fundamentalists of all types (partisans of authenticity, culturalists, Islamics, etc.) draw on opposing political theories (nationalism, totalitarianism, etc.). This is why the universalist–cultural relativist debate does not result, despite certain individuals' claims, from the confrontation between the Middle Ages and modernity. Rather, it is an exclusively contemporary conflict, that of fundamentalists speaking in the name of tradition while simultaneously projecting current ideological models into the past.

This debate resembles the eighteenth- and nineteenth-century opposition between French Enlightenment universalism and German Romantic reactionism. As a reaction against French domination over the rest of Europe, German nationalism emerged in the name of the right to be different. Nevertheless, in Enlightenment thought such as that of Hume or Kant, the theory of national characters often accompanies universalist thinking, whereas the ethnological approach of Herder, for example, owes a great deal to Montesquieu's *Esprit des lois*.[5]

It is possible that "human rights" are simply the expression of a dominant power with no need to claim the right to prejudice in order to validate its identity.[6] We could thus explain, for example, the contradictory coexistence in the colonial ideology of natural law, which prohibits repugnant customs, and of respect for indigenous customs. This apparent contradiction could be cleared up if we agreed to consider that human rights belong to the realm of principles whereas common law applies to the realm of practice.[7] In the colonial perspective, the ethnological aim must be seen as the mode by which the dominant power takes form, a mode of realization that itself leads to ethnology as a discipline. Little by little, this type of knowledge-power wielded by the dominant group was reappropriated by the dominated, who have used it as an instrument to define their own identity. The rise of ethnology thus correlates with the rise of nationalisms, ethnicisms, and culturalisms. To move beyond this point of view, one must consider culture as a "reservoir"–in other words, as a collection of practices internal or external to a given social arena that the actors mobilize as a function of one or another political conjuncture.

It is within this problematic that I shall try here to interpret the fieldwork data and archival documents gathered in Mali, Guinea, Senegal, and France.

1 Ethnological Reason

A taste for idle chatter is all Africans have received from
nature.
–Emmanuel Kant, "Observations on the Beautiful and the
    Sublime" (1764)

I like ethnography very much; as a science it possesses a rare
interest; but since I want ethnography to be free, I want it
without political application.
–Ernest Renan, *What Is a Nation?* (1882)

Ethnology has always claimed for itself a certain privilege as a weapon in the fight against prejudices of all types. But this
discipline must be more closely examined before it is acknowledged
as inherently tolerant, because the privilege accorded by ethnology
to the notion of difference could well mask, under the pretext of cultural relativism, a fundamental ethnocentrism. For this reason, it
seems to me completely illusory to want to distinguish a fundamental ethnology or a fundamental anthropology from an applied ethnology or an applied anthropology. All ethnology is "applied"; the
one designated as such is simply a more explicit version of fundamental ethnology. Ethnology is applied first of all because it is im-
plicated in the colonialist system, and second because it "applies"
as much to the definition of exotic societies as to our own.

But before we examine in detail how ethnology is consubstantially
linked to colonialism and how it has served and continues to serve
in the self-definition of formerly colonized and formerly colonizing
societies, it will be helpful to analyze the way ethnology has been
constructed from the vocabulary of Indo-European institutions and
Greek political thought.

The Relational and the Social

In Indo-European languages as in precolonial Africa,[1] some of the terms that designate social conditions are ethnic, such as terms that name foreigners or terms for those groups that appear to form a unity once they have been integrated into another society. Thus it is for the term "slave," for the term "wealth" in Anglo-Saxon—which signifies "the Celt," the conquered people–and even more so for the term "barbarian."

In all these civilizations, social distinctions are ethnic or spatial and, as a result, they bring about "chains of societies."[2] Such is Benveniste's position: "Every appellation of an ethnic character applied to past epochs is differential and oppositional. In the names a people use to describe themselves, there is, manifestly or not, the intention to distinguish themselves from neighboring peoples and to affirm the superiority that consists in the possession of a common and intelligible language."[3] From this perspective, the term "society" is merely the expression of a political distinction within a collection of societies.[4] For the Greeks, the notion of *ethnos* was a political category. It constituted one pole in the hierarchization that evolved between two principal forms of societies: *polis* and *ethnos*. If the *polis* (the city-state) was a precisely defined and valorized category, one in which the Greeks found their plenitude of being, the category of *ethnos*, in contrast, was vague and deprecatory. E. Will explains:

> They [the Greeks] use the term *ethnos* to designate human groups whose character differs in origin and distribution as well as in their political individuality, whether it concern all Hellenic peoples, the great barbarian peoples such as the Persians, the inhabitants of a city, or insignificant tribes.[5]

Thus, in *Politics*, Aristotle uses the notion of *ethnos* as much to designate those Greeks who are not organized even into villages, such as the Arcadians, as to designate the barbarian inhabitants of Babylon. In this fortified city, he sympathetically relates, three days after its defeat, an entire neighborhood was still unaware of the event.[6] The concept of *ethnos*, then, contains the idea of segmentarity, whether this be a condition of tribes, of a "tribal State," or of a "segmented State," to use Southall's expression.[7]

Both the Latin and the ecclesiastical traditions maintained the conception of *ethnos* as a form of society lacking integration, self-sufficiency, and the division of labor, which constitute the distinguishing signs of the *polis*. In Latin the term *ethnicus* designates the pagans, and in the ecclesiastic tradition the term *ethnè* refers to "nations, gentiles, and pagans in opposition to Christians."[8]

Mauss refers to this last sense of the word in *Nation* (1920). In his typology of societies, Mauss distinguishes the tribal form of society, which remains consistently organized though still segmented by the clans that subsist within it, from those forms in which leaders have permanent power, whether this power be democratic, aristocratic, or monarchic.[9]

The term "nation" is itself ambiguous.[10] When synonymous with *ethnos* it suggests the pejorative sense of "pagan." Yet until the middle of the nineteenth century it applied to all the peoples of the planet, even when a hierarchy founded on other criteria (skin color, etc.) distinguished different parts of the world.[11] For example, the sixteenth-century Portuguese explorer André Dornelas established a parallel between Spain and Sierra Leone: "All these nations are in general called 'Sapes,' just as in Spain the members of different nations are called Spaniards."[12]

The word "nation" will be superseded by the term "race" only with the idea of a classification and a hierarchical determination of different societies. This occurs under the collective influence of movements as diverse as comparative naturalism, German romanticism, nationalism, and evolutionism.

With authors such as Herder and his theory of *Volksgeist*,[13] Augustin Thierry, Taine, Gobineau, and Vacher de Lapouge and their ethnological or racial conception of history,[14] the idea of "race" as a nation's exclusive principle of identity is born. This movement of ideas accompanies European nationalism, which, as Gellner has shown, resulted from industrialization, migration toward the cities, and the integration of a "high culture" within a territorial state: all peoples who have successfully founded a state succeed in forming true nations. The others constitute ethnic minorities, where the ethnic group thus becomes a sort of nation as poor imitation.[15]

The nineteenth century saw the triumph of the principle of race during the era of nationalism, as well as the reappearance of the term "ethnic group." In his *Essay on Inequality among the Human Races*, Gobineau uses the adjective *ethnique*–the term "ethnic group" does not exist in his work–in an ambiguous manner. While he uses it concurrently with the notions of race, nation, and civilization, one nonetheless has the feeling that the word conveys to him the sense of a mixture of races and a resulting degeneration.[16]

The same basic meaning and the same ambiguity can be found in the work of Vacher de Lapouge, a theoretician of social Darwinism and the first to introduce the notion of ethnic group (*ethnie*) into French. In *Les Sélections sociales*, he attempts to account for the separation of racially homogenous populations among which certain segments have experienced diverse vicissitudes. For example, due to a prolonged cohabitation with other races, involving linguistic and cultural assimilation, these segments eventually resemble the other races more than the initial population from which they separated. These new groupings, however, which the author calls "nations," can break apart without losing the reciprocal attraction of their dissociated parts. To signify this collective cohesion, Vacher de Lapouge does not consider the terms race, nation, or nationality to be accurate; he prefers instead *ethne* or ethnic group, the first seeming more correct, but the second easier to pronounce.[17]

Both Renan and Fustel de Coulanges disagree with this racial conception of ethnography, of *ethnos* or nation. In his famous text, "Qu'est-ce qu'une nation?"–set against the Franco-German debate on Alsace-Lorraine–Renan rejects ethnographic criteria as the determining factor in the existence of a nation. A nation, he reasons, is based rather on a cohesion freely consented to and grounded in the fact of having accomplished great things in the past and the desire to accomplish more in the future, and not on such positive characteristics as race, language, or geography.[18] In the same vein, Fustel de Coulanges disagrees with modern historians who find a racial content in the notion of *ethnos* as the Greeks conceived it,[19] or who interpret the totality of French history in terms of an ethnic confrontation between the Franks and the Gallo-Romans.[20]

An ambiguity remains, however, in the thought of Renan and Fustel de Coulanges. For Renan "race" disappeared with Rome, Christianity, and the empire of Charlemagne, but continued to exist very strongly among tribes. According to the author of *La Cité antique*, the fact of being Dorian or Ionian, for Herodotus or Thucydides, carried with it no implication of inherent difference or difference in aptitude, though there were nonetheless genealogical differences between these two peoples.

Only with the development of an anthropology based on field-work, and the resulting dismantling of lineage and ethnic realities, will the definition of social collectivities be definitively separated from all racial affiliation.

The Spatial and the Political Superseded by the Temporal and the Ethnic

Although the idea that we can compare human history to the growth of a living being may be an ancient one,[21] only in the eighteenth and especially the nineteenth centuries do we find the elaboration of the great evolutionary frescoes encompassing a series of stages that all human societies have supposedly traversed (Buffon, Linnaeus, Condorcet, Ferguson, Adam Smith, etc.). In *Moeurs des Sauvages Ameriquains comparées aux moeurs des premiers temps* (1724), Lafitau proposes a vision in which modern primitives would be our contemporary ancestors.[22] Morgan will take up this perspective more than a century later in *Ancient Society* (1877). According to Morgan, human history passes through a certain number of "ethnic stages" (savagery, barbarism, civilization). In essence, these go from *societas*, a social organization founded on peoples, clans, and tribes, which parallels the Greek *ethnos*, to *civitas*, a political organization based on territory, the state, and property, which bears a strange resemblance to the *polis*. Consequently, the *ethnos* that was in Greek antiquity a form of social organization becomes,[23] according to Morgan's idea of "ethnic stages," an organizing principle of human history wherein each social stage represents merely one of the phases of an ethnological or racial itinerary.[24] The political vision of human societies is thus repressed. Whereas in Greek thought the opposition of *ethnos* and *polis* expresses a social and political hierarchy, with Morgan, Tylor, Durkheim, and Mauss the unequal spatial development of different types of societies becomes a comparative series of human communities situated at different stages in their evolution, that is, separated in time.[25]

Ethnology, in the modern sense of the term, is thus constituted only in the repression of the political or, in other words, in the idea that social and human species could be compared within an ordered scheme of the evolution of humanity. Moreover, ethnology as a discipline finds its basis not so much in the repression of history—even if evolutionism is, in a certain sense, a pseudohistory—as in the hypothesis according to which features common to all human history encompass certain backward societies, those which the Greeks defined as apolitical: the *ethnè*.[26]

It is customary in anthropological foundation stories, after having evoked the evolutionism of Morgan and Tylor, to proceed from functionalism to diffusionism, culturalism, and structuralism. Even if this procedure has the virtue of convenience, it hardly seems justified epistemologically. I would prefer to stress the ensemble of anthropological thought as well as the trends that link it to the eighteenth and nineteenth centuries, which are comparative naturalism and evolutionism. Even today, the idea on which the majority of anthropologists can agree is that different human societies are specimens or museum pieces that one can appropriately classify, compare, or label.

From this perspective, rather than consider Malinowski and Radcliffe-Brown as the founders of functionalism or Boas as the founder of culturalism, which they doubtless are, it is preferable to see them as field researchers who focused intensively on individual cultures or tribes, isolated from their spatiotemporal context, for purposes of comparison.[27]

The comparatist or "butterfly collector" approach to anthropology supposes,[28] in effect, the existence of elements separable from their intersocial fabric. It is thus not the notion of society that founds comparativism but the reverse: because I need to draw up classifications and typologies, I must have elements to classify, and if I can legitimately extract them from their context, it is because I have denied beforehand that these elements are political units situated in a sociocultural continuum.[29]

The same preoccupation can be found in an entire series of ethnologists—Boas, Rivers, Spencer, Haddon, Gillen, Mauss, Radcliffe-Brown, Griaule, and so on—which proves that a certain comparativism and its corollary, the monograph, are indeed the common denominators of ethnological thought.

Colonial Fracturing of Ethnic Groups

The invention of ethnic groups is the joint work of colonial administrators, professional ethnologists, and those who combine both
qualifications.

Initially this invention took the form of "racial politics" as it was
practiced by both the French and the English.[30] On the French side,
this political position was established by Gallieni, who followed in
the footsteps of an entire lineage of colonizers relying extensively
on the Machiavellian maxim of *divide et impera.*[31] Moreover, Gallieni was influenced by the racist evolutionism of Spencer, a theoretician of organicism.[32] According to Spencer, the passage from
simple societies to complex ones, more specifically from the ma-
rauding stage to the industrial stage, supposed that the differences
between the conquering race and the conquered one not be too
great.[33] Gallieni found inspiration in this idea to effect his "racial
politics," which drew its force from close knowledge of a country
and its inhabitants, and which was based in each country "on local
traditional authorities who enjoy the confidence of the masses by
keeping at bay the foreign intermediaries, holdovers from former
domination."[34] Binger, Archinard, and especially William Ponty will
later apply Gallieni's ideas in West Africa and will influence the
three intimately linked domains of administration, development,
and ethnography.[35]

In the territories conquered by France, such racial politics lie at
the origin of direct rule, which consists in the creation of *cercles*, administrative units presided over by the French, and "cantons," ruled
by African chiefs. On the economic level, racial filtering, brought
about in particular by the elimination of conquerors and the promotion of dominated populations, is considered in the Spencerian
tradition to be the condition of genuine economic development. Finally, in the domain of ethnography, this political position gives rise
to the establishment of an entire series of administrative, political,
and ethnic maps and atlases that serve to constitute ethnographic
knowledge, and that in turn allow the colonizer to affirm his power
over the population.[36] For the British colonies of tropical Africa, Lugard set up a classification of peoples in terms of their social organization, which includes three groups: primitive tribes, evolved

communities, and Europeanized Africans.[37] Though Lugard claims
the opposite, this classification is racial in nature. The evolved communities correspond to the Hamites, builders of empires, and the
Moslems, whereas the primitive tribes include the aboriginal blacks
who were driven back up the mountains or into the forests and who
remained at the familial stage. This racial policy concludes in northern Nigeria with the establishment of an indirect rule, that is, with
the government of Fulani (Hamite) societies by their own institutions and with their own chiefs.

Indirect rule was also adopted on the French side, by Van Vollenhoven in 1917, for example, once the disastrous effects of racial politics and the *contact direct* (direct contact) of William Ponty became
apparent. It was then decided to make use of the existing chiefs as a
means of administration. In 1932 this political position was reaffirmed by Brévié, who reinforced the traditional powers of the chiefs
against the modernized elite while the elite attempted to inflame the
population against the colonial administration. This position was
again applied by Eboué in 1942.[38] As J. Lombard remarks,[39] there
was a return to racial politics, which was in fact the fundamental
principle of both British and French colonialism, both of which al-
ternated between direct and indirect rule.

Ethnic politics in the French empire, as in the British one, was
thus a matrix common to ethnology and colonial administration.
M. Delafosse, who was both an ethnologist and an administrator,
represented this matrix particularly well. Like many of his generation, Delafosse, whose intellectual development had taken him
through studies in medicine and Arabic linguistics and a period
spent at the Museum of Natural History, models his perception of
human societies on those of animal and plant species.[40] He applies
this model to the classification and mapping of French West African
languages, which supply the primary context for the formation of
different ethnic groups such as one can observe even today.[41]

In South Africa, the *Volkekunde* of Afrikaner ethnographers inspired the politics of segregation more than did the work of Malinowski or Radcliffe-Brown (named to the Anthropology Chair of the
University of Capetown in 1921).[42] In a manner similar to Delafosse,
Radcliffe-Brown characterized anthropology as the natural science
of human society. For this reason, he distinguished several subsys-

tems–economy, kinship, politics, and so on–within different societies. With this perspective in mind, he wrote in 1940 the preface to *African Political Systems* by Fortes and Evans-Pritchard, and in 1950 he edited with Daryll Forde *African Systems of Kinship and Marriage.*

These two works constitute a sort of bible of comparative naturalism, not only for theories of kinship and politics, but for economy as well. The kinship systems within different African ethnic groups (Swazi, Tswana, Lozi, Bantu, Ashanti, Yakö, Nuba, Nuer) are compared as they were when jointly extracted from their contexts by ethnologists, administrators, and missionaries. These works were intended to "enlighten" colonial administrators and to improve their administrative abilities because knowledge of kinship relations is, according to Radcliffe-Brown and Forde, as important as knowledge of political and economic structures. But beyond this strict comparativism, these two authors reveal an essentially structuralist preoccupation, discovering that "while there is a very wide range of variation in their superficial features there can be discovered a certain small number of general structural principles which are applied and combined in various ways."[43] Perhaps this echoes *Elementary Structures of Kinship*, which appeared the previous year, even though Lévi-Strauss, in contrast to Radcliffe-Brown and Murdock, claims to perceive unconscious realities rather than conscious manifestations. But even if the notion of structure–empirical in Radcliffe-Brown, profound in Lévi-Strauss–distinguishes the two authors, their point of departure remains the same: that of ethnic group conceived as a preconstructed material. To present the Baoulé as matrilineal or the Bambara as patrilineal, for example, relieves one from having to ask just what is meant by "Baoulé" and by "Bambara," and from determining the exact number of Baoulé and Bambara who come from these two systems of filiation.[44]

Beyond this line of questioning, the typologies of kinship systems must be challenged, just as the typologies elaborated in other areas of anthropology must be reevaluated–that of politics, for example.

The classification of African political systems set up by Fortes and Evans-Pritchard was inspired by Spencer, Durkheim, and Lugard,[45] with Lugard, as we have seen, contrasting primitive tribes to evolved communities. This classification too was, of course, guided

by the concern to better administer and to better control the African
populations under British indirect rule, and that is why anthropology was called the daughter of imperialism. Nevertheless, this critique cannot be taken too far; the founders of Africanist political
anthropology were beyond a doubt far from being rabid proponents
of colonization. It is much more interesting to show how Fortes and
Evans-Pritchard, as representatives of British liberal thought, ide-
alized and interpreted from a political folk perspective the Tallensi
and Nuer segmentary societies.[46] This interpretation and this ideal-
ization were perfectly consistent with the fragmenting of the object—
which is the political system of ethnic groups—such as it was preconceived in the colonial context. But this interpretation and ideal-
ization ultimately made an abstraction of the dependence
characterizing the segmentary systems with respect to the state systems, and they obscured the centralized character of numerous lineage systems.

As I will try to show below, a rather detailed epistemological study
of the typological refinements that followed the publication of
African Political Systems leads one to see that no stateless societies
per se existed in precolonial Africa. The societies considered as such
were in fact dissident states. They were societies that, in the course
of their history, were artificially separated from their center or their
political formations and whose centralized apparatus disappeared
because of the European conquest. If the fiction of the existence of
segmentary societies could be perpetuated as long as it was in anthropology, it is because the precolonial African states possessed all
the slave-providing peripheries constituting buffer zones between
each political entity and, as a result, they appeared to have no clearly
defined borders. In the zones of weak political control situated on
the margins of each kingdom there existed satellite societies, and
they were customarily characterized as segmentary.

Yet another large domain of anthropology, the study of religions,
has not been spared by comparative naturalism, museography, and
ethnico-colonial fragmentation. The fragmentation practiced by
ethnologists in their studies at the village level led to the production
of a series of monographs on secret societies (*komo*, *do*, *ntomo*,
koré) that, taken together, allowed for the concoction of a "Bambara
religion."[47] However, this Bambara pseudoreligion is nothing but a

collection of decentralized cultural practices that transcend colonial ethnic limits and that can be found among the Minyanka[48] as well as the Mandingo and the Fulani of Wasolon. Privileging of the ethnico-village approach went hand in hand with overlooking the essentially political character of these cults. In other words, this approach neglected the fact that such practices were combinations of myths and rituals linked to diverse levels of political units: villages, chiefdoms, kingdoms, and other levels.

Moreover, the holistic anthropological vision that assimilates mythico-ritualist practices to religions such as Islam or Christianity tends to privilege the analysis of these same practices in terms of beliefs.[49] Such an ethnocentric approach masks a perhaps principal element of these polytheisms, which is their essentially pragmatic and instrumental mode of functioning.

Finally, the ethnico-village view avoids the fundamental question regarding the mode of implantation of these cults. Without returning to a diffusionist approach, it suffices to ask how a single divinity, or similar secret societies, could spread over such wide areas. In other words, far from analyzing polytheisms as universalist religions in reverse, as is done by most ethnologists, one must ask how decentralized cults that are not integrated into a church (Christianity) or even based on a book (Islam) could spread over such a large area. To privilege the analysis of mythico-cultural practices at the village level or the analysis of them collectively at the ethnic level is to forget the conditions under which they came about and were established; it is to forget that there was doubtless a force at work common to these different avatars of "Savage Mind," those local divinities or secret societies spread all along the Niger valley.[50] Perhaps this common agent must be identified with the vast political units existing in the region.

The economic sphere, among other realms, has been invaded by the ethnico-substantialist problematic. From Marx through the functionalism of the 1940s to modern economic anthropology, primitive societies were habitually characterized as self-sustaining economies in order to distinguish them from Western capitalist economies. The notion of the self-sustaining economy is in fact very near to that of "village communism," used, among others, by Bélime, founder of the Niger Office.[51]

Thus, whether it be in the domains of familial, political, religious, or economic relations, substantialist thought permeates the whole of anthropological investigations, and fashions the different representations of "primitive societies." It remains now to examine whether these representations are taken up in turn by the local actors.

The Transfer of Knowledge and the Civilizing Mission of Ethnology

Africanist ethno-historiography has been able to show that the ideas produced by the Western social sciences had been reappropriated by the Africans themselves. This is particularly apparent in the concept of ethnic group that shapes most African social or political movements. But this feedback effect occurs in other areas as well: the idea, for example, that the empires of Ghana, Mali, and Sonrai dominated a large part of West Africa. This idea, expressed by Delafosse and perpetuated by colonial schoolbooks,[52] constitutes the very principle of Malian nationalism; one of these empires, in fact, gave its name to this newly independent country. Inversely, certain Malians, who take offense at seeing their country's intellectual universe taken over by a few great but defunct historical traditions, advance the opposing thesis. In their view, the mechanisms of precolonial history were found just as much among the smaller units of chiefdoms, communities, and village confederations. Regardless of one's position, however, both views typify political anthropology as categories of colonial practice that have permeated political representations.

In the domain of religion, Frobenius, Tempels, Delafosse, and students of Griaule's disciples enunciated the idea that African rites and symbols form systems analogous to universalist religions or Western philosophical doctrines. This conception forms the very basis of the theory of négritude, such as Léopold Senghor expressed it, for example.[53] It also inspired numerous African forms of socialism.[54] This manner of opposing closed systems—négritude or Bantu philosophy versus Western thought—is strikingly illustrated by Senghor who, referring implicitly to Gobineau, pronounced his famous formula: "Reason is Greek, emotion is African."

Recently, such African philosophers as Stanislas Adotevi, Marcien Towa, Paulin Hountoundji, and Mudimbe have vigorously criticized this current of negritude or ethnophilosophy. These authors question the naive idea of elevating African belief systems to the level of their Western homologues by characterizing them in terms of religions or philosophies. In fact, far from being a project of rehabilitation, this ethnocentric projection locks African systems of thought into closed structures, congealed in a kind of absolute relativism of entities between which no communication can occur. Have the works of J. Goody not demonstrated that one cannot speak of philosophy in societies lacking writing, or "constructive rumination"?[55] Can a philosophy exist without an accumulation of knowledge and a critical look at the texts analogous to those produced in the history of Western thought?

More generally, the fact of "writing culture,"[56] of transcribing the ethnologist's field experience into the form of a story, adds something to the society studied. The ethnologist's use of allegories, tropes, and rhetorical figures that sometimes date from old travel accounts renders obsolete the idea of ethnological monographs as objective descriptions of a given terrain.

Similarly, African economists and political leaders of the 1960s echoed, but in a contradictory way, the colonial definition of African economies in terms of self-sufficiency. On one hand, the leaders of certain countries, such as Mali, used the idea of a closed economy, that is, of an archaic peasantry, to justify the socialization of agriculture. In this sense, a striking continuity exists between the views of Bélime and those of Modibo Keita, the first president of the Republic of Mali, regarding the Niger Office: both thought it necessary to break the basic unit of indigenous economy—the village community—in order to stimulate the growth of agriculture. On the other hand, the Malian leaders also believed that the nature of rural communities legitimized the setting up of forms of production—collective fields—that would furnish a surplus and thus insure an initial accumulation. Another concept originating in the economic anthropology of the 1960s was that of self-centered development or of the "disconnection" dear to Samir Amin. The latter was adopted by numerous African regimes and is today the vulgate of developers.

Thus, the circle appears closed: ethnology has perfectly accomplished its civilizing mission in that its objects of study have become themselves the emitters of ethnological pronouncements (feedback). With this sort of self-ethnology, a distinction no longer exists between the local model and the ethnologist's model because the actors define themselves in the ethnologist's terms. As we will see, this holds true particularly in the African urban milieu, since there the elite are the formulators of new ethnic labels; but this is also true in rural milieus, because urban identities spread from the city to the countryside.[57] In a sort of specular game the peasants reflect back to the contemporary ethnologist the very image of themselves they saw reflected in the ethnologist's gaze.

Ethnology for Internal Use Only

It has become banal to affirm that though anthropology claims to describe the Other, it speaks to us of ourselves and thus takes on a profoundly allegorical character. This character is particularly evident in the works of certain anthropologists who, for very diverse reasons, find a certain filiation with the eighteenth-century philosophical tale and make the Noble Savage the mouthpiece of their fixations or their disappointed hopes. If the works of Jaulin, Turnbull, and Clastres have provoked and continue to provoke debates and controversies, it is precisely because the parables they unveil question very visibly the scientific status that anthropology has acquired since the end of the nineteenth century.[58] If the ethnological monograph can no longer take on the form of the philosophical tale or moral story, it is because ethnology claimed to be an objective description of exotic societies. However (and this includes those authors who make a claim to scientific objectivity), one can find in such ethnologists' work implicit ethical elements or value judgments concerning our own society. The description Evans-Pritchard gives us, for example, of the Nuer reflects the Anglo-Saxon model of democracy, the balance of segments among the Sudanese rearers being perhaps the equivalent of the balance of powers in Montesquieu.[59] It is also evident that Margaret Mead's work on Samoa echoes her preoccupations relative to the difficulties experienced by the American youth of the 1930s. More recently, the research undertaken by R. Lee on the Bushmen as part of the Harvard Kalahari

Project is intimately linked to the problematic of American sociobiology of the 1970s.[60]

Like the other social sciences, then, anthropology cannot make a claim to objectivity, which is not to say that just any discourse regarding another population is justified under its name. A prudent attitude requires the clarification of the (more often than not) implicit preconceived opinions that run through various ethnological works, which supposes a sort of self-analysis on the part of the ethnologist.[61] In this way, one can read between the lines of these texts to find other paradigms. Though it may be somewhat abrupt, we can relate one paradigm to another and thus assemble a part of anthropology's history, just as can be done, no doubt, for many other disciplines.

There is another area where anthroplogy intervenes directly in our own self-definition, and this concerns our conception of culture. During the last few years, questions relative to the notion of identity have widely invaded the social sciences, just as they have the media. Whether it concerns our own societies and their subdivisions, or whether exotic societies are the subject, it is difficult to find an article or a book in the social sciences that does not refer in one way or another to the theme of identity: French, Breton, Occitan, Basque identities; African, Asian, Amerindian ethnic groups; identities of class, gender, and so on. No area of the social sciences or politics seems immune from a problematic that has become a kind of journalistic catchall. It is more apt, however, to place these interrogations in the framework of the rise of racism, the decline of certain powers, the internationalizing of economics, and the organization of supranational entities (Europe, for example). But the approach to these issues in terms of the multicultural society is linked directly to anthropology's emergence as a field of knowledge and, in particular, to the creation and massive diffusion of the notion of culture by ethnologists.[62]

Tylor, in particular, introduced the idea that culture is a stage in human evolution. Boas, in reference to the author of *Primitive Culture*, associates this notion with the fact that "learned behavior, socially transmitted and cumulative in time, is paramount as a determinant of human behavior."[63] This notion of culture, as Boas expressed it in reaction to evolutionism, will be used extensively by the

American cultural anthropologists (Kroeber, Clyde Kluckhohn, Ralph Linton, Melville Herskovits, Ruth Benedict, Mead, Irving Hallowell, and so on). Though Boas invented the culturalist and relativist conception of culture, however, his notion, as Stocking has shown,[64] is very near the idea of a "national character" (*génie d'un peuple*) and therefore owes much to Bastian (*Völkergedanken*) and even beyond him to Herder (*Volksgeist*) and Leibniz.[65] Consequently, it is valid to consider that, in a certain way and to the extent that it originates in German Romanticism and in the idea of an incarnation of the human spirit in its national or ethnic forms, Boas's notion of culture is definitely a transformed version of the concept of race.

It is American cultural anthropology's ambiguous conception of culture as a static entity that we find in Lévi-Strauss. Though he is justifiably considered the father of structuralism in anthropology, it is nonetheless true that an entire part of Lévi-Strauss's work depends directly on the notion of culturalism. This is patent in *Elementary Structures of Kinship*,[66] a work that remains important but in which the domain of culture, as opposed to nature, is seen exclusively in terms of the world of rules. It posits fixed prescriptions without examining the matrimonial strategies and the controlling relationships expressed on the occasion of the choice of a mate.[67] This culturalism is even more apparent in *Race et histoire* and in "Race et culture."[68] Some have opposed these two texts, seeing the first as praiseworthy in every respect but the second as influenced by biological models.[69] We can, however, find in both these works a sort of hyperrelativist cultural fixation that derives largely from museography, whose influence on the French school has always been very strong (for example, the Musée de l'Homme).[70]

Certainly, the American culturalist anthropologists were right, as was Lévi-Strauss, to focus on the specifics and relative character of values promoted by each society, given all the philosophies of history and other sagas of progress; but the corollary of this generous attitude is the erection of rigid cultural barriers enclosing each group in its singularity.

Is the notion of a multicultural society, whose ambiguities have been mentioned above, not directly situated in the tradition of American cultural anthropological thought?[71] Far from being an instrument of tolerance and liberation of minorities, as its supporters claim, this expression manifests all the problems of ethnological thinking, and this is the sense in which it has been taken over in France by the "new right."[72] To isolate a community by defining a certain number of "differences" leads to the possibility of its territorial confinement if not its expulsion. The ascription of differences, ethnic labels, or self-fulfilling prophecies not only reflects the recognition of cultural specificities; it also correlates with a thoughtless affirmation of identity, that of French ethnicity. As a result, the problematic of the multicultural society leads directly, if one is not careful, to a separate development analogous to South African apartheid, which itself issues in part from the misguided application of the notion of culture.

It is not a question of abstractly opposing human rights, which no one completely understands, to ethnic or cultural fundamentalism, explained by some as a "defeat of thought" (*défaite de la pensée*).[73] Rather, we must advance the idea of a mixture or an originary interbreeding among different groups that have formed throughout human history.

In terms of contemporary polemics, we need to be careful of the meaning we attribute to such apparently neutral categories as "genocide." Those who use this term in reference to Jews and Armenians find themselves in precise agreement on the fact that this term designates undeniably the murder, real or fictional, of a race or more generally of a descent group. But the fact that the Nazis wanted to suppress all Jews and that the Turks massacred the Armenians does not relieve us from the need to question ourselves on the appropriateness of applying the term "genocide" to all attempts to physically eliminate a human group. In fact, using this term leads irremediably to validating the idea of the existence, for example, of a Jewish race or an Armenian ethnicity. However, the Armenians do not define themselves as a *genos* any more than do the Jews; neither group defines itself as a race or descent group.[74]

The Jewish community, for example, is structured into subgroups called Ashkenazi and Sephardi, imprecise names whose current meaning is of recent origin.[75] These two categories are themselves subdivided into the many nations with which the different Jewish groups have come to more or less identify (Poland, Germany,

France, Tunisia, Morocco, and others). Beyond the multiple affiliations that segment their community, there have been countless conversions to Judaism throughout Jewish history and, conversely,
many Jews have abandoned their religion or their community in order to convert to another religion or to integrate into a secular culture. Consequently, the effort to define the boundaries of the Jewish community is a continual process of endo- and exo-ascription:
Judaism is not definable independently of the connecting forces that
permanently unite and oppose Jews and non-Jews.

Judaism is therefore not a *sui generis* quality. Not that anti-Semitism abstractly creates the Jew, as Sartre claimed in *Reflections sur
la question juive*, but the fact of being and considering oneself Jewish is inseparable from the way others, the *goyim*, perceive Jews as
Jews. In this sense, Jewish nationalism, whose ultimate form is Zionism, is a recent creation. Of course, Jews existed as a people before
the nineteenth century, but up till then they did not constitute a separate community. Though a common religion existed, the spoken
language and customs differed markedly and the rites were not
strictly identical (Yiddish, Ladino, Ashkenazic, Sephardic, and so
on). There were as many Jewish subgroups as there were Jewish national communities, even if one could distinguish the countries
where Jews had more or less assimilated (France, Germany) and in
which they became "Israelites," from those where the Jews were
subjected to ethnicization and segregation in ghettos and *shtetls*.

The idea of Zionism, as T. Herzl elaborated it, depends on the
need for a common language and land. In fact, Zionism grew out of
nineteenth-century European nationalism, which strongly intensified anti-Semitism and characterized Jewish nationalism as secondary and derivative. It is Zionism that brought the Jews into existence as a universal community functioning beyond individual linguistic, cultural, and religious variations. Zionism is thus a kind of
fundamentalism that posits an eternal and inherent Jewish essence.

Return to Exoticism

The case of the Ethiopian Falashas illustrates particularly well the
continual process of the creation of the Jewish people. As J. Abbink
has shown,[76] the Falashas or Beta Esra'el make up a population with

Couchitic (Agaw) origins, which was influenced by the Ethiopian orthodox Christian tradition which, in turn, has contained many Judaic elements since its fourth-century beginnings. For reasons that were primarily political, the Falashas opposed and inverted the elements of this tradition, both under the guidance of certain Christians who fled the Ethiopian Church and who took refuge with the Beta Esra'el, as well as under the influence of their own religious leaders of Agaw origin. This double phenomenon of borrowing and distorting Christian elements lies at the origin of the Falasha "religion."

Since their rediscovery in 1770, the connection of the Beta Esra'el to Judaism has remained problematic: only in 1975, following an intense fight on the part of their compatriots who had already settled in Israel, did the Jewish state enact the "Law of Return," finally accepting the Falashas as Jews and permitting their immigration.

The example of the Falashas illustrates the profoundly dynamic nature of ethno-religious affiliation as well as the relativity of phenomena of identification. From this point of view, the history of the Beta Esra'el, as that of all Jewish people, does not seem to differ from the mechanisms of ethnic affiliation found in Africa.

In an excellent article on the political culture of ethnicity, B. Jewsiewicki contrasts the scapegoat status characterizing the Jews in Europe with the situation prevailing in a society such as the Congo. There, several groups (West Africans, Greeks, Portuguese) occupied the position of alterity which in Europe characterized the Jews exclusively.[77] Yet the examples mentioned above manifest clearly the unity of ethnological reason in different historical contexts. Only by looking back at itself could ethnology in European society constitute itself historically as a narrative. As narrative, anthropology unfolds in the form of different paradigms—*ethnos/polis*, savage/barbarous/civilized, primitive/industrial, stateless/state—that, from the moment of their formulation, redistribute an entire series of populations into distinct categories. Certainly, each society, no matter how primitive, produces a spontaneous ethnology in that it needs a devalorized alterity to create its own identity or to found its status as a social group. In this sense, the logic of the sacrificial victim described by René Girard is verified.[78] But only in the history of Western thought does the development of ethnological reason reach its limit. German ethnophilosophy is a case in point.

Can one see in the rise of racism, following the example of Louis Dumont, a will of certain groups in modern society to overcome individualism by a surfeit of holism, founded on the purity of the *Volk*?[79] The opposition of holism to individualism reappears in the problematic of the community as, for example, Tönnies and Durkheim have expressed it,[80] which postulates the existence in primitive societies of a collective consciousness that transcends individuals. Rather than accenting the tyranny of the group and the stability of behavior in traditional societies, however, it is more appropriate to describe the ever-strengthening process of mono-identification at work throughout history. Ancient or exotic societies are in fact societies with a self-identity, not, as Durkheim says, because they are ruled by the mechanical solidarity of identical segments and that consequently their members can pass easily from one to the other, but because social states are very plastic.[81] To define the mode of identification of these societies, we could characterize them as fluid groups that, in contrast to the stereotype, leave much room for novelty and invention. Such fluidity is far from characterizing modern societies, which rigidify identity to such an extent that it no longer evolves.

The process of mono-identification presents an obvious contrast with the rise of the literate bureaucratic state that records all identities with more and more precision. But the obsession with identity inevitably produces the opposite effect: the exclusion of those who cannot claim the majority identity. Nineteenth-century nationalism valorized a "high culture" based on writing, a class of professionals of power and the sacred, and a territorial state. Under the influence of this tradition, ethnological reason disqualified other societies and other individuals living in the midst of European societies. All groups, whether exterior or in the minority, not fully part of the territorial nation-state are henceforth relegated either to exotic races or ethnic groups or to domestic minorities.

2 Tensions Within Culture

> A company of porcupines crowded themselves very close
> together one cold winter's day so as to profit by one another's
> warmth and so save themselves from being frozen to death.
> But soon they felt one another's quills, which induced them to
> separate again. And now, when the need for warmth brought
> them nearer together again, the second evil arose once more.
> So that they were driven backwards and forwards from one
> trouble to the other, until they discovered a mean distance at
> which they could most tolerably exist.
> –Schopenhauer, *Parerga et Paralipomena* II, Part XXXI,
>   "Apologues and Paraboles"

The essential characteristic of cultural anthropology is its representation of the world as a plurality of cultures without an established hierarchy: in other words, cultural anthropology is based on what is commonly termed "cultural relativism." According to this conception, each society or culture is deemed to have developed certain institutions or cultural traits. Hence our society has focused on technological development, while a primitive culture might place emphasis on kinship, art, or religion. Thus compared, different existing cultures become principally "incommensurable"; they are organized along the lines of self-contained and arbitrary distributions with no communication between them.

This type of approach trivializes the origin of the notion of culture, as well as the role played recently by anthropology and cultural relativism in Western history. As pointed out by Kroeber and Kluckhohn, the concept of "culture" was first broadly used by the Germans.[1] At the end of the nineteenth century the German nation, because of its lack of political unity, stressed cultural development, while France and England concentrated on economic growth.

This situation explains why, in German, the term *Kultur* takes on two very different meanings.[2] The first is found in the writings of

Kant, where the notion of *Kultur* assumes a universality even when disseminated by individual, privileged nations such as France, for example. The second connotation, on the other hand, as expounded by Herder, is an ethnic one that gives expression to the sense of inferiority felt by the Germans and the Russians vis-à-vis the more advanced nations.

It is this second connotation that has been attributed to the word *Kultur* by American anthropology; it can furthermore be expressed in German by the term *Volk*—often a synonym for "German people."[3] In a similar vein, *Völker*—the plural of *Volk*—tends to designate cultures in general and primitive cultures in particular, *Völkerkunde* being ethnography or the science of primitive societies.

Thus, the term *Volk* can mean both "the people," in the broadest sense possible, and an Other stripped of all value. Mayer points out that *Volk* is synonymous with *goyim* and *gentes*, terms that originally meant "people" in Hebrew and Latin, but which subsequently acquired the meanings "pagans," "Gentiles," and "nations."[4] According to Tönnies, *Kultur* is likewise a synonym of *Volkstum* (nationality, national character) as opposed to *Zivilisation* or *Staatstum*.

This German conception of culture is found in E. B. Tylor's work. In his *Primitive Culture*, Tylor defines culture in the modern, anthropological sense of the term as follows:

> Culture or Civilization, taken in its wide ethnographic sense, is that complex whole that includes knowledge, belief, art, morals, law, custom, and any other capabilities and habits acquired by man as a member of society.[5]

This definition is similar to that expressed by Boas, who says of culture that it

> embraces all manifestations of the social habits of a community, the reactions of the individual insofar as he is affected by the habits of the group in which he lives, and the products of human activities insofar as they are determined by these habits.[6]

This Tylorian and Boasian notion of culture, the cornerstone of American cultural anthropology, would influence a string of researchers such as Kroeber, Kluckhohn, Benedict, Mead, Linton, and Herskovits, most of whom were students of Boas.

The bulk of the work done in American cultural anthropology

rests on the premise that culture comprises three elements: (1) a people's notions of the way things ought to be; (2) their conception of the way their group actually behaves; and (3) what does in fact occur, as objectively determined.[7] Cultural anthropology thus agrees on the general meaning of the term "culture" and on the equality of societies past and present, viewed on the same level. This, however, obliterates the fact that the notion of culture is the outcome of an unequal development or an asymmetrical relation of forces between different political structures.

The notion of culture could only arise in Germany and Russia, due to the inferiority experienced by the aristocracy as compared to France and England.[8] This was not because, as Dumont would have it, the French are men first and French second while the Germans are German first and men second,[9] but rather because, in eighteenth-century France, "people" and "nation" were notions applied to civil society as opposed to government.[10] But in Germany, these words were employed by Herder and Fichte as bounded terms of exclusion imbued with sentiments at once anti-French, anti-Catholic, and anti-Semitic.[11] Having drawn up an outline of the origin of the concept of culture and shown the ties linking it to the notions of race, ethnicity, people, and nation, we should note that American cultural anthropology has been strongly tied to this concept.

Bastide points out in *Anthropologie appliquée* (*Applied Anthropology*) that American cultural anthropology developed within the framework of European colonialism and as a reaction to it.[12] With the decolonization process underway, American cultural anthropology took an evolutionary turn (L. White). Bastide states that the stress placed on cultural relativism by American anthropology follows a period during which the assimilation of the Indians was to have been brought about by a "development policy," that is to say, a policy of governmental aid to communities. It was precisely the failure of this policy of intervention that pushed American leaders to develop a new policy, this time based on cultural relativism. From this perspective, Bastide concludes:

> Each community is . . . endowed with a culture of its own, which is historically formed as a result of the actual interaction between the evolving human group and the external milieu which enable the needs of the group to be satisfied.[13]

The differences between Indian and American cultures do not pre-
clude political and economic integration, but this integration is subject to free choice, and funds are distributed to the Indians in such a
way as to enable them to acculturate and Westernize, should they so
desire.[14]

The attitude of American leaders concerning the Indian communities is not unlike that prevailing in the West as regards developing countries. For decades stress was placed on the creation of large-
scale development projects administered by international organizations and local governments. Recently, however, the transition was
made to a concept of development based on peasant initiatives and
nongovernmental organizations. As in the American case, the relative failure of the development projects–because their benefits were
mainly reaped by the ruling groups whose power was dependent on
the control of the state structures–has made apparent the need for
peasants to assume responsibility for themselves, and has led to the
promotion of small projects set up by nonstate organizations.[15]

In both cases, if differences are respected and communities allowed to take responsibility for themselves, development will take
place under optimal conditions. This leads to the "dilemma of cultural relativism": according to Bastide, under the pretext of re-
specting the autonomy of each culture, practicing cultural relativism amounts to assimilating and integrating, with as little effort
as possible, those communities that had at first to be constituted as
different.[16] That this approach should have taken root in the United
States as a result of a failure does not alter the fact that, in practice,
cultural anthropology results in an applied anthropology, such as
that of Herskovits, and is typified by the very ethnocentric vision it
seeks to combat.[17]

The subsequent course of events does not entirely validate
Bastide's stand, since, far from disintegrating along with colonization, culturalism has, on the contrary, developed to a considerable
extent in American anthropology. Sahlins, for example, after un-
dergoing a Marxist period around 1968 and expounding a theory of
the "domestic mode of production,"[18] subsequently turned to other
areas. A more recent work is fully devoted to refuting Marxist
thought on the basis of ethnological data and also through data
drawn from our own society.[19] According to Sahlins, it is in fact cul-

ture, distinct from practical or utilitarian reasons, that is the foundation of any society; a culture is built on a system of symbols that is the integrating schema of that culture. Taking fashion in American society as an example, Sahlins maintains that its different elements constitute a system of oppositions that correspond to the different social classes. An object will thus have no inherent use-value, or rather, its use-value will not be comparable to that of another object; this use-value is in fact seen as purely symbolic and therefore arbitrary. With acumen reminiscent of Baudrillard in *Le Miroir de la production*,[20] Sahlins denounces the futility of any political economy that is not a political economy of the symbol. Any transhistorical interpretation of the course of humanity, and particularly the evolutionism traditionally associated with Marxism, is thus cast aside. Each culture supposedly harbors the keys to its own interpretation, even if there are means of passing from one to the other.

Geertz likewise falls into this category; he states that in order to explain social phenomena, one must situate them within the frameworks of local consciousness in such a way as to clarify forms of comprehension that are not our own.[21] Ethnography thus relates to literary criticism, even to hermeneutics, whereas anthropology consists of translating other cultures into our own cultural system.[22] Rather than defining Geertz's position as a form of structuralism, it would be more correct to call it a sort of transculturalism or comparativism that relies on an intimate knowledge rather than the unconscious perception of several cultures.

Whether the issue be structuralism or transculturalism, the anthropological operation consists of comparing cultural objects constructed to meet the requirements of the theory in question. This Leibnizian approach, which allows one to move from concrete to abstract universals, in fact presupposes the existence of a universal abstract (God or knowledge), in other words, a comparativist matrix that generates the different elements to be compared. In this sense, one can concede along with Dumont that all societies are holistic, for does not comparativism itself provide a unified global vision of the different cultures?[23] It is not, therefore, the existence of different cultures that leads to comparativism, but comparativism that constitutes different cultures as such.

Does postulating the existence of isolated cultures not neglect the fact that these cultures cannot exist independently of one another? The boundaries of each culture are in fact fixed by an outside party playing the role of observer and thus depend on the point of view employed. The image that springs irresistibly to mind is that of the zoom lens of a camera, alternately enlarging and narrowing the operator's field of vision.[24] In effect, if one can define a custom or a tradition as belonging to one culture, it is because such a culture has been constituted, or that one constituted oneself as a bearer of this culture. When belonging to a given culture, one is not conscious of living that culture as such. Lacking the benefit of an outside perspective, the members of society X or Y merely carry out various dispersed practices that are not subsumed by a specific culture. The designation of one or another culture thus results from an objectifying external viewpoint. This in turn creates the scale of "Others" that history has categorized: the Savage, the Barbarian, the Pagan, the Gentile, the Infidel, the Negro, and so on.

Leiris demonstrates how the concept of African art does not exist for the Africans any more than that of European sculpture exists for Westerners. The apparent cohesiveness of African art is no more than an optical illusion; it exists only by virtue of its opposition to European art and is no more than the product of an aesthetic appropriation, by European painters of the first half of the twentieth century, of magico-religious objects taken out of context and placed in the same category.[25] This objectifying and globalizing position is the product of power relationships: it suppresses cultural differences to the extent that one can conceptualize a Dogon, Bambara, or Chokwe art form. Returning to the image of a camera, the enlargement of the photograph, and later the ethnologists' focus on smaller details and more defined cultures, makes the new classification just as controversial, although it appears to rest on a greater degree of scientific objectivity.

Granted, the delineation of different cultures as "imagined communities" is not absolutely arbitrary.[26] This is not because different cultures exist "objectively," as it were, but because their establishment is a recent historical process, itself a result of the relation of forces between those who determine and those who are determined.

As Anderson suggests, the birth of certain European nations can be attributed to precisely these principles.[27] Prior to the period

1800 to 1850, Bulgarian was no different from Serb, Croat, or Slav; Ukrainian was a different form of Russian; and Swedish was spoken in Finland. A large number of European languages and cultures have, in fact, been created by intellectuals (historians, lexicographers, grammarians, philologists, writers, musicians, and so forth). By transcribing languages, customs, folklore, and music, and by spreading their writings, these intellectuals contributed to the emergence during the eighteenth and nineteenth centuries of European nationalism, as well as its "by-products," the cultures of ethnic minorities. The Arab emergence in Lebanon, for example, is part of the same process. It is clear that the production of different nonliterate cultures of the world is the work of European domination and its corollaries: writing, schooling, urbanization, the emergence of a literate class, and the creation of new nations.[28]

Consequently, one of the principal acquisitions of anthropology is the cultural logic that results from the dominance of the literate cultures over the oral cultures. We think in terms of cultural relativism today, not because we acknowledge the originality or singularity of different cultures, but because our predecessors defined a limited series of societies for us.

Some of the unities have disappeared, not because their members or descendants no longer exist, but because they did not capture the imagination of the social actors. They were not in demand by individuals situated outside these societies (migrants, intellectuals, town-dwellers, and so on); they did not become "cultures." For culture to become a culture, it must be capable of appealing to certain social actors who share a common response to its symbolism. This applies to those cultures that have triumphed and flowered into nationalisms, as it does to cultures that have been conquered and relegated to the rank of ethnic groups or cultural minorities.

Thus the course of history, at least that of the last few centuries since the age of capitalism, could be analyzed not just in terms of the class struggle, as Marx understood it, but also in terms of the struggle for recognition of identity under conditions of scarcity. One merely needs to look at certain recent events to realize how easily one can slide from the vertical order (the class struggle) to the horizontal order (the existence of juxtaposed cultures) as in, for example, Soviet Armenia and the Baltic countries. Yet one could argue

that although all these cultures may merely be products of the imagination, of ethnography and colonialism, and that their external
representations may well have been reappropriated by the social actors themselves, the fact remains that they do exist. The practices
of excision among the Bambara,[29] or that of cannibalism among the
Tupinamba of Brazil, both clearly manifest cultural differences that
distinguish these societies from our own. It would be simplistic to
maintain that these differences cannot be denied. In any event, anthropology defends the validity of its fields of observation by an inventory of precisely these differences. It is not so much the existence
of these differences in itself that causes the problem, but rather the
way the anthropological field represents them and accounts for
them. What constitutes a culture? The question cannot be asked independently of the interrelationships existing among different cultures, nor of the fixing of such cultures in writing and by the emergence of a particular form of state: the centralized bureaucratic
state.

Culture as the Result of a Relation of Forces

A particular culture can be conceived, in the first place, as a set of
scattered cultural traits; yet this definition is problematic in that it
favors the diffusionist's approach. In effect, cultural traits are not
distributed haphazardly: for a culture to "set," it must constitute a
symbolic schema that can be recognized and can trigger feelings of
emotion in a subject. In this respect, the comparison that naturally
springs to mind is that of language. A language is articulated and
each language has a grammar, that is to say a set of rules, written or
unwritten, appropriated by a subject and thereby making that subject a "locutor." The model of language as a grammar has, up to now,
consciously or unconsciously, influenced the way anthropologists
apprehend the culture or cultures they study. However, in addition
to the fact that it has not yet been ascertained whether this conception of language as a set of rules can fully account for linguistic phenomena—as has been shown by sociolinguists—language is also a social state resulting from a relation of forces between dominant and
subordinate groups or between juxtaposed groups. It would therefore appear that this viewpoint is even less applicable to culture.

Culture, as opposed to language, can only be considered as a set of incorporated rules by not taking into account how it has come to be, and by erasing the conditions of its very creation. To lay cultures "flat" is to "photograph" them at a given instant and to refuse to consider them as living entities. It is precisely by overlooking the conditions of production of a culture that one can treat a culture in such a way.

The production of culture contains two aspects: an external production as well as an internal one. A given culture cannot be grasped as such unless it has been singled out arbitrarily and dissociated from the intercultural tapestry into which it was woven. Cultures are not situated one next to the other like windowless, doorless Leibnizian monads: they fall into place within a whole that is itself a structured field of relations. If one envisages a given cultural area—a revealing geographical metaphor—one cannot gratuitously assume that the cultures present in this area are simply juxtaposed, or that links established between them are purely fortuitous.

The definition of a given culture is, in fact, the result of a relation of intercultural forces: the culture that dominates spatially maintains the ability to assign other cultures to their respective places within the system, thereby making them into subordinate or determined cultures. Thus there are cultures that have the power to name other cultures and to circumscribe their own field of expression, while others are only capable of being named. Nevertheless, the system is by no means static; formerly subordinate cultures become dominant while others, like stars, are born only to disappear. The modification of the relation of forces within the field, as well as the blossoming and disappearing of cultures, accounts for the changes that occur in each subcultural system taken separately.

Although traditionally a given culture was associated with either a patrilineal or matrilineal kinship system, we know, for example, that a society can experience several kinship systems during its history. It may move from a patrilineal system to a matrilineal one, thereby reversing the order of succession adhered to ever since the emergence of evolutionist theories.[30]

The recognition of the evolution of kinship systems goes some way toward addressing the cultural-structuralist paradigm. The latter consists in selecting elements in each culture with comparativist aims in mind, thereby preventing any understanding of the dynamics of these systems, not to mention the relation of forces that explains the passage from one kinship system to another.

What holds true for kinship certainly applies to religion as well. Different cultures, in particular the more primitive ones, display striking religious dynamism. Here too intercultural relations condition the development of religious life. Primitive religions are actually systems of pragmatic, plastic, and political mythico-ritual practices. Granted, the very term "ritual" invariably evokes the strength and permanence of tradition; but the trade in fetishes and masks, which many ethnologists have recorded, provides ample proof that religious innovation is of much greater importance in primitive cultures than in our own.

The same can be demonstrated in the political field, for example, for the same society can move from a centralized political system to a segmentary one and vice versa.[31] As for material culture and the economy, these sectors are likewise subject to changes, notably those concerning the adoption of new techniques, new monies, and new products. Borrowing of cultural traits notwithstanding, this should not be worked into the framework of a diffusionist type of analysis that could only consider them as the product of a purely mechanical hiving off of the population. Nor does it suffice to emphasize the dynamic character of culture, as does Herskovits, after having studied it as a static phenomenon.[32] The error made by cultural anthropologists consists in not treating culture as an unstable medium, the perpetuation of which is essentially random and aleatory.

Each culture, in addition, results from a relation of internal forces. The struggle for identities among groups occurs and unfolds in a debate concerning their distribution within a given culture, in other words, a social unit conceived as a political formation. The struggle for identity is of course particularly strong in class-based societies, where the competition for social status is clearly defined. Nevertheless, this battle for social recognition also exists in segmentary and lineage-based societies, which contain divisions between "first settlers" and "conqueror," between free men and slaves. This opposes the Durkheimian view that in these societies, a sole ideology or "collective consciousness" encompasses the totality of the culture. The "collective consciousness " or cultural community is, in reality, merely a retrospective optical illusion resulting from a codification arranged from the exterior.[33]

The so-called primitive societies should more generally be viewed as much more open than ours for the following reasons. They are not, as Goody demonstrated, constrained by written records and, above all, they are not subject to centralized bureaucratic states that capitalize on the written word and serve both as the guarantor and witness of social changes. Once again, tradition and culture are merely optical illusions resulting precisely from the paucity of written sources relative to "primitive societies" and the lack of interest anthropologists have shown in this problem. Nothing could be less traditional than a primitive society, and to impute tradition to such societies is merely to push them into the background and to exclude them from our own society. Just as evolutionist anthropology fabricated contemporary ancestors, it also ascribed tradition, that is to say orality, to certain societies in order to better deny them their own historicity. The best-known example in which tradition is imputed to such societies appears in the use anthropologists make of the comment "Because we have always done so," which they get in response to the question: "Why do you do such and such a thing?" This question and answer provide anthropologists with the comforting conviction of the strength of tradition, just as they reinforce the power of the elders. In fact, the ethnologist has detected the latest stage of tradition or even the result of a "negotiation" of a relation of forces, which may be called into question at a later date; in reality, social status or position is constantly subject to transaction. Far from being fixed entities embedded in immutable categories, they are renegotiated continually according to locally prevailing situations.

Let us take the example of precolonial western Sudan and, in particular, what is called the Mande or Mandingo cultural sphere. The analysis of this example will allow for more than just a general outline specifying our perception of culture or identity as transactional. This Mande cultural sphere is a construction manufactured by ethnologists, Maurice Delafosse in particular. It derives from the decontextualization and the artificial synthesis of the various political units that are the only concrete entities that can be observed at a given moment. These political units may take the form of a village, a confederation of villages, a chiefdom, or kingdom. It is the mode of constitution that explains the political organization, not the economic system. In precolonial western Sudan, therefore, slavery as a mode of production will not reveal the nature of each political unit; slavery, in fact, can be imposed from the outside in the same way as the political unit under consideration. Both are the result of a relationship of intersocietal forces.

Each chiefdom (*kafo*) is simultaneously the same as, and different from, its neighbors. The differences are due to the hazards of history, that is, the particular combination of elements that existed at the time of each chiefdom's formation. On a more abstract level, however, all chiefdoms have this in common, namely, that they appear to result from a hierarchy of lineages. The classical or standard expression of this hierarchy of lineages takes the form of an opposition between the lineages of first settlers or agriculturalists and the dynasties of conquerors, the holders of political power. These first settlers are "first" in name only, and were themselves preceded by a whole series of populations that were the object of successive expulsions.

In the Keleyadugu chiefdom in southern Mali, for example, it would appear that the group stretching back the furthest in oral tradition is that of the Kuruman.[34] This group was annihilated, expelled, or absorbed by the Tarawele, who arrived at a later stage to take power. The Tarawele were subsequently subjugated by the Bagayogo, who demoted them to the rank of "animistic" priests (*somaw*) and of landowners (*dugukolotigiw*). In this way, a division of tasks was established between the Bagayogo and the Tarawele, consolidated by a pact of *senankuya* (a "joking relationship") that prohibits phyical contact, sexual relations, and, of course, matrimonial relations. These *senankuya* pacts also codify the ties between certain nobles and certain castes, suggesting a functional and perhaps historical homology between the first occupants and the people belonging to certain castes.

This bifunctional ideology thus places the first settlers, the landowners and ritualists, in opposition to the conquerors, holders of power. It would perhaps be possible to come up with a realistic reading of this bifunctional ideology. Perhaps the "first settlers" do in fact correspond to a prior stratum of population. It would be more to the point, however, to view this division as a structural schema, a category of local or regional political thought (Bambara, Mossi). From this "cultural structuralist" perspective, such a division would simply serve to reinforce power relations at a conceptual level.

First settlers and conquerors are entirely necessary, since the exercise of power throughout the Sudano-Sahelian area rests on an alliance between the people of power and the people of the earth. Real, genuine power—the power of the savanna bushland outside the villages—is actually considered to belong to the people of the earth, who are also the masters of ritual. In oral tradition, the first settlers are always described as devils, creatures with long hair, people with powerful charms; and access to their haunted villages is described as very dangerous. The terms may change; these people of the earth may have been the ancient wielders of power. Regardless, it is the relationship between people of power and people of the earth, and the permanence of this division, that must be taken into account.

Can one bypass this cultural-structuralist vision of things? In one sense the structuralists will always be in a better position than the historians, for history, Lévi-Strauss has shown, is an infinite regression.[35] The only means of transcending the structuralist position is to proceed to a simulation and comparison with related phenomena. In reality, the archetype of first settlers/conquerors, like all archetypes, can function as such only because it has been disconnected from the temporal flux and the spatial whole into which it falls.

The archetype has been perpetuated merely because the conditions for its creation have been forgotten. In the same manner, the pact (*jo*) or the joking relationship (*senankuya*) appear to be the outward expression of a social contract or institution only because the underlying relation of forces has been obscured.

In this context, institutions are simply canonized practices that, far from having functioned for all eternity, should be understood as deriving from a complex and fluctuating relation of forces. The problem lies in reproducing a norm as a sanction or transaction of a relation of forces. The postulate that tradition is perpetuated by a sort of characteristic inertia must be discarded; rather, one must look into the reasons for its relative persistence. When an ethnologist isolates a norm or an institution, he is isolating a practice that has been consecrated by the society. By presenting this norm or institution in the guise of tradition or custom, he merely reinforces this canonization.

It is possible that binary oppositions, such as that of the people of power/the people of the earth, are structural oppositions analogous to the Indo-European ideology of the three functions analyzed by Georges Dumézil. Perhaps this opposition is characteristic of all the great empires in this region (Mali, Sonrai)? Perhaps it has been transmitted from one empire to another through the various exchanges that occurred between these political formations? One can safely assume the existence of a common civilization throughout Sudano-Sahelian West Africa, a common civilization of which one finds traces in the form of cultural traits and linguistic terms spread throughout several entities that the field of anthropology considers as distinct cultures or ethnic groups: Minyanka, Senufo, Bambara, or Mossi. Perhaps one could even go so far as to hypothesize an original indistinction, a common base of cultures that have subsequently diverged.[36]

For this perspective to be applicable, a radical change of method is called for. In particular, the whole would be favored at the expense of the various parts, so as to establish a sort of Benvenistian "Glossary of West African Institutions." Yet even if such a culture or civilization were to be identified, its permanence or traditional character would still be left unaccounted for. This is precisely where the shoe pinches, since anthropologists have always tended to depict tradition as an intangible notion, whereas in fact it represents the end result of all previous negotiations. In this sense, the "tradition" of anthropologists, like the *longue durée* of historians, amounts to retrospective or self-fulfilling prophecies.[37]

In reality, this "product" is constantly reproduced, perhaps because the general conditions of its production have remained unchanged for centuries. Thus the theories of power in Mali today, for example, differ little from those of the past, no doubt because the present Malian state is analogous to that of past political formations: the relations of force between people of power and people of the earth (the peasants of today) remain fundamentally unchanged. They continue to be defined and characterized by the plundering of peasant wealth. By inverting the relation of the past to the present,

one thus arrives at a conception of culture as a contemporary construction rather than a heritage of the past.[38]

Culturalism as Fundamentalism

The perception of social facts through "traditions," "customs,"
"cultures," or "nations," in other words in terms of essence or substance, requires, as Renan saw, that one overlook the conditions of
creation of the entity in question, and that one project the present
into the past.[39] In any form of culturalism, as in any form of nationalism for that matter, an element of fundamentalism lies dormant.
The term "fundamentalism" initially designated the American
Protestant sects seeking to preserve the purity and timeless truths
of the Scriptures against the threat posed by liberalism, socialism,
and communism.[40]

Ever since this notion was popularized by Barr, it has been applied to a whole series of religious (Islam, Judaism, etc.), political
(nationalism), ethnic, and cultural phenomena.[41] Fundamentalisms
are the result of an external viewpoint, but they are also used by the
actors to designate themselves. Fundamentalisms are part of modern life and therefore presuppose the existence of the state and the
nation. Based on the sacred texts, they strive to establish a doctrine
of truth and hence appear to be essentialist. Finally, confined within
themselves, fundamentalist movements grow rigid in their opposition to global society.[42] Fundamentalisms thus represent the quin-
tessence of culturalism, since they make use of the written word and
inject the present into the past. One can thus compare the religious
fundamentalisms flourishing today to nationalisms, ethnicities,[43]
and more generally, to all invented social categories–"the people,"
for example–that make extensive use of the diffusion of the written
word in order to exist.[44] Capitalist development via the printed word
and the bureaucratic state leads to the proliferation and fetishiza-
tion of all identities.

It would not be invalid, therefore, when looking at Mali, for example, to compare the relations between "first settlers" and "conquerors" in the Mande cultural sphere to those between Moslem
"reformists" and "traditionalists." The categories of "first settlers"
and "traditionalists" are not absolutes: they are constructions of the

mind and exist only within the framework of a binary opposition. Only within this opposition can the notion of "first settlers" or of "traditionalists" take on its full significance and so become relative. The "conquerors," on the one hand, and the "reformists" on the other, create these categories themselves so that one will always be someone else's "first settlers," "traditionalists," or "pagans." The existence of the Mande political culture as well as that of the Moslem Malian culture are therefore the result of a permanent tension that lies at their very basis.

Granted, one could raise the objection that these two fundamentalisms, if indeed there be fundamentalism, diverge on one essential point: Moslem culture is a culture of the book, while Mande culture is largely oral. Our hypothesis is, however, that today it is virtually impossible to speculate about nonwritten cultures, as present-day identities are defined almost exclusively by literate actors. To a certain extent, this allows for the assimilation of the Mande culture into the Moslem one.

The only noticeable difference between religious and cultural fundamentalism in Mali is this: although the "first settlers" were originally conquerors, and although the history of settlement in the area may appear to be that of a succession of population expulsions, the category of "traditionalist," even in a pejorative context, refers back to a state that did not in fact exist or prevail prior to the spread of Islam.

While the traditionalists are viewed as mere "mixes" and pagans in the eyes of the fundamentalists, the fact remains that paganism, in a pre-Moslem setting, did exist in Mali, even though it does not follow that one can infer from this the existence of some original "Bambara religion."[45] The fierce insistence of the Wahabis on distinguishing themselves from other Malians, Moslem or not, can best be understood if seen in terms of the recent conversion of numerous Malians to Islam. At the same time, it requires constant reference to the great empires (Ghana, Mali, Sonrai) as political formations linked to this area.

Any anthropological study of a Malian population that does not take into account such phenomena will fail to grasp the role of each society, culture, and ethnic group or identity as elements determined by the whole. Only by taking the state, the nation, universalist religions, and printed matter as starting points can one grasp the different cultures of today. The cultures of this planet, dispersed as they are, can exist as such only because of the repression of the truths presiding at their inception. It is not memory, therefore, that creates culture, but the obscuring of the tensions that made living entities of these different identities. In this regard, a culture never manifests itself as strongly as when it is in the process of disappearing. What then is the situation of precolonial cultures or cultures prior to the large-scale diffusion of writing? The modes of precolonial gatherings, identities, societies, or cultures were the subject of constant negotiations and debate. Possibly this debate on the appearance of a culture is what actually constitutes it as an identity. For there to be an identity, society, culture, or ethnic group, it is not necessary for all parties to agree on what defines this culture; it is sufficient that they are able to establish the terms of identity as a problem about which they can debate or negotiate. Put differently, one could hold that identity is the agreement on the very subject of disagreement.

Each culture has a point of reference–Fulani, Bambara, Malinke, and so on–that can be appropriated by a particular social category to which it will lay claim or that it will defend. The "cultural structuralist" would consider this referent to be a category that endures through time, even though the identity in question is the subject of debate, or the result of a relation of forces. However, nothing points to this referent remaining identical throughout the course of history. The fact that this referent may extend to groups that did not previously lay claim to such an identity, or that it was abandoned by other groups, amply proves that at issue is an historical product. The referent is therefore more than an immediate fact of social life; it is the stake over which social groups enter into struggle. Individual identities (last name, first name, nickname, and so on),[46] as well as collective ones, are constantly defined by the internal and external relations within a region. The ability to name, to give a first name, surname, or nickname, is of course essential; it reveals the rifts and the relations of forces at work within a given social field. Social stakes constantly manifest themselves in this ability to name and the possibility of refusing to be named.[47]

Culture as a collective identity, as a classification, is thus continuously the subject of a political struggle, of a struggle for recognition that takes the shape of an incessant reclassification, such that even the appearance of the society must be subjected to constant re-definition.

If, as stated by Georges Balandier, every society is open to reappraisal,[48] then this is due to the conflicts inherent to it. These have the effect of endlessly redefining the terms under which the agents envisage the debate over the ties that bind them to each other. The social contract is the common area of conflict, the minimal antagonistic space that ties the social actors to one another. In the absence of these ties, there is no culture, no society.

3 Fulani, Bambara, Malinke: A System of Transformations

> What if the names of real or fictional ancestors constituted in their onomastic substance the only indisputable fact?
> –Berque, *L'Intérieur du Maghreb*

Populations classically recognized as Fulani, Bambara, and Malinke inhabit the region we have studied. They have customarily been considered three ethnic groups merely juxtaposed in space. We propose to demonstrate that they constitute in effect a system of transformations. This threefold schema of identity appears as "onomastic emblems" that the actors appropriate and abandon in aleatory fashion according to political contingencies.[1]

Fascination with the Fulani

The history of Fulani studies is a long disappointing pursuit of a chimera: the phenotype of a pure Fulani race that can be assigned to Fulani societies that existed historically. The construction of the Fulani race or ethnic group cannot be analyzed independently of nineteenth-century and early twentieth-century historiography and anthropology, both of which accent the confrontation of races and the theory of conquest.[2]

Just as European history has been broadly interpreted as the history of Aryan or Indo-European domination, French history has been reconstructed as the conquest of the Gallo-Romans by the Franks and their ensuing conflicted relations. The principle of racial struggle, promulgated by nineteenth-century European historians, has contaminated historiography in general, including the Dorian-Ionian conflicts in ancient Greece. Even Africa did not escape this theoretical affliction. We base our idea of Africa on an image of different *types* of societies in existence on the continent, as well as of the *stages* of development they have reached. This image derives from the view that a certain number of races occupied successively the positions of conqueror and conquered.

The theory of races and conquest explains the fascination that Europeans, particularly ethnographers, have continually felt for populations classified as red or white, Berber or Semitic. By assigning a historical role to such populations (Fulani, Moors, Tuareg), it was possible to explain the differences between savage or barbarian and civilized, primitive tribe and evolved community, anarchist and empire builder, paleo-Negroid or Sudanese and Hamite, pagan and Moslem, and stateless societies and state societies.[3]

Attempts to identify the pure Fulani race began as a long expedition in the nineteenth century with the physical anthropologists and the specialists of *Völkerkunde*.[4] It continues to this day. Certain anthropologists freely include skull measurements in their data, or suggest a continuity between the herders depicted in the Saharan Tassili n'Ajer frescoes and the nomadic Fulani of West Africa today.

The pure, true Fulani is the red, nomadic Fulani, *Badaado* with nappy hair who considers himself white and who practices *pulaaku*, that is, the manner of conducting oneself as Fulani. This manner, a sort of Spinozist *conatus*, is characterized by resignation (*munyal*), intelligence (*hakkillo*),[5] courage (*cuusal*), but especially discretion or reserve (*seemteende*). As M. Dupire has remarked,[6] the first three values are found in many other African societies, but so is the last one as well. These values characterize all aristocratic West African societies, whether sedentary or nomadic. They could in no way genuinely define anything unique to the Fulani. If it is difficult to identify the Fulani by something other than the language, which has many dialects, the task becomes even more complicated when one considers seminomad or sedentary pagan Fulani living among blacks and speaking a language other than the one assigned to them.

For this reason, Crozals, an essayist fascinated by the Fulani, disputes Caillié's claim to have met Fulani people in Ouassoulou who "did not speak the language of the Foulah" and who "worshiped fetishes, the moon, the sun, and the stars."[7]

The innumerable historical expressions of Fulani essence are perceived as so many cases of treason in relation to the model, because the identity of the group can be defined only in a system of relations involving neighboring identities. The term Fulani (*Peul*) is itself ambiguous. According to Boilat, it should be Wolof.[8] "Fula," which gave the fifteenth- and sixteenth-century Portuguese Foul, Fulos, or Fulas, is a Mandingo category according to Monteil, just as is the term *pullo* (plural *fulbe*).[9]

In analyzing the concepts and institutions that supposedly characterize the Fulani as an ethnic group, one finds numerous terms to be of Arabic origin or common to other languages in the region, such as the terms *satigi*, *saltigui*, or *siratik*, which designate the sovereigns of certain West African Fulani kingdoms. At first glance, this expression, borrowed from the Mandingo language and meaning "master of the road," refers to the herders or tenders of the flocks, the traditional activity of Fulani chiefs.[10] But how accurate is it to see this as a borrowing? Before asking if the Fulani have borrowed from the Mandingo or the Mandingo from the Fulani, we must first question the validity of any idea of borrowing that follows from a partition between Fulani and Mandingo.

What was just said regarding the notion of *satigi* can apply to many other Fulani cultural traits. Dupire notes that the eastern Fulani nomads fight with a Tuareg spear and that the *bori* cults of possession are also found among the Hausa.[11] These examples, to mention only a few, show what several anthropologists have observed, namely, that one can become Fulani or Toucouleur,[12] and that, inversely, the Fulani will convert ethnically to become Hausa or Bambara.[13]

Rather than asking, for example, how the Fulani archetype–the Bodaado pagan practicing ritual flagellation (*soro*)–hybridizes to give rise to other avatars of the Fulani ethnic group: black, Islamized, city dwellers, and so on, it would be more appropriate to postulate a primary multiethnic situation that would include, for example, those people speaking the related languages of Fulani, Serer, Wolof, Mandingo, or the Volta languages.[14] A primary multiethnic situation would have given rise to the different ethnic entities in the forms eventually fixed by colonial thought.

Of course, in the case of the Fulani as well as the Tuareg or the Nile-Hamites, it is much easier for ethnologists or essayists to give free rein to their fantasies since their subjects are for the most part nomadic herders of flocks and these have always excited the imagination of authors craving pseudo-historical narratives. It is known since Khazanov's work, however, that nomadism guarantees neither autonomy nor purity.[15] As he has shown in a broadly comparative study, nomadic societies function in an extensively heteronomous fashion and cannot be understood independently of the surrounding context. In this respect, the Fulani nomads do not constitute a self-sufficient enclave or a prehistoric holdover any more than do the other herding peoples. Quite the opposite situation prevails. They are the result of a complex historical grouping that includes sedentary agricultural societies, long-distance trade, and political states. What astonishes researchers is this rigid conception of a Fulani essence, given the ubiquity of the Fulani themselves, who, though sometimes part of peasant societies, define themselves at other times as empire builders.

Since the Fulani are a social production, it is impossible to assign a single referent to this ethnonym. In fact, as many meanings of the term Fulani exist as there are actual expressions of a Fulani essence. These run from a tentative integration into a chain of sedentary societies for nomadic Fulani, to their disappearance as a semiautonomous ethnic group, and to their integration into the statutory network of a large state.[16]

Contrary to the racial and ethnological perspective defended by a certain number of Fulani specialists, no Fulani substance exists that eventually gave rise to the different avatars of Fulani-ness by degenerating, and interbreeding with neighboring dark-skinned people. As historical beings, the Fulani result from a double process of absorption and elimination, or of coming together and expulsion,[17] which encapsulates a large part of West African history just as it does probably of many other cultural units. It is all the more true, then, that the past of this subcontinent cannot be analyzed as the product of a confrontation between the Fulani and other populations. B. Barry has shown that, in the case of the Futa Jalon, for example, the *jihad* of 1725-50 cannot be understood in terms of a Fulani-Jallonke conflict, but rather as the constitution of a class-structured society based on Islam, a movement in which the Mandingo marabouts actively participated.

An examination of Fulani history from any region, but specifically the history of the Wasolon, requires, then, a total reversal of perspective: the most ancient texts regarding the whole of the area under investigation need to be consulted. Of course, fifteenth- and sixteenth-century West African Fulani history is difficult to reconstruct because, except for the *Tarikh*,[18] we possess only the meager sources left by the Portuguese.[19] However slim, these sources, combined with information in the oral tradition, suffice to challenge an essentialist and substantialist vision of the Fulani.[20] The different accounts convey the impression of a primary mixing from the earliest beginnings, and this makes it absurd to even pose the question of Fulani identity.

The history of the spread of the Fulani, that is, the history of their migrations, cannot be understood independently of two major events: Sonni Ali's struggle against the Masina Fulani and the wandering of Tengela and Koli Tengela throughout the western Sudan. It must be noted that in the *Tarikh*, as well as in the Portuguese authors, it is never a question of the Fulani per se, but rather of the *Fulan* or *Fulani*, terms of Sonrai, Hausa, or Arabic origin.[21] In certain cases, we find the expression *Beïdan*, which means "the Whites."[22] Fulan, Fulani, or Beïdan are specifically involved in the extortions committed by Sonni Ali, sovereign of the Sonrai from 1465 to about 1492. This king reputedly disliked the Fulani and was depicted in the *Tarikh el-Fettach* as particularly impious:

> There were no enemies he [Sonni Ali] hated as violently as he hated the Fulani and [he] could not stand to look at a Fulani without killing him, no matter who he was, educated or ignorant, man or woman. He accepted no educated Fulani in either the political administration or the magistracy. He decimated the Sangaré tribe, allowing the survival of only as many as could stand under a single tree.[23]

Sonni Ali's drive to exterminate the Fulani might appear to be the result of an ethnic confrontation between the Fulani and the Sonrai. However, on a closer reading of the *Tarikh el-Fettach*, it seems that Sonni Ali's hostility toward the Fulani has less to do with them as Fulani than with their being Moslem. The passage following the one cited above supports this view: "He would seize a free Moslem and present him to other Moslems, claiming thereby to liberate them."[24]

In reality, if Sonni Ali objected so strongly to the Fulani or the Beïdan, it was not because they were all Moslem—far from it—but because among them there were numerous educated men, such as môddibo Ouâra, whom he killed at Dâ.[25] His hostility toward this clerical class extended to the whole group. Whatever his motive, the Fulani extermination most certainly pushed those who were defined as such to leave Masina for Wasolon or for other areas.

The great migration undertaken by Tengela and Koli added to this dispersal and modified the political balance among different western Sudanese populations.[26] Led by Dulo Demba, the Foul army crossed upper Senegal and Gambia around 1450 and then went south as far as the Rio Grande where it was defeated by the Beafada. The survivors regrouped at nearby Futa Jalon. With this dispersal originated a new political venture and a refoundation. An escapee from the first wave or an earlier immigrant, Tengela became king around 1460. He and his adopted son Koli[27] founded the dynasty known as Denyanké or Denyankobbe, names that apparently came from the Jolof region where they spent some time.[28] At the head of an army of Malinke, Badyar, and Bassari slaves,[29] Tengela (according to tradition, the son of Sunjata) and his "son" Koli left their base in Futa Jalon, ravaged Wuli, and attacked Mali.[30]

Around 1510 the Denyanke became rulers of Galam, which Koli left to subdue the Futa Toro where, like his descendants, he took the title *satigi*, *saltigi*, or *siratique*, which in Mandingo (as we have seen) means "master of the road."[31] For his part, Tengela went to Kingi, which he subdued but was unable to rule for long because Askia Mohammed, sovereign of Sonrai, defeated him in 1512.[32] The Jakite Saabashi of Gwanan, already shown to be "false Fulani," nevertheless claim Tengela for their ancestor, just as do the Jalo of Sananfula, who are in fact Banmana Samake, of Kurlamini provenance.[33] The large-scale housecleaning provoked by the events just described—anti-Moslem persecutions, formation of states, conflicts between kingdoms, and so on—as well as those taking place later (the jihad of Futa Jalon, the *dina* of Seku Amadu in Masina), offer a clearer account of the history of the peopling, or simply the history, of a peripheral region such as Wasolon than an explanation in terms of ethnicity.

From this point of view the Wasolon appear essentially as a community of expelled groups that, in turn, took in the Fulani, who were expelled from their region of origin (Futa Jalon, Masina) by different groups striving to settle the area and enact reforms of their own.[34] To privilege the ethnic factor, as did the late Y. Person,[35] for example, makes a primary issue of the fact that the Fulani were nomadic herders whose migrations, therefore, were governed by the single imperative of their pastoral mode of life.

But the Fulani were not motivated solely by the immutable wanderings of their flocks. They were part of social groups in movement and they mixed with societies who defined themselves by other labels (Malinke, etc.). They were just as much subject to a history that shaped them as they were controllers of their own destiny. In other words, what appears in the social consciousness of Africans and ethnologists as a distinct Fulani entity is in reality the result of a continual modification of political formations and an evolution of the relations of forces between Islam and "paganism."

The only way one can possibly speak of a Fulani cultural sphere distinct from a Bambara-Malinke sphere is to discern a particular inflection of the Fulani language in one or another region. If the idea of cultural categorization has any meaning at all, it can be expressed in relative terms only: one is more Fulani than Bambara in certain zones and, inversely, more Bambara than Fulani in others.

In Mali the signifier "Fulani" has practically ceased to mean anything ever since the French conquest. Under colonization and especially since independence, it was superseded by the referents "Bambara" and "Malinke," leaving the category of Fulani to specify the limited role of an ethnic minority. This role is all the more difficult to play since the Fulani of Wasolon, for example, speak Bambara-Malinke and must maximize their small differences from these groups in order to be considered an ethnic group.

How Does One Become Bambara or Malinke?

The French word "Bambara" is a heteronym of Fulani and Arabic (Moorish) origin that is never used by the people to whom it is applied.[36] The term used by the actors claiming such an identity is *banmana*. This category applies to an extremely vast field and concerns an entire series of positions occupied by the agents at the heart of the cultural and linguistic sphere of the same name.

It would seem that this appellation originates in Minyanka society, which does not differ markedly fron the Senufo society or societies.[37] The term "Minyanka" is, in fact, a name applied by those exterior to the peoples who characterize themselves as Banmana and who speak the language of the same name (*banmana djomo*). This conception is not shared by the groups that, since colonization and especially since the work of Binger and Delafosse, are classically recognized as "Banmana" or "Bambara" and whom the Minyanka consider as speaking the language of slaves (*blo djomo*).[38]

The term *banmana*, then, belongs to a fragmented society with extremely undetermined contours, living essentially from agriculture, being weakly Islamized, and serving as a slave reservoir to the kingdoms of Segu and Sikaso. Moslem merchants in the cities of Djenne and Timbuktu and Islamic aristocrats understandably applied by extension the term *Banmana*, denoting a population of *pagani* (peasant/pagans), to the idolatrous communities of warrior/peasants in the region.[39]

Subsequently, the term designated all the groups negatively defined by their relation to the dominant classes. For the city dwellers of Sikasso, Senufo peasants were known as Banmana, speakers of the Banmana language; for the long-distance traders, they were the Mande-Soninke who spoke the Jula dialect of Banmana.[40] Thus, the educated Moslems from Kankan considered Jeri Sidibe, a Fula of Wasolon and leader of the "war of the sons of the dream," as "Bambara" or "Cafri," that is, pagan.[41] Finally, for the Islamic Soninke, the term "Banmana" even became a synonym for slave, and thus fixed once and for all the sense of this word as a negative category.[42]

"Banmana" designates, then, the savage, the pagan (*banmana fin*), but also the black or the autochthon, the first inhabitant as opposed to the conqueror, the city dweller, the Moslem, the red man, or the white man. It was up to colonialist thought to transform this toponym or this functional category into a racial or ethnic one, which it did to historicize it and justify conquest. According, for example, to Dr. Collomb, a naval doctor posted at Bamako and correspondent for the Lyons Anthropological Society, the mixture of the Bambara race with the Fulani race gave rise to the Markha race:

[This was] an aboriginal race [the Bambara] that spread over the entire vast territory running West and East, from the Atlantic ocean along the Niger river, and from the North to the Kong Mountains of the southern Sahara. An immigration of tribes coming from upper Egypt, the Fulani or Phulani, eventually mixed with the aboriginal race to form powerful empires, but could not wipe out the first race, whose features constantly reappear in anthropometrical studies.[43]

Collomb's concern for precision went so far that, not content with measurements according to nation or ethnic group (Bambara, Malinkhe, Soninkhe, Phoul, Sourakha, etc.), he applied Broca's rules literally and measured the skulls and height of members of different "tribes," that is, those known by various regional praise names (Diara, Traore, Coulibaly, etc.), which, by the way, he found in several countries. At the end of this long labor of physical anthropology, Collomb could not fail to recognize that "the mixture of these diverse nations was quite extensive . . . and that the anthropometrical and ethnological differences distinguishing them are minimal."[44]

Labouret supported this conclusion in his view that the Berbers play the same role as the Fulani and by Tauxier in his explanation of the formation of "the Segou and Kaarta kingdoms":

The two monarchies constructed by the Fulani over a large area of Bambara in Segou and Kaarta distinguish at last the social Bambara from the true Negro unable to rise above the stage of the autonomous village or district. The real Negro way is the anarchy of autonomous villages and districts, not the rigorous despotism that exists here and there (Achanti, Dahomey, Benin, Segou, Kaarta, etc.) but which always presupposes a superimposition of races by foreign conquest.[45]

A reading of these texts shows clearly that in the ethnological and physical anthropological tradition, the Bambara is a sort of absolute reference or degree zero of civilization. The same holds true in the local tradition, in Wasolon, for example, where the opposition of Fulani to Bambara refers to no real historical process but to a representation that, in effect, opposes Nature to Culture. A mutually reinforcing relation exists between the history of the spread of a people in a local area, as ethnologists depict it in a schema of "first settlers" and "last comers," or "people of the land" and "people of power," and colonial racial theory. They do so by tranforming the structuring schema, that is, the relations of force between peasant and ruling classes, into an imaginary confrontation between populations belonging to different ethnic sources. Positing the fact of a distinct essence separating those enslaving from those reduced to servitude allows one to transform the permanence of power relations uniting layers of an originally mixed population into a narrative of origins.

The population distribution in the region under study here reveals that to be Bambara is not an immutable condition, but rather a status one acquires. This analysis counters the view of several authors, such as Tauxier, Zahan, and Pâques, who have stated that only Bambara populated the Bougouni region.[46] Though the existence of the Banmana as a race, people, or ethnic group seems self-evident, some of these authors nevertheless stress the profound heterogeneity of the development of this group, emphasizing quite appropriately that it is the institution of chiefdom that unites these different peoples.[47]

Table 1 shows that the Bambara people, such as they are described by scholars operating in the colonialist tradition, are in fact merely a conglomerate of disparate elements united only by features common to the political network of the small chiefdoms (*kafo, jamana*) spread throughout western Sudan.

The different cases of identity conversion figuring in Table 1 can be divided essentially into three groups: ethnic conversions, statutory conversions, and religious conversions.[48]

The ethnic conversions, for example, concern the passage from Fula or Senufo identity to Banmana. At first glance, it seems to be a case of a simple change of group, or of a simple transition, analogous to the way a German national could take on French nationality. It would be difficult to maintain, however, that these ethnic conversions have no effect on the status of the groups in question. Identity change always occurs in terms of power relations, resulting in the individual's inscription into a position of dominant or dominated. If one adopts the praise name (*jamu*) and/or ethnonym of the group one has vanquished, it is to better integrate oneself and legitimize one's presence in the region. In this sense, the different categories of names (nickname, praise name, ethnonym) form a central element in the ideological stakes proper to a given political arena. Because the Kone fled Gonkoro and dominated the Cendugu

TABLE I
Identity Conversion Table

Chiefdom	Ethnic Group or Status	Praise Names	Ethnic Group or Status	Praise Names and Lineage
Kelayadugu	Sonrai or Muslim Arabs	Bagayogo	Banmana	Bagayogo
	Maninkas Moslem	Tarawele	Banmana	Tarawele
Jitumu	Fula	Sangare	Banmana	Samake Somala
	numu	Jabate	Banmana	Samake Numuniziela
	fina	Kamara	Banmana	Samake Npiebala
	jon	Sako	Banmana	Samake Furabala
Banan	Markajalan	Niobla or Markajon	Banmana	Niambele
Kokun	Maninka	Niambele	Banmana	Niambele
Ntinkadugu	Fula	Jakite	Banmana	Fonba
Cendugu	Fula	Jakite	Banmana	Suntura
	Shiena (senufo)	Kone	Banmana	Kone Gonkorobi
Cemala	Shiena	Kone	Banmana	Samake

SOURCE: Information on identity conversions comes from my own fieldwork as well as, for Cendugu, Samake, *Pouvoir traditionnel et conscience politique paysanne*, p. 33.

people, they abandoned the Shiena (Senufo) language for Banmana, thereby changing their ethnic affiliation. Similarly, because the Fula Jakite of Banan vanquished the Banmana Fonba, they appropriated the latter's praise name and identity.

Cases of identity conversion accompanied by a statutory change are numerous, even though information regarding this subject is difficult to obtain. In Jitumu, for example, the ancestors of the Jabate *numu* (blacksmiths), the Kamara *fina* and the Sako *jon* (slaves) were incorporated by the dominant lineages of Samake. They adopted the Samake praise names and gave rise to the lineages under Samake patronage of the Numuniziela, Npiebala, and Furabala, who supply chiefs to a certain number of villages.[49] This represents an ascendant social mobility, but the opposite occurs also. At the end of wars in Wasolon, for example, the noble families who had been reduced in numbers or who were poorly armed passed themselves off as *numu* in order to escape death or slavery. Their marriage with *numu* women established a new social status for the nobles, who abandoned their Soninke or Banmana identity for the opprobrious designation of Kooroko.[50]

Moreover, examples of identity change amounting to religious conversion are equally numerous in the region that concerns us. But it is striking to note, and here the notion of a Banmana cultural sphere remains pertinent, that all the conversions occur in the direction of abandoning Islam and returning to "paganism." Thus, the chiefs of Tarawele in Keleyadugu claim Maninka origin and they associate this characteristic with the fact of having acquired fetishes in Mecca. They say that they became Banmana as a result of migrations and their contact with other populations, which makes them fetishist priests, *somaw*.

The Bagayogo, who conquered this same chiefdom, proclaim that they were Arabic or Sonrai marabouts who became Banmana, that is, pagan warrior/peasants, after having abandoned their Moslem faith. In Kokun, a neighboring *kafo*, the first Markajalan inhabitants, the Marka secs, or Markajon (slaves of the Marka) Niobla, originally from Tengrela, also define themselves as Islamized Banmana who were subjected and later absorbed by Niambele coming from the Mande area. (The expression "Marka secs" is a literal translation of the Markajalan, a subgroup of the Marka people. It is a pejorative term.) This integration led to their adoption of their conquerors' praise name and to their becoming, or returning to being, pagans, that is, Banmana.

The few examples mentioned above show the difficulties of finding an ethnic conversion that did not result in a statutory change, which is most often, if not always, linked to a migration. To understand how identities are continually renegotiated, one must envision the spatial relationship of a chain of political units. It is difficult not to characterize identity as a political phenomenon or as ratified by the powers that be. Moreover, these identity conversions are quite often kept secret, as if they in some way were linked to an enfranchisement.[51] This is why one cannot define identity as a substance, but as an unstable condition translating the permanent struggle between those who define themselves as Banmana and those who define them as such.

The referent "Bambara" did not disappear with the colonial conquest. On the contrary, it spread so extensively that it encompassed practically the entire territory of Mali, except perhaps for the Tuareg. There were, nevertheless, various stages in the history of this semantic expansion.

The term "Banmana," which as we have seen had a fluid meaning before colonization, was hypostatized by Delafosse as the ethnonym "Bambara."[52] The term henceforth became widely used by Monteil, Tauxier, Dieterlen, and N'Diayé, who conferred a sort of semiofficial status upon the different ethnic groups of Mali.[53] As in the case of several other African regions, the invention of an ethnic group was accompanied by the production of dictionaries to codify the language, by collections of proverbs, tales, and legends, and by the constitution of a press in Bambara linked to a general literacy.[54] Thanks to radio and television, the Bambara language has in effect become the second official language of Mali and is spoken by most members of the state administration. The domination and massive imposition of Bambara on practically all of Mali has transformed the speakers of other languages, and in particular speakers of the more segmented groups (Bobo, Minyanka, Senufo, Dogon, etc.), into as many ethnic minorities.[55]

In contemporary Mali the term "Bambara" can thus be equated with the dominant class, or, more precisely, with the administrative class. But other distinctions have in turn come to light, such as the opposition between the "true Bambaras," the elders whose lineal power extends beyond the framework of village society to that of the dominant class, and the "false Bambaras," considered as uninitiated and belonging, politically speaking, to the dominated class.[56]

The French term "Malinké," as is the case for many other words ending in -ké, originates in Fulani and Soninke.[57] In the Mali empire, for the people of Djenne, it designates warriors as opposed to merchants, called Ouangara.[58] Gallieni, for example, refers to the word in the same way, affirming that Samori became Malinke, that is, ceased being *dioula* (trader) to take up the warrior's career.[59] When they characterize themselves as such, the actors use the terms "Mandenka" (Mande people) or "Maninka" (Mani people). These

terms derive from Mande, the region stretching from Kurusa in
Guinea to Wayewayanko near Bamako, and from Kita to Kama, a vil-
lage located on the banks of the Sankarani.[60] The city of Mani would
be located near present-day Nyamina, with the sovereign Belemun
Koman Keita as its leader. His descendants were the Tangara, the
Bware, the Sinare, and the Koare from Segu.[61]

The term "Mandenka" or "Maninka" most likely produced the
Portuguese "Mandinguas," the English "Mandingos," and the French
"Manding" or "Mandingue."[62] Colonial thought fixed this last category as Mandingo language, culture, and people, which spread over
several West African countries.[63] The mode of existence of "Mande-
ness" was further strengthened by the organization of large groups,
such as the Congress of Mandingo Studies (London, 1972) or the creation within the American African Studies Association of the Mansa
group (1986). These groups created an institutional pressure group
lending credit to the idea that populations, languages, and cultures
whose similarities do not at first glance seem self-evident can easily
fit into the mold of "Mandean civilization."[64] There too, in a self-fulfilling prophecy, scholars create the object they claim to study. Let
us recall, however, that one is not eternally Mandingo; one becomes
it and one ceases to be it. The Jakite Saabashi were well aware of that.
On leaving Gwanan, they abandoned their Fula ethnicity to create
an offspring chiefdom bearing the same name as the one they left,
and they adopted the Maninke identity as well as the Konate praise
name.[65]

Both the Maninka and the Banmana categories are dynamic. They
underwent phases of expansion and contraction due to various
choices made by the actors, that is, those defining themselves as
Maninka and those defining them as such. In this sense, the
Maninka category plays an important though secondary role in the
definitions of the Malian ruling class. Coupled with the term "Bambara," it allows the bureaucracy to identify itself; but it remains an
accessory appellation, the subject of occasional jokes.[66]

As can be seen from the examples mentioned above, the trinity
Fulani-Bambara-Malinke is a system of transformations with a logic
of its own. Identity is found in this logic, in the relations among the
concurrent terms, and not in ethnonyms considered in isolation.
Identity is thus defined as a variation or as a difference. Further-

more, identity melts into ethnicity when conditions of social and political production are forgotten. Political formations are divided into ethnic forms only because their modes of appearance, functioning, and disappearance are lost in the mists of time. This memory loss allowed ethnologists, colonial administrators, and present-day leaders to negate the historicity of African societies and to obscure the common features of their customs. Though the Malian state apparatus is today identified with the category Banmana-Maninka, that does not mean that the majority of political personnel is recruited from the Bambara and Malinke ethnic groups. It means simply that the Banmana-Maninka identifications were considered, for historical, political, and institutional reasons, more important than, for example, Fulani or Tuareg identities. From this perspective, the facts of ethnicity have more to do with an essentially political reading. It is, thus, the elucidation of political mechanisms, which in Africa means the dialectic of the state and the segmentary, that allows one to account for the different identities claimed by the actors.

4 The State and the Segmentary

It is said of Babylon that its capture was, two days later, still unknown to a part of the city.
—Aristotle, *The Politics*

If in African studies an area of congruence between a discipline and a geographical specialization exists, that area is political anthropology. The seminal moment for this discipline occurred in 1940 with the publication of *African Political Systems*, edited by M. Fortes and E.-E. Evans-Pritchard.[1] Other works, such as Lowie's,[2] had certainly approached this subject. But no work caused such a stir as *APS*, which has become a classic and continues to shape anthropological thought to this day.

The opposition it detected between stateless societies and state societies has become so obvious for the entirety of the anthropological profession, that those holding the most widely divergent views invariably make reference to it. This typology, its origin both evolutionist and functional, even influenced scholars who had no explicit theoretical affiliation but who seemed to consider it self-evident that their research involved either a segmentary society or one with a centralized political power. All currents of thought of an anthropological stamp have adopted this distinction.[3] This is particularly so for Marxist anthropologists, who apparently had no trouble applying an old opposition to areas previously neglected by classical anthropology.[4] Does not the title of a work that appeared a few years ago—*Guerres de lignages et guerres d'Etats en Afrique* (Kinship wars and State wars in Africa)[5]—provide a striking illustration of the influence of Fortes and Evans-Pritchard's inaugural work? Though contrasting with the Marxist current, the writing of P. Clastres, notably, also makes reference in its own way to *APS*.[6] So does the thought of other anthropologists who uphold analogous and inverse theses while evoking the propensity of certain societies to construct a state.

Could the opposition stateless society/state society be the limiting factor of political anthropology, or of anthropology itself? We need to return to the source, to *APS* itself, particularly the preface written by Radcliffe-Brown, an anthropologist of the preceding generation who lent his authority to the project of his spiritual heirs.

According to Radcliffe-Brown, anthropology is the natural science of human society and, for this reason, it must use the scientific method, for this comparative method allows one to perceive universal characteristics behind apparent differences.[7] To meet the comparative requirement, certain criteria must be selected, such as economic, kinship, or political systems. The author of *Andaman Islanders* wishes to define what he calls "political society," particularly in societies where the absence of a state makes this task difficult.

An essential characteristic of such societies is their foundation on a territorial structure that furnishes not only the framework for political organization, but also other levels of social organization, such as an economy. In contrast to Morgan, who maintained in *The Ancient Society*[8] that an entire part of human history consists in the passage from a social organization founded on people (*gentes*), phratries, and tribes (*societas*) to a political organization based on territory, the state, and property (*civitas*), Radcliffe-Brown saw no essential difference between lineage societies and territorial ones: the first are no more primitive than the second.

In general, Radcliffe-Brown defines political organization as the foundation and maintenance of social order within a territorial boundary by means of an organized coercive authority that includes the power to use physical force. This forms the basis of both a judicial system and repression of internal revolts within the territory, and an armed confrontation with other, external states. Law and war must thus be distinguished from each other, but so must the intermediate forms, such as predetermined modes of vengeance that attempt to minimize losses (vendettas, feuds).

Wars play a major role in the history of political development, notably in the case of conquest wars, which are the very origin of the foundation of certain states. But the state proceeds also from differentiation and complication of roles (age, sex, noninstitutional specialization, and so on), so that gerontocracies and societies where power issues from age sets naturally evolve toward state societies.

In their introduction to *APS*, Fortes and Evans-Pritchard adopt Radcliffe-Brown's comparative and naturalist method. They compare eight representative societies of African political systems according to a certain number of criteria: the role of kinship in political organization, the influence of demography, livelihood, conquest theory, territorial factors, balance of power, the function of organized force, differences in response to colonial administration, values associated with the political system, and the problem of territorial limits.[9] Beyond its overall importance, this book's essential contribution consists in its formulation of the major opposition between societies with a centralized political power, or primitive states, and societies without centralized political power, or stateless societies.

According to Fortes and Evans-Pritchard, these two systems differ first of all in terms of kinship. Whereas an administrative organization prevails in the first type, a segmentary lineage system dominates in the second. As for livelihood–though it is difficult to observe a link between this and political structure, since the whole of the African continent was subjected to a system of self-sufficiency and redistribution–the authors maintain that segmentary societies are economically egalitarian and homogenous, whereas state-controlled societies produce an elaboration of systems of rank, status, and occupations not regulated by differences in wealth.

As have German authors such as Gumplowicz or Oppenheimer, Fortes and Evans-Pritchard consider that the transition from segmentary societies to state societies takes place through conquest. Culturally or ethnically heterogenous societies result from conquest; the state's purpose is to control them through the institution of castes or classes. Regarding territoriality, Fortes and Evans-Pritchard adopted Radcliffe-Brown's idea that the two types of societies possess a spatial armature for the same reasons.

An equilibrium, however, characterizes these two political organizations, again for the same reasons. State societies have a balance between centrifugal and centripetal forces as well as a system of compensatory powers to balance power and authority on one hand and duty and responsibility on the other.[10] The stateless societies possess a balance among the various dominant lineages. Generally, in African political systems the chief rules by consent of the people. When he no longer has this consent, he is replaced, but his position itself is not called into question. M. Gluckman explored this theme in considerable depth in his work on rebellions.[11] As for the use of organized force, Fortes and Evans-Pritchard hold, from a Weberian perspective, that the state alone can control its own administration, whereas different "segments" possess this power in stateless societies. In societies with a centralized power, the king or the chief plays the pivotal role, in the framework of British indirect rule, between colonial power and its subjects. In acephalous societies, the colonial powers named chiefs arbitrarily, and this profoundly altered the functioning of the segmentary system.

Fortes and Evans-Pritchard insist on the bonds uniting African political systems to religion and the supernatural. An entire current originating in Frazer's *The Golden Bough* will later come out of this perspective, making very prominent the sacred or divine character of African kingdoms.

APS, then, is a seminal work for anthropology, and it inspired a considerable amount of research. However, it obscures the problem of territorial limits in different political systems. Fortes and Evans-Pritchard were able to establish such a radical distinction between two types of societies because they disassembled the precolonial "chains of societies," and because they failed to analyze the many relations existing between segmentary societies and state societies. To the degree that the *APS* decontextualized African societies, it is linked to a precise historical conjuncture: that of colonialism.

What Is a Segmentary Society?

While everyone knows pretty much what a state is, since we all have an immediate experience of it, the same does not hold for segmentary societies.

Let us recall that in *The Division of Labor in Society*, Durkheim draws on Hebrew, American, Australian, and African examples to distinguish three types of primitive societies: the horde and the clan, on which we will not dwell, and segmentary societies based on clans. About these societies, Durkheim writes:

> they are segmentary in order to indicate their formation by the repetition of like aggregates in them, analogous to the rings of an earthworm, and we say of this elementary aggregate that it is a clan, because this word well expresses its mixed nature, at once familial and political.

He goes on to say:

> For segmentary organization to be possible, the segments must resemble one another; without that, they would not be united. And they must differ; without this, they would lose themselves in each other and be effaced. According to the societies, the two contrary necessities are satisfied in different proportions, but the social type remains the same.[12]

Fortes and Evans-Pritchard refer implicitly to Durkheim in their definition of type B, that of acephalous and stateless segmentary societies, which they apply to the populations they studied: the Nuer of Sudan and the Tallensi of North Ghana.[13] Though they draw on Durkheim, however, Fortes, Evans-Pritchard, and their successors enlarge considerably upon the notion of a segmentary society, particularly as regards the relativity of political groupings, equality among the segments, and the predominance of leadership over authority. In the wake of *APS*, and independently of the many monographs devoted to specific societies, most theoretical reflection focused on typological refinements of the two categories singled out by Fortes and Evans-Pritchard.

Two types of refinements stand out: a typological refinement from below and a typological refinement from above.

Typological Refinement in Segmentary Societies

Two works illustrate particularly well the current of thought concerning stateless societies. *Tribes Without Rulers*, edited by J. Middleton and D. Tait, brings together research on African segmented systems in the tradition of *APS*; R. Horton's "Stateless Societies in the History of West Africa" explores the historical role played by such societies.[14]

Middleton and Tait distinguish three types of segmentary lineage systems, but these do not encompass all the societies observed.[15] In the first group a single all-encompassing lineage genealogy accounts for significant political identification with a territorial segment, since the political system is constructed on an agnatic framework forming a single pyramidal network of relationships. Such a system can be found among the Tiv, the Lugbara, and the Nuer. In the second group, political units are composed of small descent groups, gathered into intertwined clusters that often form congregations of cults or are held together by quasi-familial bonds. The third constitutes the "aggregate," "associate," or "polycephalous" type, which characterizes the Dinka and Mandari societies. There, one finds neither the dominant clan of the Nuer nor the all-encompassing genealogy of the Tiv. Even in some of these stateless societies, however, one can observe an opposition between dominant clans and dominated clans, just as one finds an affiliation between the chiefship and the dominant clan, such as exists among the Mandari.

These observations reveal the impasse of all typological approaches, which, by nature, require one to neglect a certain number of societies and to include cases representative of the opposite type. In many respects, Horton's now classic work, which bears a striking resemblance to *Tribes Without Rulers*, runs into the same difficulties. He distinguishes two kinds of life in segmentary societies: sedentary agriculture, which characterizes most stateless societies, and nomadic pastoralism. Horton identifies three types of sedentary agricultural modes: segmentary lineage systems, territorial dispersed communities, and village communities. As in *Tribes Without Rulers*, the proposed typology leads Horton to categorize as belonging to the segmentary societies–those he calls "territorial dispersed communities"–those societies characterized by an opposition between people of the earth and people of power, whereas these societies could for this very opposition just as well be placed in the category of state societies. By the same token, if one accepts Horton's view that "village communities" are linked to the obligation to defend themselves, one must then accept that this type cannot be conceived independently of an "exterior," which is most often represented by a predatory state.[16]

Horton finds a particularly strong link between the second type, that of nomadic pastoralism, and Fulani societies, among which must be included the Tuaregs and the Moors. But this arrangement is manifestly cumbersome for Horton, for whom the pastoral peoples are invariably organized into segmentary lineage systems. He fails to take account of Fulani states, which have played a major role in the history of this region. Nor does he take into account the dependence of numerous nomadic groups on those engaged in sedentary agriculture.[17]

Horton does not establish a radical gap between stateless societies and state societies; rather, he sees this continuity as an evolutionist. In fact, in "territorial dispersed communities" and in "village communities" he sees the germs of a state. His work, then, does not represent a step forward in relation to Fortes and Evans-Pritchard's book. His work reveals the same naturalist concern for classification as theirs has, and he does not always resolve the difficulties raised in the transition from one type of society to another.

Typological Refinement of State-Controlled Societies

The typological refinement of state-controlled societies is essentially Southall's model of the "segmentary state" among the Alur of Uganda. The political system of this society combines a lineage segmentation with specialized institutions, making the chiefdom and kinship complementary organizational forms.[18] Here is his definition of this intermediary situation:

> The distribution of power in the segmentary state is characterised by the fact that, within any one segment, at any level of the pyramidal structure, there is at any one moment a certain degree of monopoly of political power, development of administrative staff and definition of territorial limits, whereas, within the system as a whole, the political relations of the various segments are determined by much the same factors as in the case of segmentary societies which have no political specialisation at all.[19]

For Southall, the segmentary state system characterizing Alur society represents an intermediate form between segmentary societies and state societies. According to his typological and evolutionist perspective, this system possesses in embryo the attributes of a state as described by Weber and Nadel,[20] namely, territorial sovereignty, centralized government, specialized administrative personnel, and the legitimate monopoly of the use of force.

In his desire to fill the gap between stateless societies and societies with a state, Southall enlarged the range of concepts in political anthropology. But to the degree that the notion of a segmentary state can apply to any society, it does not offer much help. The same goes for efforts to refine the analysis of ancient and precolonial states.

H. Claessen and P. Skalnik define three types of ancient or early states: the pristine state, the early typical state, and the transitional early state.[21] R. Cohen distinguishes two forms of developed political oranization, the chiefdom and the state, whereas M. Fried opposes primary states to secondary ones.[22]

One could multiply ad infinitum the examples of typologies of political systems without learning very much. In fact, a study of the defining processes proves more useful than the resulting definitions of notions that, though useful in the institutional context, do not really shed much light on the situation.

The Break with Typologies: Edmund Leach and the Political Systems of Highland Burma

To pinpoint an area of progress in the history of political anthropology, one must look to Asia rather than Africa. Edmund Leach's masterful book constitutes a radical rupture with the "butterfly collector" approach of political anthropology and of anthropology in general.[23] In his work devoted to the Kachin in the highlands of Burma, Leach reconstitutes several years of fieldwork, during which he observed with perhaps more precision and insight than his Africanist predecessors the processes of political change at work in a society.

Leach does not set out to identify a Kachin political system or to discover what it means to be a stateless society or a state society. He singles out two political systems or poles in this society: the aristocratic system *gumsa*, based on a chief, and the democratic *gumlao*, based on the village community. According to Leach, the alternation of these two systems can be understood only by placing them in a larger framework, bringing into play the Shan kingdoms of the neighboring plains as well as the Chinese empire, which exerted an influence from a distance.

This book represents something of a rupture with functionalist and typological political anthropology because Leach's fieldwork, in contrast to Evans-Pritchard's in particular, took place over an extremely long period of time. Consequently, he was in a position to discover processes that many of his Africanist colleagues were unable to during their shorter periods of research. But aside from duration, the geographical vastness of his fieldwork, which included societies that were neighbors of the Kachin, enabled him to define this society in terms of a contradiction.

The most salient aspect of Leach's work opposing him to the founders of African political anthropology is his recourse to history. Actually, *The Nuer* offers very little historical information, and this is true in general for Anglo-Saxon anthropology of the 1940s, probably because at this time functionalism dominated intellectual life. But this "denial of coevality"[24] resulted just as much from these anthropologists' experience of the prevailing colonial environment of indirect rule.

Without calling into question Fortes and Evans-Pritchard, it seems nevertheless impossible to oppose, as did G. Leclerc, an "ethnology-techne" to an "ethnology-theoria" and not to implicate the work of these two authors in the colonial phenomenon.[25] It is not so much a matter of knowing if the government anthropologists were conscious or unconscious servants or parties to British colonization, as to establish if the object they described or developed owes anything to the colonial context.[26] But that does seem to be the case, as Fortes's study of the Tallensi shows. He made this society into the prototype of segmental lineage societies by cutting it off from its historico-political environment and obscuring, in particular, the Tallensi dependency on the Mamprusi kingdom.[27]

One could just as well reevaluate, as Southall has done, the analyses of the Nuer-Dinka, such as those provided by Evans-Pritchard.[28] In an extensively documented article, Southall applies a historical analysis to Evans-Pritchard's findings and demonstrates convincingly that, far from being an opposition between two societies or two ethnic groups, the Nuer (Naath)/Dinka (Jieng) represent a single binary system consisting of two groups of the same origin pitted against each other as raiders (Nuer) and raided (Dinka). In effect, each group produces a particular inflection of the social system: the

Nuer possessed an aristocracy and were more political; the Dinka, who institutionalized mastery of the spear, were more ritualistic.

Following Southall's example, we can legitimately compare the Nuer-Dinka pair to the two poles of *gumsa* and *gumlao* that Leach identified among the Kachin.

Polarized Models

Looking from a certain perspective at the history of anthropology during the last thirty years, one remarks that Anglo-Saxon functionalist anthropology was remodeled by Marxism to produce economic anthropology, "mode of production" style, but that it now tends to neglect such large explanatory structures and looks toward historical anthropology, that is, toward an understanding of singular social networks situated in a precise and limited chronology. By avoiding evolutionist fictions and emphasizing concrete and identifiable historical processes, one can ignore certain unanswerable questions, particularly regarding the origin of the state, which have endlessly obsessed generations of anthropologists. Rather than worrying about the precise moment the state appeared in one or another context, one can focus more on just what is meant by "state." In other words, rather than establish the pseudo genesis of institutions defined a priori, we can spatialize and contrast intersocial relations. This leads to a view of history not as a process tending toward certain ends–the emergence of the state and capitalism, for example–but as a "pump" that both draws in and centralizes politically, that is, constructs states and suppresses or peripheralizes segmental societies. In a parallel metaphor, we can see a mass that alternately contracts and dilates in the interior of a given space, thus allowing the passage from the state to the segmentary as well as the inverse.

Thanks to the work of certain anthropologists, we have documented case studies based on a polarized model. Cohen's application of the method of controlled comparison to the series Kanem-Borngwé-Pabir-Bura and Fombina from the north and middle east of Nigeria will furnish a useful example to our demonstration.[29]

Cohen based his working hypotheses on the idea that no simple causes explain the phenomenon of the formation of the state. It results from a "funnel-like" process: following unsolvable conflicts, certain prestate systems are forced to evolve toward higher levels of political hierarchy. The Bornu empire was founded in the fifteenth century by a clan of Moslem immigrants, the Magumi, originally from Kanem, a region located northeast of Lake Chad. In Cohen's view the nature of this formation is not clearly established; but Kanem was probably formed by a confederation of chiefdoms itself composed of nomadic and seminomadic clans, though they differed from a true state because of its tendency toward fission. However, this political system was linked to trans-Saharan trade and was influenced by Moslem culture and religion. In the middle of the thirteenth or beginning of the fourteenth century, the Magumi lost control of Kanem. They left the region and settled in Bornou, where they became sedentary, built fortified cities, and constructed an empire. Known henceforth as Kanuri, they progressively absorbed the plain's population.

Other groups took refuge in the mountains, hills, and forests of the south, where they built fortified villages on the borders of the empire. The southern kingdom of Pabir in Biu was forced to develop a more centralized form of power due to the growing strength of the Kanuri state and their continual raids in search of booty and slaves.

To the south of Pabir, the Bura inhabited a mountainous region, difficult of access. Their favorable geography permitted them to continue living in small, independent villages, where they escaped the raids by Bornou horsemen and were spared the necessity of building such fortifications as Pabir had to construct. The Fombina state originated by a somewhat different process. In this case, the nomadic and seminomadic Fulani grew tired of the exactions levied upon them by the agricultural population. So they followed the example of the Sokoto empire, uniting with a Moslem warrior chief to found a kingdom that became something of a dependency of their powerful neighbor to the northeast.

According to Cohen, these three episodes of state formation are secondary elaborations:[30] the Magumi of Kanem-Bornou were in contact with the Moslem states; the Pabir maintained ties with the Bornou; the Fombina were linked to the Sokoto empire. Only a few of these peoples constructed states; the others successfully maintained segmentary forms. From these case studies, we can distinguish several characteristics of state formation: (1) Islam often in-

tervened in the creation of states in this zone; (2) their formation
resulted from migration or incursions by nomadic peoples into agricultural village societies; (3) the agricultural peoples' defense reactions to warrior expeditions from neighboring states often resulted
in the creation of a state; and (4) these states were all the product of
a phenomenon of contact. Cohen's detailed study brings to light
what we could call the infinite regression, in time and space, of the
state's origin and the aporia of every attempt to pinpoint its beginning or emergence in positive terms. From this point of view, Cohen's opposition–between the chiefdom defined by fission and the
state characterized principally by centrality–hardly seems satisfactory. Aside from the fact that a state doubtless also undergoes fission in periods of decline, it does not seem possible to define it as
other than the most developed pole of a hierarchized space, that is,
as the result of a chain reaction or an intersocietal realignment.[31]

   In this, one finds Cohen's distinction between sovereignty, defined as the territory in which the state exercises its authority, and
hegemony, or the zone of its long-distance control.[32] Examples
taken from the history of western Sudan illustrate this process at
work because in this region it is very difficult to assign a precise origin to the state. Of course, one can look to the well-known empires
of Ghana, Mali, and Sonrai, but it is difficult to see exactly how they
differ from the political organizations that preceded them. Moreover, one can consider that the subsequent period of feudal or segmentary disintegration (from the end of the sixteenth to the beginning of the eighteenth centuries) gave rise to chiefdoms that were
no more than contracted forms of an empire or kingdom. Some were
also segmentary states, or vassal provinces furnishing booty and
slaves to the central kingdoms.[33]

   This is why the definition of the state, as well as that of the process
of its emergence or dissolution, cannot be analyzed in positive
terms. One must imagine a sine curve in which a period of grandeur
and expansion, leading to the formation of an empire, would be followed by a period of decline or contraction during which the empire
would crumble, and then a new period in which the state would
emerge (Segu, Futa Jalon, Samori, etc.). Thus the history of the
emergence of the state has itself a history: all states are to a certain
extent secondary states.[34]

Nonpolarized Situations or
Segmentation as a Point of View

One could object that the model of polarity applied to ancient civilizations or societies of precolonial Africa, America, and Asia[35] is not universal. Societies exist in Africa or New Guinea, for example, in which no polarity obtains and which are merely in a relation of contiguity to each other. In this case, no one element exercises power over any other element, whether nearby or far away.

This would be a series of nonstate situations or periods preceding the emergence or the reemergence of the state: western Sudan between the collapse of Sonrai (1591) and the advent of the kingdom of Segu (1712), southeast Cameroon before the Fulani jihad at the beginning of the nineteenth century,[36] or pre-European New Guinea.[37] Placing such different situations in the same category is perhaps absurd. The first case corresponds to a period preceding the emergence or reemergence of the state (in the western Sudan) during which a feudal regime ruled; that is, it corresponds to a period of disintegration. The other two examples deal with societies dominated by "big men" (as in New Guinea) or those in which the power of these "big men" does not extend beyond the interior of the extended kinship unit and its allies (as in Cameroon).

Beyond the question of the size of the entities considered–seigniory or chiefdoms on one hand, and tribes on the other–a strong similarity exists in the relations among the groups themselves. In contrast to the examples mentioned above in which the model of polarity defines the relations among societies, here relations of contiguity are in effect. In Sudan as in Cameroon or New Guinea, there is a juxtaposition or opposition of similarly sized social units that define themselves in relation to each other. On the whole these units make up a continuum of social structures that constitutes their real matrix of social and political production.

In all the cases just analyzed, relations of contiguity, juxtaposition, or opposition represent the phenomenon of segmentarity in its broadest sense, that is, the predominance of vertical relations over horizontal ones. Accordingly, segmentarity, as has often been pointed out, can be defined only in relative terms: it is nothing more than a specific type of bond linking each group to the other that can operate at different levels (lineages, clans, states, etc.).

In conclusion, it appears difficult to define segmentary societies in opposition to state societies because one can consider lineages, villages, or states as small states or, inversely, one can consider states as large lineages. But the merit of political anthropology is to have drawn our attention to a level of analysis previously neglected, which can apply to exotic domains as well as domestic ones. Are not football games, youth groups, political parties, and the like new areas of investigation for this discipline?[38] In other words, the opposition between polarized and nonpolarized situations reproduces the distinction between "societies without history" and "historical societies." A kind of Brownian motion characterizes the first, caught as they are in a repetition of the same. Only the second undergo cumulative processes leading eventually to the emergence of the state.

If we have to accept that differences between these two situations exist, we must also account for the presence of these nonpolarized and segmentary areas in the larger clusters—in the "held together," to use Castoriadis's formulation[39]—that gives them shape. We must also note that these groups of societies can give rise to more elaborate forms of political power.[40] Regarding the Mkako of Cameroon, Copet-Rougier shows that ephemeral chiefdoms managed to form before the Fulani jihad but that, in the absence of elements that would assure a dynastic continuity, their duration was uncertain.[41] In these nonpolarized situations, we notice a phenomenon identical to what was observed in the model of polarity: the process of political contraction and expansion.

Political Anthropology or Anthropology of Powers?

If one stops thinking in typological terms and considers segmentarity as a point of view, the idea that a political anthropology devoted to classifying political systems operates at the expense of an anthropology of powers immediately vanishes.

Phenomena of power must be conceived in this new configuration. For a long time in political philosophy, reflections of power went hand in hand with reflections on the state and its inverse, civil society.[42] When exotic societies had to be accounted for, it was the notion of civil society–a fiction of political philosophy–that served as the implicit model for the concept of the segmentary society, which was also defined in essentially negative fashion as a stateless society.[43] Such a filiation explains the later driftings of political anthropology toward the problematic of the "society against the state,"[44] or its opposite, the "society for the state."

In both cases, the state continues to be considered as the only referent, whereas "other" societies should, in fact, be thought of in terms different from those used to conceptualize our own societies. In this regard, the very success of the notions "stateless society" and "society against the state" is not foreign to our need to characterize our own societies in opposition to other political structures. Since we are white, European, and live in states, there must be blacks, Africans, or Indians who live in stateless societies. The definition of our own identity would be facilitated by the existence of an entire range of radically different societies. Here we find a logic of attribution omnipresent in processes of identification: what the positing of negative categories–stateless society, illiterate society, tribe or ethnic group–allows one really to do is affirm the superiority of our literate United Nations. The anthropology of powers has the merit of avoiding the fateful pair society/state since it does not tackle the problem of the political arena–that is, the state or its institutions.

If sorcery, illness, benediction, or malediction remain as important for social production as the relations of production or the chiefdom, or rather, if sorcery and illness are also relations of production, political relations, and ideological relations, then there is no need to ask if we are dealing with a state or a stateless society.

As a result, we witness the disappearance of the entire spectrum of distinct social levels that justifies the subdivisions of political, economic, or religious anthropology. Henceforth, one of anthropology's tasks is to identify the forces at work in a given society as well as their spheres of influence or control.

Whether it concerns a healer, a religious leader, or a sovereign, one can reconstitute a whole network of patients, disciples, or subjects that defines a sphere of power. By making analogies with other areas of power, one can delineate an interlacing of social relations that will define the properties of these various powers or, in other words, their position in the social space.

In this way, the anthropology of power can link with the more fruitful approach of political philosophy, which studies forms of power, decision, and action.[45] We must find our position in the tradition of Machiavelli in such a way that we cease thinking of other societies as the inverse of our own. If anthropology wants to get out of a vicious circle, it must renounce cultural relativism, which could very likely be just another facet of ethnocentrism.

5 A Retracted State: Gwanan

> Conversely, according to recent understanding, royalty in the
> high Middle Ages, and particularly in the Carolingian period,
> acquired its meaning apart from an anachronistic conception
> of the State; the feudal king no longer derived his power in
> spite of the feudal system but from the very nature of the
> system itself.
> –Jacques Le Goff, *L'Imaginaire médiéval*

In the framework of our reflections on political realities
and ethnic groups, we will examine two chiefdoms–Gwanan and Jitumu–that represent intermediate political types between the state
and the segmentary. We will also look at cases of collective identity
that overlap the Fulani, Bambara, and Malinke cultural spheres.
These two types of organization call into question the typologies of
political anthropology and the classifications of ethnography.

Gwanan is one of the chiefdoms of Wasolon, a region considered
part of the Fulani world but which could just as well be classified in
the Mande world because of its spoken language and customs, the
subjection of the Fulani to Islamic penetration, and the identity
changes the people have experienced.

An entire series of data exists in the Mande cultural sphere–epics
recited by the griots (*jeli*), family traditions told by the elders–that
should allow us to reconstitute local history. In a previous publication, I reprinted an epic narrating the feats of the Jakite Saabashi
lineage of Gwanan and also presented collected familial traditions
from the elders of other lineages in this chiefdom.[1] Of course, independently of their eminently hagiographic character, these materi-
als must be handled carefully because we do not know when they
were written. Though they supposedly refer to very ancient events,
it is not impossible that they were recently composed and thus rep-

resent the projection of Samorian and colonial situations onto the period preceding the great conquests. It is equally possible that those who narrate the "traditions" transpose into a Moslem and state-supporting perspective a reality that, in fact, is much less rigid and much less pagan than it appears. Such questions are all the more well-founded because the prestigious lineage, the Jakite Saabashi, whose exploits the epic recounts, gave to Samori a general, to France three *chefs de canton*, and, in addition, engineered the Islamization of the region.

This narrative gives the impression that the Jakite Saabashi have exercised power for all time and that they went through a phase of pagan obscurantism before being miraculously enlightened by Islam. The epic overlooks entirely other prestigious lineages, such as the Jalo Malikishi, as well as certain Jakite Saabashi who opposed Farabalay or who, as *chefs de canton*, were not originally from Madina Jasa. These phenomena of concealment can be explained by the institutionalization, territorialization, and Islamization of power resulting from Samorian and colonial conquests.

During the period preceding the Samorian conquest, chiefs were not installed or laws implemented. Power was in the hands of the strongest, of those who could subjugate the others.[2] The Samorian conquest and, even more so, colonial power modified this state of affairs. To assure its domination over Wasolon, the Samori named military generals to the position of regional governors. Under colonization, power was related to a territorial space, to the chiefdom of a "canton," that is, to an institution controlled by juridical rules and bound, in theory at least, to rigid principles.

The Jakite Saabashi maintain that their ancestor Saaba ruled all of Wasolon, from Kankeri to Menian and from Bawulen to Niantanina. A certain stability of territorial limits could thus have existed during the reign of this king. Nevertheless, during a good part of this country's history, the borders of Gwanan must have been singularly blurred and fluctuating, reflecting the domination of military leaders. In fact, before the Samori, territorialized spaces did not exist. There were only lineage spaces and spaces of segmentation. Each principality (*jamana*) was a micro-region where a certain number of lineages and armed bands entered into conflict.[3] There was no power assigned to a specific territory.[4]

This state of affairs had nothing to do with any type of inability in
Wasolon society to construct a state, or any lack of desire to do so; it
is simply a matter of fact. Likewise, it is not accurate to think that
this shared, segmentary, or dispersed power derived from a situation prior to the construction of the state. It was a lineage phase
within a continual process of composition, decomposition, and re-
composition of the state that had affected this region for centuries.
The lineage phase also had to do with the environment of state control among the Wasolon (Kabadugu, Futa Jalon, Segu) that almost
entirely limited the institution of centralized political power and favored internal disputes and internecine wars.[5] Whereas the epic of
Jakite Saabashi describes the ancestor Saaba as a pagan prince, his
power was probably legitimized by Islamic beliefs that had already
infiltrated the area. It is, in fact, difficult to accept that this religion,
which had been present in West Africa for centuries, could have
failed to affect local belief systems. The presentation of Saaba as a
magician is, therefore, a construction a posteriori by the griots ex-
plainable by the career of his descendant Farabalay, who contributed largely to the Islamization of Gwanan and, generally, to all
of Wasolon. The Jakite Saabashi's political legitimacy is currently
closely linked to Islam. Similarly, the claim of a Fulani ethnic and
cultural identity, and the separation this claim implies regarding
the Banmana, cannot be dissociated from the Jakite Saabashi's belonging to the religion of the Prophet.[6] As we have seen above, the
colonial theory of races, which associates a Fulani nature with Islam, reproduces to a certain extent the local theory of identity that,
for the Wasolon as for others, links religious specificity to ethnic
particularity.[7]

Gwanan

Gwanan is traditionally attached to a region, Wasolon, whose borders are difficult to locate. Several etymologists claim to account for
the name "Wasolon." According to certain authors, it derives from
the name of the "Bambara" king Solon.[8] Others have established a
link between Wasolon and Solon, *kafo* of the Niger's right bank, in-

---

Opposite. Wasolon and Neighboring Chiefdoms

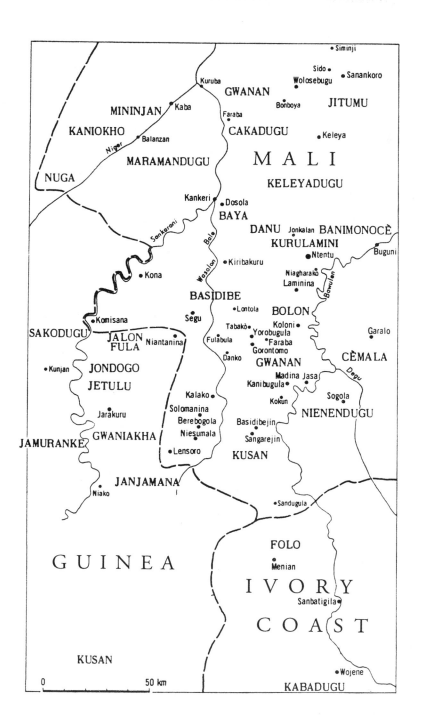

• Siminji

Sido •
Wolosebugu • • Sanankoro

Kuruba
GWANAN
JITUMU
Bonboya
Faraba

Kaba
MININJAN

KANIOKHO
CAKADUGU

• Keleya
Balanzan

Niger
M A L I
MARAMANDUGU

NUGA
KELEYADUGU

Kankeri • Dosola

BAYA

DANU Jonkalan BANIMONOCÈ
KURULAMINI

Sankaroni
• Ntentu
• Buguni

Bale
• Kiribakuru
Niagharakò
Laminina
•

Bowulen

• Kona
Wasolon

BASIDIBE

• Lontola
BOLON

• Komisana
Segu
Tabakò • Koloni •

Koni
Garalo

SAKODUGU
JALON
FULA
Niantanina
Fulabula
Yorobugula
• Faraba
Gorontomo

Danko
CÈMALA

• Kunjan
JONDOGO
GWANAN

JETULU
Madina Jasa
Degu

Kanibugula •

Jarakuru
Sogola

Kalako •
Kokun
NIENENDUGU

Solomanina
Berebogola
Basidibejin

GWANIAKHA
Niesumala
Sangarejin

JAMURANKE
• Lensoro
KUSAN

JANJAMANA

• Niako

• Sandugula

FOLO

G U I N E A
• Menian

I V O R Y

Sanbatigila •

C O A S T

KUSAN

0   50 km

• Wojene

KABADUGU

habited by the Fulani Sidibe, Jakite, and Jalo, who later expelled the Dunbiya who had come from Ginbala.[9] According to a third hypothesis, the term originates in a Janjamana village called Wasolontigila.[10] This last etymological interpretation is supported by the fact that, on his crossing of this *jamana*, R. Caillié wrote his description of Ouassoulo (Wasolon), but we must not forget that these different etymologies are actually symbols disputed by the various groups living in the region.[11]

The French conquerors associated the Wasolon with the Samori empire; yet we now know with certainty that it composed only a small part of that empire.[12] Before the Samori conquest, the region was made up of about a dozen chiefdoms (*jamana*): Janjamana or Sananfula, Jetulu, Jondogo, Jamuranke, Folo, Basidibe, Jalonfula, Gwaniakha, Bolon, Kusan, and Gwanan. These chiefdoms were composed mostly of groups claiming a Fulani identity (*fula*) but speaking Banmana-Maninka and having adopted the elements essential to this culture. They were in opposition to the neighboring Maninka and Banmana *kafo*.

Other *jamana* exist inhabited by the Fula, however, such as the Banimonoce, Cemala, and the Nienendugu, which are not part of Wasolon. Thus the existence of a network of overlapping social relations, whose cohesion is reinforced by pressure from stronger political groups (Futa Jalon, Kabadugu, Segu), contributes more to the identity of the Wasolon Fula than do cultural and linguistic characteristics.

The cohesiveness of the Fula of Wasolon never appears as distinct as when they confront an external danger and the lineages and chiefdoms have to form a united front. Such occasions revive the myth that all these groups descended from the "four sons of the Fulani woman" or that they are "sons of the four women of Tinkalan [Tengela]," a symbolic figure in West African Fulani history.[13] Placing the Wasolon in a "chain of societies" would be, then, the key to this phase of identification; it would also be a genealogical and racial (*shiya*) form that the society applies to itself. But it is equally possible to see in this Fulani unanimity a reconstruction a posteriori by the oral tradition, that is, the effect of a particularist claim that has meaning only in reference to a present conjuncture.[14]

The Construction of the
Jakite Saabashi "Political Charter"

The "indigenous" theory of power emphasizes the superposition of several layers of population, each corresponding to a migratory movement, as does the colonial theory of races. This view legitimizes Fula supremacy over the rest of the Wasolon population. Also, rather than seeing a consecutive arrival of different groups, a more accurate view depicts a relation of precedence that reveals the permanence of the fundamental social relation: opposing the peasants to the state.

According to this indigenous theory, before the arrival of groups identifying themselves with the Fula, the Wasolon included elements that the Fula called Bambara, Bambaran, or Bambaraw, a name that, as we have seen, is the Fulani term for Banmana. In reality, this term has no precise ethnic connotation. It is a generic term encompassing populations that did not necessarily speak the same language or have the same practices. It could refer, for example, to groups who spoke Bambara-Malinke or Senufo. More precisely, in the minds of the conquerors, some of whom were Islamized, it most certainly designated an indistinct mass of pagan peasant-warriors. This would make the name the functional equivalent of the terms *kado* (plural *habbe*), or *ceddo* (plural *sebbe*), applied by the Fulani to such polytheistic peoples as the Dogon, to the mountain people in northern Cameroon, and to blacks in general.[15]

This earlier population left multiple traces, particularly in terms of toponymy. Many villages and *jamana* were named after their founder or the Bambara chief living there. Such is the case for Gwanan, whose name came from a Bambara king named Nfa Gwanan.

Gwanan, then, experienced successive periods of domination, with each new dynasty subduing the preceding one and inventing distant foreign origins for itself in order to better establish its power in the chiefdom. Such is the case with Saaba, ancestor of the Saabashi and last founder of Gwanan, who was the probable source of an epic whose aim was to conceal his Senufo origins behind a Fulani genealogy springing from Tinkalan.[16] Similarly, one should not believe, as certain informants have stated, that the different powers completely eliminated their predecessors by expelling them, killing them, or absorbing them. True, the Saabashi and their allies wanted to make a clean sweep of everything existing before them, and these groups certainly could have been destroyed, repressed, or assimilated. Nevertheless, descendants of the "first inhabitants" still live in certain villages.

The Saabashi were able to impose the idea that the Shielenkaw (people from Shielen) form the earliest layer of population to settle in Gwanan. According to the foundation story, these were Banmana, who took the praise name Kone and who originally came from Solon. After being expelled, these Kone moved to the region of Senu near Bamako, where some of their descendants still live. According to the Jakite Saabashi, there are no more Shielenkaw in Gwanan, either because they had all fled this chiefdom, or because, more probably, they were absorbed into the succeeding dynasty. The ancestor of this dynasty, Gondo, was also known by the praise name Kone but, unlike the Shielen, he is considered to be Maninka.[17] According to the official version, this group was also almost entirely expelled or absorbed by the next group to arrive.[18]

People from Kolon were the next to the last group in power before the arrival of the Jakite Saabashi in the region. Originally from Futa Jalon, Kolon was apparently known by the praise name Jalo or Jakite. The uncertainty regarding his patronym is surely connected with the manipulations of identity practiced by Saaba. One can legitimately suppose that when Saaba took power, he claimed for himself Kolon's praise name and forced him to adopt the Jalo one. Whatever the case may be, it is certain that Saaba did not create the chiefdom in Gwanan, for it already existed.

The Four Gwanan Men (*Gwanan Mogo Naani*)

The Gwanan "political charter" derives from the association of four men: Saaba Jakite, Maliki Jalo, Maliki Jakite, and Korika Sanba Jakite. They are the forebears of the dominant lineages and the four basic, generic figures for the foundation narratives. The epic relating the life of Saaba, for example, echoes the life of the founding heroes of the kingdoms in this region, in particular Sunjata, the most well known among them.[19]

The legend's different episodes constitute a theory of power more than an account of real events. The themes of the hero's destiny, the settling of conflicts, sacrifice, alliances, and magic power, not to mention the journey itself, are meant to lend credit to the idea of a peaceful and inevitable takeover and to encompass the whole of the Kolobakari Jara or Konate in an identical genealogical mold.[20]

In this myth, several inversions and dissimulations occur: the case of places frequented by Saaba, which were actually later founded by his descendants, and the case of slaves described as brothers. This shows once again the limitations of these mythic tales and the oral tradition in general as historical sources. It also demonstrates their essentially symbolic value.

A Predestined Hero

Saaba and his men took power in Gwanan after the Shielendaw, the Gondokaw, and the Kolonkaw. Saaba is the nickname of a man who was in fact named Tonkere and who had the praise name Jara or Konate. Saaba means "big snake," which symbolizes, as do the names of many of the chiefs,[21] the pillaging nature of their power, but also their magical abilities, since it is said that Saaba could transform himself into a snake. According to certain versions, he was a powerful, even terrifying person who took power in Gwanan more with his magical abilities (*barka*) than military might (*fanga*).

According to the Jakite Saabashi genealogy, Saaba is himself the great-great-grandson of Tinkalan who, as we have seen, was Tenguella, king of Futa. Somawulen, the great-grandson of Tinkalan and father of Saaba, apparently came from an undetermined location to settle at Jafunu; there, he had twelve sons, the next to the last of whom was Saaba.

According to the principal commonplaces in this type of tale, Saaba was incorrectly placed in the order of familial succession and yet he was destined to seize political power in one place or another. His half-brothers (*faden*) took umbrage at his ambitions and drove him off. He left Janfunu with his mother, his "brother" Mori, his wives, his children, his griots (*jeli*), his blacksmiths (*numu*), and his slaves (*jon*). His little troupe passed through Murja, Kuruba, and Gwala at the confluence of the Niger and Sankarani rivers. From

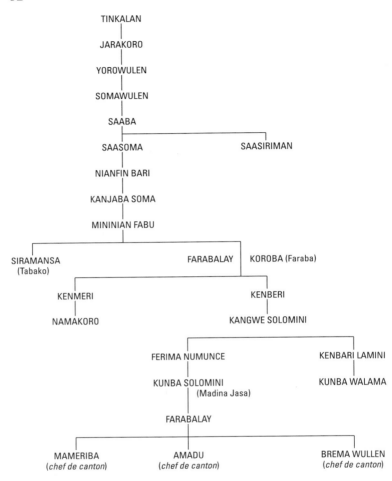

FIGURE I

Genealogy of the Jakite Saabashi of Madina Jasa

there, Saaba and his entourage went to Gonkoro, a Banmana fin or
Senufo village, where Saaba settled a dispute between two brothers
over a groundnut plant.

From Gonkoro, Saaba went to Tamase and Kologo in Cemala, but
did not stay there long. He then went to Niagharako, where he separated from his brothers, and continued on to Kiribakuru in Ba-

sidibe. His journey ended at Gorontomo where he found Kolon Jakite, the local chief (*yorotigi*), who offered him hospitality. Saaba seduced his host's daughter, Bawasa, whom he subsequently married. She revealed to him the secret of power: he should sacrifice a he-goat with no odor before Kolon had the chance to do so. Thanks to this feminine treachery, Saaba was able to sacrifice the he-goat and gradually seize power.

The Gwanan foundation myth is clearly an invention by the griots, whose purpose was, by making reference to the mythic ancestor Tinkalan, to emphasize the Fulani nature of the Saabashi and to thus legitimize their roots in Wasolon. It is likely that Saaba never made such a long journey and that he more probably came from Banmana fin or Senufo in Gonkoro, a large village near Wasolon that produced many of the region's dominant lineages.[22]

Saaba and his troupe took power in Gwanan (*ka fanga mine*), but his power remained precarious for a long time. According to Touze:

> For a long time the countryside was not safe. Bands of pillagers, descendants of Kolon and Banzan Diakité, the first inhabitants and who were based in the south near Odienne, prowled the area setting fires and wreaking havoc. . . . Even though the Diakite Sabasi from Tabako fought these pillagers and brought peace to the country, it was only with Kaba Toure [circa 1860], and especially his lieutenant Bintou Mameri, that the highwaymen were eliminated. They were practically all destroyed.[23]

We can, then, imagine Saaba and his army waging war and extending their domination over a progressively larger area of Wasolon, from Kankeri to Menian and from Bawulen to Niantanina.[24]

Association

Saaba's alliance with the ancestors of the other three dominant lineages formed the skeleton of the Gwanan "political charter," which resulted from an aggregation of the traditions of different lineages. This stemmed from a stable situation, that of the *pax gallica*. The basic agreement among the different segments regarding their common history gave Gwanan the image of a "nation" that included lineages descending from four ancestors: Saabashi, Malikishi, Serifuneshi, and Sanbashi. These lineages possessed the chiefship of a certain number of villages, but the political significance of this function was certainly not the same as it became under colonialism, where it was sanctioned by state authority and no longer challenged by the continual armed conflicts that formerly took place in the region.

The griot Jeyoro Kuyate of Yanfolila said: "There could be several warlords [*kelemansa*] per village"; and each "village contained its own destroyer within the village itself."[25] Power could fall to the oldest member of the senior generation of the dominant lineage, to the council of the elders in general, and also to the warriors, since, at this time, power lay in the arrow and the spear.

In light of these power relationships, theories of power currently formulated in Gwanan that stress, for example, the alternation of the chiefdom between the eldest lineage, the Saabashi (Tabako), and the youngest one, the Madina Jase, or between the Malikishi and the Saabashi, are merely projections of the political climate prevailing during colonialism onto the precolonial period. During colonialism there were, in fact, a Malikishi *chef de canton*, two *chefs de cantons* from the senior lineage (Saabashi), and three from the junior lineage.

The ancestors of Maliki Jalo claimed to be Fulani from the Timbo region and from Kuin in Futa Jalon, whereas they were more likely, as we have seen above, Banmana Samake from Kurulamini who settled in the Mande region of Niani. Maliki Jalo's descendants stressed the Fulani character of their ancestor and his role in the integration of the Jakite Saabashi with the Fulani of Wasolon,[26] as the following legend reveals:

The founding ancestor of the JanJamana and brother of Maliki Jalo's father, Fulamusajan Jalo, set off to war. Zantigi Turamagan Tarawele, king of Niani, took advantage of his absence to sack the Jalo village and kill Fulamusa Tumani, father of the young Maliki Jalo. The child managed to escape with his mother Kurian Sidibe and they joined a traders' caravan.[27] The small band arrived at the home of Koronba Kuyate, the griot of Saaba Jakite. He informed his master of the arrival of a caravan with a woman and child who, it seemed, were Fulani. Saaba ordered them to remain with him, threatening to make slaves of them if they tried to flee. He expressed his desire to marry Kurian, but she at first protested, saying she was not free and that her family might come to rescue her. Eventually, however, she married Saaba.

In the meantime, Fulamusajan returned from his military expedition, found his village sacked, and set off to find his brother's wife and her son. Leading an army, he attacked the village of Gorontomo. Kurian saved the villagers by passing them off as Fulani Jakite. Fulamusajan left Kurian and her son with Saaba. Maliki grew up and left for Mecca to seek fetiches or sacred earth that would protect Gwanan. Upon his return, he met a man of the same first name, Maliki Jakite, from Djenne. He presented this man at Gorontomo to Saaba, who agreed to let him stay. The name of the lineage came from Maliki Jakite's son, Serifune.

Saaba gave his first daughter, Tobi, to Kolon, the king he had dethroned, so that she could marry his son, Yerifunewulen, but he was killed at war. So Saaba decided to have her marry Maliki. Saaba's marriage to Kurian, Maliki's mother, as well as the union of Maliki with Tobi, Saaba's daughter, reinforced the relations between the Saabashi and Malikishi lineages. Tradition states as well that the two men extended their domain, fighting side by side. Nevertheless, Maliki's return from Mecca provoked a conflict among the Saabashi. Saasiriman, powerful warrior and youngest son of Saaba, doubtless jealous of Maliki's prestige and the favors he received from his father, asked for his share of griots, blacksmiths, and slaves. He left Gorontomo and waged war on his way to the confluence of the Niger and Sankarani rivers, where he founded Gwanan of Kuruba, a daughter chiefdom of the Wasolon.[28] Once again in the Maninka milieu, Saasiriman Jakite took back his former patronymic [of Konate], which his descendants go by to this day.

Korika Sanba Jakite, ancestor of the Sanbashi, originally came from the village of Kuin in Futa Jalon. Along with his young brother Flabu, his young sisters Fatuma and Seben, and his cattle, he went to Dabaran in Gwaniakha, on the left bank of the Wasolon Balen, where he found the Kuruman, who controlled the area but answered to Saaba. These Fulani asked permission to settle, but the Kuruman sent them to ask Saaba's permission and advised them to practice geomancy beforehand. From this divination, they learned that they were to sacrifice a paralytic girl in order to have their wish granted.[29]

It so happened that one of the Kuruman had a paralytic daughter, so he gave her over for sacrifice. She was immolated in the waters of the Wasolon Balen with kola and millet cream (*dege*). The Kuruman and the Jakite swore loyalty to each other and the Kuruman then asked Maliki Jalo to receive the Fulani. He accepted and used a stratagem to avoid letting Saaba make captives of Korika Sanba's group:

he presented Korika Sanba as Maliki Jakite's brother, who had brought the news that his parents would join him. Saaba agreed to welcome them into his community and married Seben, one of Korika Sanba's sisters.

Successors to Saaba and the Gwanan Wars

Saaba was a great warrior chief who, probably through his political skill for arranging matrimonial alliances, extended his domination over a large part of Wasolon and even beyond. Information regarding his successors, however, is very scant. We know practically nothing about his son Saasoma and very little about his grandson, Nianfin Bari, except that he ruled in this region (*o ye yoro nin kunnasigi*).[30] There is most likely a relation between this fact and the shrinking of Saaba's sphere of influence following the arrival in the region of Baya and Solon of the Dunbiya, who claimed to have pushed the Fulani toward the southwest, that is, into Wasolon.[31]

In the epic of Jakite Saabashi, a conflict between Siramansa and Farabalay gave rise to the different lineages of the elder Tabako and the junior Faraba. Kunba Walama's military prowess is evoked, but nothing is said of Serence Namakoro of Faraba who, according to Gallieni, was one of the most powerful war chiefs in all of Gwanan history.[32] In a rare convergence between written sources and oral tradition, numerous sources confirm this power. It is clear, in light of the documentation referred to here, that all of Gwanan history is contained in the history of its wars, whether they were wars to reconstitute the chiefdom, or wars of hegemony or fission (*fadenkele* or *badenkele*), all of which were both internal and externally promoted by neighboring states.

Saaba's wars of conquest figure among the first type of conflict.[33] Saaba's efforts to extend his control led him to occupy a large part of Wasolon, where he established an immense chiefdom that, in the context of political fragmentation characterizing the period, possessed certain features of a state.

Later wars, notably that of Konde Brema and the "war of the dream," exemplify the second, hegemonic and defensive type. In the first case, Konde Brema tried to establish hegemony over all the Wasolon and thereby present a strong "polytheistic" barrier to the Islamic expansion represented by the theocratic power of Futa Jalon.

But the Almami defeated Konde Brema,[34] whose failed efforts were possibly due to the military expedition undertaken at the same time (1776) by Ngolo Jara, king of Segu, against the neighboring area of Menian in Folo.[35]

In the last years of the eighteenth century, in fact, Wasolon was a source for booty for the kingdom of Segu. Around 1795, Monson raided Wassela (Wasolon), taking numerous slaves, whom he sold at Kangaré, Kangaba, Bamako, and Nyamina.[36] At the beginning of the nineteenth century, during the reign of Da, this area of conflict shrank and Segu's domination stopped at the confluence of the Sankarani and Wasolon Balen rivers.[37] Between 1851 and 1854, Demba defeated Wasolon, Birgo, and Ganadugu. The "war of the dream" (*sugo kele*) occurred during the reign of the next king. This would be analogous to Konde Brema's war except that it was fought by soldiers possessed of genius. Jeri Sidibe led this anti-Moslem war, inflaming all of Wasolon, but did not achieve a durable hegemony over the region.[38] Jeri Sidibe's army was defeated first by the *kafo* of Baya,[39] before Segu intervened on Jeri Sidibe's behalf, and a second time by Torokoromari.[40] Jeri was also defeated by Vakaba Ture of Wojene, then held off by Kankan, whom he unsuccessfully attacked. He lost his life in this conflict, in 1855.[41] Most probably on this occasion Torokoromari conquered Gwanan and consolidated the power of the Jakiti Saabashi.[42]

The Fulani War (*Fula Kele*) or the War of Kaba (*Kaba Kele*)

As its name indicates, the Fulani war was internal to Wasolon. Since units of equal size (*kafos*, lineages, villages) fought against each other, it was a war of fission that superficially differed markedly from those preceding it, but which, in fact, was merely one phase in a process of political expansion and contraction. This war provoked immediate intervention by *kafos* and neighboring states. Thus, in the context of the period (second half of the nineteenth century) and the region, this war was typically segmentary in that it exemplified the controlled competition among lineages fostered by more powerful units, the states, as a form of domination.

As the following story shows, the origin of this war was itself typically segmentary in nature. It concerned a conflict between the two dominant lineages, Saabashi and Malikishi, though Namakoro's challenge was actually nothing more than his will for power:

> There was once a king [*masake*] called Serence Namakoro.[43] He was the one they offended at Ferekeli Bagan's funeral by shooting off their guns too near him. People told them they were annoying the king, but Namakoro said to let them be since it was one of his uncles.[44] Afterwards, he sent a message to which no brave men could fail to respond. At the same time he sent a message to Kunjan Jemori Sako of Sakodugu[45] asking for help in bringing to heel certain troublemakers in the region. Kunjan's army came to Lontola. Namakoro let the people of Lontola defend themselves, then arrived when the battle was over. Kunjan's warriors had sacked the village and left with their booty. Namakoro got angry because he thought the Kunjan would share the booty with him. There are still children of our Fulani women in Kunjan.

Namakoro was a powerful king who united several war chiefs by offering them his daughters or other relatives in marriage.[46] He possessed a fortress at Danko and fought with Yorogwe Jalo, a Malikishi who entrenched himself at Fulabula, a village surrounded by nine walls (*jin*).

To get revenge on Kunjan Jemori Salo and eliminate the Malikishi Jalo of Fulabula, Namakoro called on the aid of "all the livestock holdings of the Fulani woman," that is, the war chiefs of Banimonoce, Cemala, Kurulamini, Janjamana, Jetulu, Gwaniakha, Basidibe, and Toron.[47] They attacked Fulabula several times, but failed to take it.

At that point, Namakoro sent his son Namakoro Jara and his relatives, Kunba Walama and Farabalay, to look for the Kabakele (war or army of the Ture of Wojene). The three men spent the rainy season at Wojene, during which Namakoro Jara was able to have a love affair with the king's wife, who became pregnant. Using this as a pretext, Namakoro informed another relative, Kunba Solomini, of his son's misconduct and of his own desire to see the Wojene army withdraw. At that moment, the Kabakele, led by an ally of Namakoro, the war chief Bintu Mameri Ture, arrived at Sandugula (Kusan), whose doors were closed. The Wojene army laid siege to Sandugula and finally took the village. The Wasolon Fulani broke into two opposed forces: one gathered around Namakoro and Kunba Walama, the other taking as their leader Bintu Mameri, ally of Farabalay and Yorogwe Jalo. At the beginning of the hostilities, Kunba Walama and Namakoro prevailed: they took Kokun, Ferela, and Sirakoroba, where Kunba Walama was killed. The Wojene army went to Yoroncena and there the situation reversed: the two Fulani groups reconciled, drawing on the myth of their common ancestry as descendants of "the four sons of the Fulani woman" or "the sons of the four women of Tinkalan." As a result, they appeared on this occasion to be an ethnic group.[48] The Fulani united against the Kabadugu people and pursued Bintu Mameri all the way to Siratogo in Banan. Bintu called on Segu for reinforcements. Amadu, the son of Al Hajj Umar, sent an army but refused to help fight the Fulani of Wasolon. Bintu Mameri was brought to Segu, where he remained until the end of the Samorian wars.

The story of the "Fulani war" sheds light on the deeply segmentary character of the pre-Samorian Wasolon. As long as this region was autonomous, the numerous small states that shared the same political space were continually at war, fueling the internal trade in slaves.[49] Only with the threat of intervention from without did these states confederate and assume the Fulani "label" to stand unified in the face of adversity.

Samori

In a similar way, Samori was able to peacefully rule Gwanan by manipulating internal divisions and lineage alliances.[50] Though Al-mami had to conquer the rest of Wasolon, he was able to subdue this *jamana* by using the existing alliance between Yorogwe Jalo and Farabalay Jakite, the Saabashi who had come to Wasolon with the Ture army from Wojene. Even though Samori made contact with the Gwanan people at Sanankoro, it was at Nyako, in Janjamana, that he received from Farabalay the submission (*dege min*) of Gwanan and the five other *jamana*: Kurulamini, Bolo, Cemala, Nienendugu, and Banimonoce.[51] To reassure Samori, who was anxious to know if the Kurulamini and the Banimonoce, with their large stocks of arms (*forobagwasa*) and powerful armies, were truly subdued, Farabalay tested them by asking that they supply soldiers for the war against Sagajigi Kamara of Gwankundo.[52]

Samori thus brought to heel the six *jamana* by dangling before them the prospect of a victorious military expedition–and a sizable

booty—against one of the region's premier war chiefs. All the warriors of the six villages were placed under the command of two
keletigi: Namakoro, Fode Jakite, one of Serence Namakoro's sons,
and Dabi Sanba Jalo, a Malikishi from Yoroncena. After nine months
of combat, they took Gwankundo, amassing a booty composed
chiefly of captives.

Samori used the same stratagem a few years later when he wanted
to take Sikaso. There too, he brought about a military alliance, a
joint venture destined to destroy villages and amass a large booty.
The six subdued villages each sent a contingent of soldiers under the
command of six war chiefs recruited locally. Upon their departure
for Sikaso, Farabalay turned the command over to Yamaga, Namakoro's son,[53] and ordered Bujan Jalo, a Malikishi, to take care of
the supplies for the Gwanan troups fighting in the Samorian army.
But Farabalay betrayed Samori and hid out at Ceba during the siege
of Sikaso. There he stayed until 1898, when Ceba was taken by the
French.[54] Farabalay was replaced by Jinamansa, son of his older
brother, who became war chief but who did not remain in power for
long. In fact, the siege of Sikaso and the resulting deprivations un-
dergone by the conquered regions provoked the great revolt of
1888–90. Unable to prevent the uprisings of the Kurulamini, the
Bolo, the Cemale, the Banimonoce, and the Nienendugu, Jinamansa kept control only of Gwanan.[55]

This was the situation until 1893, when Samori sacked Ntentu and
fled to the Ivory Coast, pursued by Bonnier's troops.[56] At that time
the inhabitants of Gwanan split into two groups: one part remained
in Gwanan and hid while awaiting the arrival of the French; the others, with Jinamansa as their leader, retreated or were forced to re-
treat with Almami. Jinamansa perished in the Ivory Coast during
the last years of the Samorian epic.

Colonization

With the 1893 arrival of Commander Bonnier's troops, all of Wasolon surrendered.[57] The French then called all the inhabitants of
Gwanan together and asked them to choose a "messenger." A
Saabashi, Flabu Jakite, was chosen. The colonizers consented to this
choice, but Flabu Jakite dealt in slaves,[58] so he was replaced by Bujan Jalo, a Malikishi originally from Berele, the same one who had

been ordered to take care of supplies for the Gwanan troups laying siege to Sikaso.

At this time, the Gwanan people who had not followed Samori to the Ivory Coast did not return to their lands, remaining instead at Faragwaran under French protection for fear of Almami's return. This is the context in which Bujan attempted to unite all the Wasolon people around Faragwaran. He sent emissaries to Gwanan, Baya, Basidibe, Gwaniakha, and Kusan, asking the inhabitants of these *jamana* to place themselves under French protection. The Kusan people, living to the south of Gwanan, asked to be grouped with Gwanan in order to escape the too heavy requisitions because, they said, "work is business of white men."[59] That explains why colonial documents, particularly the *Monographie du cercle de Bougouni* established by R. Touze, included the Kusan with Gwanan and why this *jamana* currently numbers fifty-five villages.[60]

When in 1898 Sikaso was taken by the French, Farabalay returned to Yorobugula, in Gwanan, and found Bujan Jalo at the head of the *chefferie de canton*. Unwilling or unable to assume this position because of his Samorian past, Farabalay returned to Madina Jasa to take up agriculture.[61] Bujan Jalo remained *chef de canton* for two or three years before being imprisoned for reasons that remain unclear. Since Farabalay had proven his goodwill toward the French, he took the position of *chef de canton*. It was the alliance of Yorogwe Jalo with Farabalay, Farabalay's nomination of Bujan Jalo as steward of Gwanan, and his succession of Bujan Jalo as *chef de canton* that lent credence to the idea of an alternation between Malikishi and Saabashi in Gwanan, or to the idea that a Saabashi chief would always have at his side a Malikishi advisor.[62]

This is, in fact, a fixed colonial structure—that of a *chef de canton* who would obey certain rules regarding elections, nominations, and so on—projected onto a pre-Samorian period that, aside from certain principles of relatively fluid lineage and dynastic succession, knew no other law than that of warfare. One finds the same type of false archaism apropos of Farabalay's successors, the Saabashi of the senior lineage. After having occupied his position for some time, Farabalay was dismissed for having struck his subjects.[63] He was replaced by Sanba Jakite, then, in 1916, by Numori Jakite, both of the senior family branch and residing in Tabako. But Sanba, and especially Numori, had difficulties with Farabalay who, though excluded from his position as *chef de canton*, continued to exert considerable influence. As former *chef de canton*, descendant of a prestigious lineage, and fervent Moslem, he enjoyed the support of the district's primary spokesman.[64] He continually undermined the authority of *chefs de canton* from the senior branch, which brought the district commanders to reconsider and entrust the leadership again to a Saabashi from the junior family branch.[65] But the return to power of the Saabashi of Madina Jasa did not bring an end to the difficulties of colonial administration. In fact, Mameriba, *chef de canton* in 1930, was involved along with his brothers in an affair of unauthorized levying of fines. Mameriba's authority was further weakened by the fact that some of the Gwanan people did not recognize his legitimacy since he was descended from a slave.

At the time, the district commanders attributed their problems with the *chefs de canton* to the fact that most of them were not chiefs by virtue of their lineage, but men of humble origin.[66] What was needed, then, was to empower men of the correct lineage. Thus, when Mameriba Jakite died in 1931, an authentic Saabashi of Madina Jasa, Amadu, succeeded him.[67] Amadu maintained the best of relations with Lasausse, the district commander who spared Amadu the difficulties of supplying rubber and rice for the war effort by not undertaking "investigations during the census of 1942 that could have recorded a considerably larger number of inhabitants." Thanks to Lasausse's support, Amadu was also able to construct one hundred and fifty kilometers of roads that allowed the country to be "opened up."

These practices displeased a large part of the population in Gwanan because of the many deaths occurring in Madina Jasa, including the 1943 death of the *chef de canton*, which were attributed to poisonings. Brema Wulen, half-brother of Amadu, succeeded him as *chef de canton* and remained in that position until the chiefdom was terminated in 1959.

Good relations continued to exist between the district officer and the new canton leader, which allowed the chiefs and notables of certain villages to increase their wealth by taking advantage of the difference between the actual population numbers and those accountable for taxes. Discord within Gwanan intensified because of the denunciations to which these profiteers were susceptible. Several factors made the canton ungovernable: the 1946 appearance of "politics," that is, electoral competition between the Sudanese Party for Progress (P.S.P.) and the Democratic African Party (R.D.A.), compounded by the undermining carried out by the unsuccessful rival of Brema Wulen for the 1943 election, the interpreter Cewulen Jakite.

In 1947, the administration worried about the "turmoil" stirred up by a marabout in the canton's southern portion. The district officer intervened and forced the marabout to go to the Ivory Coast. In 1950, to take matters in hand, the district officer decided to hold a census in order to increase tax revenue, but especially to reestablish order. This move entailed numerous "palavers," in-depth conferences, census taking, and, in 1953, the preparation of village monographs.[68] Nevertheless, the authority of the *chef de canton* remained precarious due to his propensity to set up sinecures. Originally a member of the P.S.P., he went over to the R.D.A. during the 1956 elections. The P.S.P. then accused him of treason and blamed him for strengthening the R.D.A. influence in the district.[69] In 1957, following the nomination of a Jakite as village chief in Yorobugula, the local Jalo, who were Malikishi, asked to form a separate canton.[70] Their request was not granted and Gwanan remained unchanged until 1959, when the *chefferie de canton* was suppressed. This only intensified old feuds among the segmented groups, however.

There were continual feuds between Malikishi and Saabashi and between Saabashi members of the senior branch and those of the junior branch. The colonial administration, the Saabashi lineages of the junior branch, and the Malikishi who took advantage of disputes among the Saabashi interpreted these feuds as indicative of the structural nature of the alternation among rival segments. In the social consciousness, this permanent feuding took the form of a "political charter," that is, an alliance of power bringing together the descendants of the "four men of Gwanan." Colonization thus made the condition resulting from relations among war chiefs into a model of segmentarity.

This series of events illustrates one way in which segmentary societies appeared in Africa. Following the peace established by the colonial political apparatus, chiefdoms based on warfare and slavery disappeared to become agricultural village communities.

6 A Dominated Segmentary State: Jitumu

The two chiefdoms we have chosen to study, the Gwanan and the Jitumu, differ significantly in their origins. The "Fulani" chiefdom of Gwanan resulted from the crumbling of the great empires of Mali and Sonrai, while the Jitumu originated in the eighteenth-century intervention by the kingdom of Segu in the Upper Niger Valley, an intervention which produced a dominated segmentary "Bambara" state. By "dominated segmentary state," I mean a form of political organization intermediate between segmentary societies and state societies. These political formations were the offshoots of large kingdoms, characterized by the significance that revolts and interlineage conflicts (*fadenkele*) held for them. It is primarily from and by these conflicts that the central kingdoms drew their force, such that the state produced and reproduced itself largely in segmentary entities. Though the mode of constitution and the ethnic affiliation of these two chiefdoms differed, it is clear that in both cases the segmentary pole and the state pole formed two complementary aspects of a single reality.

In trying to retrace the genesis of a political whole such as Jitumu, one invariably confronts the impossibility of writing the history of a population's expansion. This is not for lack of information—in which case anthropology, as Malinowski declared, would have to give up history and produce only "mythical charters"—but rather because what looks like a collection of lineages takes on all the features of a structurizing archetype.

In other words, in order to function, local political theory needs a limited number of categories, essentially that of the first settlers and that of the conquerors.[1] The history of different *kafos* thus becomes an extremely spare scenario consisting of two elements, one superimposed upon the other: a layer of landowners (*dugukolotigiw*) and priests (*somaw*) overtaken by a wave of conquerors who dominate them and seize political power. As we have already seen regarding Gwanan, however, this category of first settlers is an intellectually convenient fiction that allows one to formulate the theme of alliance (often of the "joking relationship" type–*senankuya*) between the landowners and the possessors of spiritual power on one hand and the possessors of physical power (*fanga*) on the other.[2] It turns out that the first settlers were first in name only and that they were preceded–as much as we can determine from the oral tradition or archeology when it exists–by an entire series of groups whose position is irrelevant for the region's history or political hierarchy.

Another element enters the picture: Banba Saganogo, who came from Kong and appears in several legends about the founding of Bamako,[3] dominated the area between Demeni, in the *kafo* of Morila, and this village. Demeni is now populated by the Dunbiya, who originally came from Kemeni near Segu,[4] and the Tarawele, native to Kong, who, under the command of Mori, took power in this area.[5] There are other villages in the area, Worofara, near Jela, Soba, or Folona in Keleyadugu, or Demeni, none of which plays a role in the structure of the local political discourse.

On the other hand, of three villages that do play a role–Bonboya, Ferenan, and Jakokoronin–two have today disappeared. The hamlet Bonboya is today peopled by Dunbiya, whose taboo is the "metallic blackbird" (*molo*) and who are joking relatives (*senanku*) to the Komagara from Ngolobara in Solon. Ferenan was inhabited by Dunbiya different from those of Bonboya.[6] Their taboo is the panther (*warakalan*) and they are related to the Dunbiya of Demeni and to those who preceded the Tarawele to Keleyadugu. The descendants of the Dunbiya of Ferenan who now live at Siminji and those of Demeni are all *senanku* of the Bagayogo who founded Keleyadugu in the eighteenth century.

According to certain versions, the Dunbiya of Solon lived in the two villages of Ferenan and Jakokoronin when the Kulubali arrived there. According to other stories, the Kulubali were Bitonshi fleeing Segu around 1750, at the time the Jara took power; they met up with the Dunbiya at Solon and came with them to the area that would become Jitumu. The Dunbiya founded Ferenan, the Kulubali settled in Jakokoronin. In fact, according to the colonial administrator, M. Riou,[7] it seems that Joman, who commanded the Dunbiya of Ferenan, dominated the country politically and had Mori, chief of the Kukubali, as his marabout. These contradictory versions refer to the positions of different groups jockeying for local political power. But it is important to emphasize that one of the groups of first settlers, the Kulubali, was itself the product of a "state dissidence,"[8] extending ad infinitum the problem of an original layer of autochthons.

<h2 style="text-align:center">Origin of the Samake and
Foundation of Jitumu</h2>

Similarly, the foundation of Jitumu by the Samake seems to have also resulted from a distant "state dissidence." To pinpoint the genesis of this *kafo*, one has to go back to the kingdom of Toron. According to the foundation myth reported by Riou, who received it from the dominant lineages:

> The Samake (Ture) ancestors were two brothers, Duba Ngolo and Duba Zan. They were vassals or slaves of the king of Toron, a region situated near Kerwane in what is now Guinea. The two brothers had settled at the foot of two hills named Masanyaman and Jitumu, which were part of Rabajala, the king's residence. According to the legend, Duba Zan was the ancestor of the Samake from Kurulamini and Duba Ngolo the ancestor of the Samake from Jitumu. Duba Ngolo's wife, Kulun, gave birth to Kulu Ngolo and Kulun Npie, ancestors of the two dominant Jitumu lineages: Serimana and Fabunela.
>
> Having become powerful, the two brothers tried to overthrow the king of Toron. They attacked and pillaged Rabajala, seized magical objects of war, but could not take control and were forced to flee. With a small troop, they went to Jonkalan in Kurulamini where they rested but, with the Toron army at their heels, they had to move on, taking with them part of the Kurulamini people.

During their flight, they crossed Keleyadugu and were saved only because of the *kafotigi* Keleyamansa Bagayogo, who told the king of Toron that he had not seen them, thereby sealing a durable alliance between Keleyadugu and Jitumu. Having escaped the king of Toron, the little band settled in Ntenkoni in Ntinkadugu (Banan), where both Kulun and her youngest son, Npie, died. The eldest brother, Ngolo, found himself leader of the family. Taking Jitumu Musa, Npie's youngest son, he fled the wartorn Ntinkadugu.[9]

For both Jitumu and Gwanan, as we saw earlier, the myth of origin functions to unite groups of people with the same name around a common ancestor, in this case, the Samake of Jitumu and those of Kurulamini. Though the authenticity of this long migration is not questioned, it patently synthesizes several epochs and generations, thus dissimulating the fundamental heterogeneity of the whole of the Samake, both of Jitumu and of Kurulamini. In all likelihood, the conquerors of Jitumu must have already been settled at Ntenkoni in Banan for some time when, upon the arrival of the Jakite-Fonba, they had to flee.

Here is more of the legend recorded by Riou:

Ngolo, Jitumu Musa, and their entourage arrived at Ferenan, where they asked Mori Kulubali of Jakokoronin to take them in. He refused, but Joman Dunbiya accepted. Ngolo and Joman pledged their loyalty [*jo*] to one another. Joman took Ngolo to a place where they could settle, and there they founded the village of Jela.

Ngolo cared deeply for his brother Npie, and was inconsolable at his death. He cherished his brother's son, Jitumu Musa, who became his most trusted child advisor. Ngolo asked Musa to consult the oracles on the fate of the region. Sacrifices were required: a virgin, a live boa, and the construction of a hut made of earth kneaded or moulded with shea butter. Ngolo's sons, Siriman and Somable,[10] each had a virgin among their children, but both refused to hand them over for sacrifice. Only Jitumu Musa accepted, but not before having his brothers swear to acknowledge his primacy. The amulets were Makogoba and Nangologo, and remain the national amulets of Sanankoro.

Musa's brothers, Siriman and Somable, feared for their future and wanted to get rid of him. They asked their father to send him as representative to the king of Segu. They then secretly asked Damonzon to keep Musa prisoner, as a danger to the country. Damonzon put Musa in irons. The old Ngolo grew worried about Musa's prolonged absence and sent another brother, Semion, to take Musa's place. Musa hurried home to Jela, where Ngolo died the following day. Joman of Ferenan remarked Semion's absence and told Mori of Jakokoronin. Both intervened and obtained his release.

Musa was no more noble than the other children of Npie and Ngolo. A source of benediction for a child is the material and moral support he gives his parents during their old age. Thus, Musa's father agreed to accompany and support their aged mother during their flight. Musa remained with her at Ntenkoni until she died in his arms. This good mother was not indifferent to her son's actions. She obtained for him the blessings of the old Ngolo, her uncle, whom he supported in his old age. He was worthy of his country not only for having risked his life in numerous delegations to Segu, but also for having alone accepted painful sacrifices. Gifted in the occult sciences, particularly geomancy, which he learned from his slave Nanburama, he labored for the prosperity of Jitumu, which still bears his name (Jitumu Musa). This is why his primacy and that of his direct descendants have been recognized throughout the country.

In this narrative, three themes conceal what was actually a seizing of power by the youngest lineage from the eldest, led by Ngolo.

The first two reappear constantly in foundation myths of *kafos* or states in this region: divination (geomancy) and magic are almost always associated with a power takeover because they are naturally linked to the mastery of supernatural forces ruling the world. It was because Jitumu Musa was both a great soothsayer and a great magician—he did not die, but disappeared—that he could seize power, not because he used force (*fanga*).[11] Beyond its fixed and recurrent form, this motif takes on a particular meaning here: soothsayers pronounced the name of Jitumu Musa, one of the greatest geomancers of the region, during incantations accompanying sacrifices, making reference to his fight against the secret society of the *komo*:

> Old Bala of Jitumu
> pursued the *komo* of Jitumu, cut off its defenses
> by the force of the blacksmith's sand.
> This earned him power and fame.

Other narratives emphasize the fact that Jitumu Musa used geomancy to the detriment of the *komo* established by the first settlers, and that, as a result, his power was linked to another type of ideological domination, that emanating from the Arabic and Islamic world. In this foundation narrative, the theme of Segu's intervention is more concrete, thus indicating that no power could be established without at least the tacit approval of the kings. But this version is obviously unanimist, since it emphasizes Ngolo's role in obtaining Jitumu Musa's release and return home, thus legitimizing the complementary roles of the senior and junior lineages in governing the chiefdom.

According to V. Pâques, after having killed Ngolo, Musa seized power over Jitumu.[12] A conflict quickly arose between Jela and Ferenan, however, since the Samake had stolen goods from Ferenan Joman. The incensed Joman commanded Mori Kulubali to set in motion occult forces against Jela, whereupon a torrential rain destroyed the village. This event provides one of the possible etymologies of the *kafo*'s name, since in Bambara "Jitumu" means "destruction by water." Another is the Toron hill, at the bottom of which resided the Samake.

The hospitality Ngolo asked of the indigenes, their resistance through magic, and the destruction of Jela are so many symbolic elements that barely conceal the institution of a new power (*ton*) in the region.

One informer, Nkoro Dunbiya of Siminji, confirms this fact:

> When Ngolo arrived at Ferenan, the Bambara ruled [*banmana fanga*]. If you hear talk of *faama*, it means extortion [*binkanni*] and war. Ngolo despoiled and ravaged the people. We had nothing, but spoliation is an old practice. Stealing the belongings of another and selling them for profit. At that time, a person could steal a woman and her baby to sell them at the market. That is why we had to leave Ferenan to settle here.

The institution of this new power resulting from Jitumu Musa's victory over Ngolo also provoked a division within the dominant group. Ngolo's son, Seriman, left to settle at Beneko, which became the first village ruled by the senior lineage, that of the Serimana, whereas Npie's son, Jitumu Musa, settled at Nfamusala between Sanankoro and Bagayogobugu. With Musa's death, his son, Fabune, acceded to the leadership of the chiefdom, founded the village of Sanankoro, and gave rise to the junior lineage, that of the Fabunela.

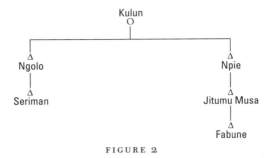

FIGURE 2

The little group of fugitives led by Ngolo and Npie included slaves and dependents. They either left Toron with the Samake or joined up with them during the peregrinations that took them to Jitumu. In the course of identity conversions, these groups, originally of very diverse origins including some of very humble status, were assimilated by Samake belonging to dominant lineages.

For example, the chief of the Samake's slaves was named Furaba Sako. Once arrived at Jitumu, he abandoned his patronymic and took the Samake patronymic of his master Fabune. Furaba founded Segesonan and his descendants formed the Furabala lineage. As for Jitumu Musa's Fulani shepherd, he was called Soma Sangare. According to certain tales, when Jitumu Musa's wife discovered him practicing geomancy, he was required to teach divination to his master. He took his surname from Musa because of his attachment to him and went on to found the village of Konia and to become the ancestor of the Somala or Koniadugu lineage. Similarly, Npieba Kamara, a *fina* originally from Beledugu and a member of Ngolo's and Jitumu Musa's entourage, exchanged his patronym for that of Samake. He set himself up at Kaban, which became the primary village of the Npiebala lineage. Finally, Nzie Jabate headed a group of blacksmiths (*numu* originally from Ntenkoni in Banan) who followed Ngolo and Npie in their flight to Jitumu. He too took the name of his host (*jatigi*), founded the village of Nzielabugu, and gave rise to the Numuniziela lineage. The whole of these major patrilineages (*faso*, *fabon*, or *kabila*) that divided into a multiplicity of minor matricentered (*babon*) patrilineages formed the uppermost layer of the chiefdom. Two lineages dominated, the Serimana and the Fabunela, who are linked in the expression *Npie ni Ngolo ci* (the traces of Npie and Ngolo). Just below in the social hierarchy are the dependent lineages, whose makeup is heterogenous (slaves, Fulani, statutory groups). As we have seen, they acquired the *jamu* Samake and are not considered authentic Samake by the Serimana and Fabunela. Yet the origin of these dependent lineages is not immediately apparent to outsiders, and this mystery strengthens the *kafo*'s identity to the outside world (*an be kelen*), all the while assuring a strict hierarchy within.

These two groups, the dominant lineages and the dependent ones, do not make up the totality of the Samake. The Dogotu and Kantene Sama must also be included. The Dogotu, originally from Kurulamini, were chiefs of two villages, but played no political role in the operations of the chiefdom. They were to a certain extent nonfunctional, a little like certain villages that existed in the region when the Samake first arrived. The Kantene Sama or Samanisenjan, however, who were the joking relatives (*senanku*) of the Serimana and the Fabunela, did not head any village. It seems that these Samake, who lived both at Kurulamini and Cemala, were freed slaves. In the past, Samake of dominant lineages did not intermarry with them.

Since they were not endogamous, the Samake needed potential allies in villages and lineages with patronymics different from their own. Hence the importance for them of villages and lineages with which they were affined or matrilineally (*furunyogon* or *belenin*) connected, to which they provided wives and from which they took wives.

These are villages of the "first settlers," that is, people whom the Samake found when they themselves arrived in the region. Bonboya led by the Dunbiya, Ferenan led by other Dunbiya, Jakokoronin, whose chiefs were Kulubali, as well as other village communities, made up the indigenous population. The Samake willingly maintained that they came later. At the bottom of the social hierarchy were the slaves (*jon*) and their descendants (*woloso*), who formerly must have been relatively numerous but who were later considerably reduced in number, either because many left or because they were integrated into the larger group.[13]

Consequently, the striking feature of the Jitumu social hierarchy is its extraordinary plasticity and its capacity to integrate many pop-

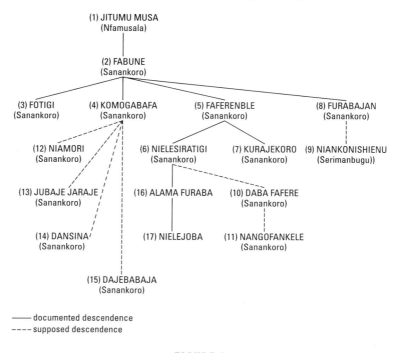

FIGURE 3

List of the Jitumu 'kafotigi'

ulations with very diverse origins. Thus, during the course of name changes and incorporation into dominant Samake lineages, groups with a relatively low status could have a certain upward mobility. In spite of this mobility, however, political life in the chiefdom was nonetheless confined to the interior group of free men, that is, dominant, dependent, and affined lineages. As numerous as the slaves were, they were excluded from membership in what constituted the Samake "nation."

Functioning of the Chiefdom

Though Jitumu was a province of the kingdom of Segu for a relatively long period, it is possible to study the chiefdom as more or less autonomous. In fact, even though Jitumu as a *kafo* was to some extent a production of the kingdom of Segu, with a resulting exogenous morphogenesis, Jitumu nevertheless continued to exist after Segu fell and has remained in existence throughout diverse historical vicissitudes to this day.

Segu thus knew civil war (*fadenkele*), which resulted in Ngolo, the first *faama* of Jitumu, ceding power to Jitumu Musa. According to the principal informers, all the *kafotigi* of Jitumu, up to Samori and including Ngolo, issued from the junior lineage, Fabunela, that takes its name from Fabune, son of Jitumu Musa.

This list of *kafotigi* up to the creation of the canton chieftaincy in 1914 is the only one I have been able to obtain orally. While the names of Jitumu Musa and Fabune are accepted by all the people of Jitumu, only two other names on the list, Kurajekoro and Furabajan, have been confirmed by other informers. Aside from them, the name of Fotigi Samake, a Fabunela who, according to Binger, ruled Jitumu, Keleyadugu, and Jalakorodugu and who, according to Person, resided at Sido, does not figure on the list, nor do the names of two other Fabunela, Tle and Semioba, who became famous in the chiefdom's history, as we shall see below.[14]

Given the large number of chiefs from Sanankoro, it is logical that almost all the informers indicated that village as the capital of Jitumu. Besides, the village is the home of two magical objects: the Makungoba and the Nangoloko, neither of which I have ever been allowed to see.

If power remained in the Fabunela lineage, as it has in all likelihood, it is due in part to the fact that the members of this lineage descended from Jitumu Musa. His exploits reflected on his posterity, thus giving his descendants a sacred legitimacy. As we have seen, Jitumu Musa most certainly sealed his power by the practice of geomancy, an Arabic divinatory technique, and imposed it to the detriment of the secret society of the *komo*, prerogative of the "polytheistic" autochthons. Leaving behind marks of geomancy–the imprint of his foot and that of a child on a lateritic–he disappeared at Nfamusala under mysterious conditions, abandoning his spear and scrip. Every seven years, all the lineages of Jitumu sacrificed kola nuts, chickens, goats, and bulls in order to demonstrate cohesion within the *kafo* and at the same time to mark the preeminence of the Serimana and the Fabunela, who alone had the right to approach the altar.[15]

The Serimana and Fabunela were also closely associated in organizing the funeral for a chief and the enthronement of his successor. The Fabunela immediately informed the Serimana when a chief died. The funeral services included the sacrifice of an ox, with parts of its body distributed corresponding to the order of succession to the chiefship: the immediate successor received the chest portion, the next in line received the heart, the third the liver. The remainder of the meat (*wolosogo*) went to the affines.

Three months after the death, a successor was chosen. The Serimana designated two of their men from Sanankoro and asked the Fabunela to chose one of them as *kafo* leader. The one chosen had to be perfectly pure (*yerewolo*), that is, not illegitimate. As soon as the Fabunela agreed on their choice, all the villages in the *kafo* were informed. The Fabunela announced the successor before all the lineage heads and village chiefs gathered at Sanankoro. In principle, the successor would be the oldest member of the major patrilineage, but he did not have to live at Sanankoro.[16]

The Serimana gave their assent, cattle were sacrificed, and libations were offered, accompanied by the sound of war drums (*kelemasadunu*). The *kafotigi* sat on the royal skin, that of the ox killed for his enthronement. Upon the command of the Serimana, the Dunbiya of Bonboya, an affined lineage and the inhabitants of the oldest village in the region, had the chief sit and stand three times on the royal skin (*masagolo*). The new *kafotigi* inherited his predecessor's regalia, particularly his emblem of leadership (the tail of a cow). If the new leader was not from Sanankoro, he thereupon returned to his village, and would in time be buried there.

Though accounts of nominations of chiefs give the impression of great stability, a stability evidently reinforced, as with other political developments, by the institution of the canton chieftaincy, the power of the Fabunela chiefs did not have an infallible legitimacy. Lineage or dynastic continuity was disrupted several times by civil or internecine wars (*fadenkele*). Rivals (*faden*) united the people against two despotic *kafotigi*, who were subsequently eliminated. One of Jitumu Musa's sons, for example, Tle of Cesana, was guilty of multiple extortions from the people of Sanankoro. He seized the goods of several deceased villagers and pillaged the area on two occasions. In revenge, the ally of the rest of Jitumu, Sanankoro, destroyed Cesana village and brought his power to an end.

His successor, Semioba of Farala, had similar habits:

After the millet harvest [*foboda*], all the villages gathered to honor the elders with chickens, millet, peanuts, and gourds of honey. When they went to honor the *kafotigi* of Semioba, one of the griots expressed surprise at their coming. He claimed that the villagers did not come to pay their respects but to commit an act of treachery. In order to kill them, he invited the delegation leaders to meet beneath a tree outside the village. All the villagers went there to attack and kill Farala.[17]

These two stories of *fadenkele* show that the power of the *kafotigi* was despotic in nature. Only rivals, those who aspired to the chiefship themselves, stirring up rivalries among lineages and villages, were in a position to end the arbitrary rule of certain *faama*.

Certain practices, such as those concerning justice, were part of the normal wielding of power. The *kafotigi* of the junior Fabunela lineage and his entourage formed an association (*ton*) that arbitrated in the frequent conflicts within the chiefdom. It was not uncommon for one village to challenge and then attack another. Those judged guilty had to pay a fine. A portion of the *kafotigi*'s revenues came from such transgressions. However, the *kafotigi* also took part in both internal and external conflicts of the *kafo*. Leading his army, the *faama* would pillage a village on the request of another village community, calling upon the aid of another *kafo* if necessary. The warrior confederations that worked against the Fula of Segu, for example, originated in these types of aggressions. War, often difficult to distinguish from justice, represented another appreciable source of income for the chief. The army was composed primarily of hunters (*donso*) armed with guns (*marifa*), bows (*kala*), arrows (*bien*), and spears (*tama*). Its layout on the battlefield reproduced the structure of the chiefdom. It was led by a war chief (*keletigi*) from Serimana and included three units: the "chest," located in the center and including the Fabunela, Npiebala, Furabala, and Numuniziela warriors, symbolized the portion of the ox given to the chief upon his enthronement; the "left," where the Serimana were grouped; and the "right," where the Somala gathered.

The booty (*konson*), composed of captives, cowry shells, livestock, strips of cotton, and beads, was divided into five parts: the Serimana, Npiebala, Furabala, and Numuniziela each had a share; the Fabunela and Somala split the last part between them. In fact, it seems that a large part of the booty went to the *kafotigi*, who sold it as collective property (*forobanafolo*). In this way, he was able to accumulate a larger quantity of goods than the other warriors. Cowries, livestock, and slaves thus became indications of his preeminence.

Booty, fines, and gifts brought in tribute by the villagers for harvest and New Year festivals (*jonmine*) constituted the *kafotigi*'s primary source of income, since no fees or taxes were actually levied. This was so, no doubt, because such fees were collected by the *faama* for the king of Segu.

Segu's Indirect Rule

The relations between Jitumu, as well as the region's other *kafos*, and Segu were extremely ambiguous. Though Segu played a role in the constitution of Jitumu as a chiefdom, it never occupied it physically. It is difficult to date with any precision Segu's seizure of the region, or, more precisely, the period during which Jitumu fell within the domain of this kingdom. It is unlikely that this occurred during the Kulubali rule. Most probably it was under the Jara that this loose incorporation occurred.[18]

Segu had no need to send an army to convince Jitumu to capitulate. This kingdom was sufficiently menacing for the heads of the various chiefdoms to proclaim their obedience to the supreme chief of their own accord. The legend told above contains an element of realism regarding the arrival of Jitumu Musa in Segu to offer the allegiance of his village.[19]

C. Monteil described Segu's attitude toward the peripheral provinces: "The suzerainty stretched very far, but remained precarious because there were not enough troops to enforce its position. Its subjects had to pay taxes more or less regularly, the nature and amount of which was set when they became subjects."[20] The payment of a tribute, "the price of honey," but also "the price of life" or "of fear" (*disongo, ni songo*) was the basic sign of submission. The nature of the tribute varied, depending on the resources of the region in question. Jitumu, an essentially agricultural province, had to pay in cowries and millet. The payment of cowries required the sale of certain goods (livestock, gold, slaves, millet, etc.) and consequently stimulated the development of a mercantile economy.

It was the *kafotigi*'s duty to collect the *disongo* and send it to Segu for the New Year (*jonmine*). Each year he summoned the lineages to send their share to his residence, where the goods were collected. When the *kafotigi* had taken a portion for his own use, a delegation left for the kingdom's capital to deliver the cowries and millet to the king.

The delegation members took millet and cowries to cover their needs during the trip, which significantly reduced the amount received by the sovereign. In fact, the tribute was largely symbolic, the act of allegiance it represented being more important than the quantity of goods given.

The sending of warriors (*tonjon*) from Jitumu was another aspect of the kingdom's domination in the region. The people of Jitumu took part in expeditions led by the *faama* of Segu and, in certain cases, they settled in the capital. The grandfather of one of our informers, Allah Ye Min Ke (What God wills), was a slave at Segu. He was in charge of the cowry and millet storehouses and was remunerated by the king. To the Jitumu people who came to visit him, he claimed that his life in Segu was far better than what his life would have been had he remained in his home village. This is not an isolated case among men from other *kafos* who settled in Segu. Thus, the incorporation of Jitumu into the kingdom offered considerable possibilities for upward social mobility and reinforced the bonds between the center and periphery of this political sphere. Joint military expeditions (*jubo*) by Segu with one of the Jitumu villages were another form of intervention by the empire. In cases of civil war between two villages or of revolt against a tyrannical *kafotigi*, one of the villages in the dispute would make a remuneration (*kelewelefen*) in exchange for help from Segu warriors who would loot the other village. The king received the booty and the defeated village could pay a ransom to reclaim the men who had been taken prisoner.

This rather supple system allowed Segu to insure its domination over large stretches of territory without physically occupying the country. Divide and conquer: such could have been its motto. Relying on the divisions among lineages, villages, and *kafos*, Segu prevented the emergence of any power that could challenge its hegemony. It thus practiced a policy of indirect rule before the fact. As soon as a local *faama* became too strong, Segu used neighboring *kafotigi* to assert its power over him.

For vassal *kafos*, the paying of *disongo* was not sufficient to protect them from raids; nor was receiving tribute a simple substitute for pillaging. A docile chiefdom that became too powerful would immediately be the object of a segmentary, leveling operation on the part of the kingdom.[21]

Autonomy

With the conquest of Segu by Al Hajj Umar in 1861, a new era began for Jitumu, as it did for the neighboring *kafos*. The fall of the kingdom at the hands of the Fula[22] gave the vassal provinces more autonomy than they had ever had before. Of course, the Fula did not stop at Segu but extended their conquests to the southwest and created a fortress at Tajana to assure communications between Segu and Dinguiraye. In contrast to the *faama*, however, they did not demand tribute from the neighboring *kafos*. They merely pillaged and looted the region (*soboli*), often at the request of a village that wanted the Fula cavalrymen to help in destroying an enemy village.

The endless raids finally wore out the region's *kafos* and with the passage of Gallieni and the approach of Samori, the people saw the chance to get rid of the Fula. The Fula decided to require a tribute from the population of Jalakoroba.[23] When the Jalakoroba people rebelled and called for help, a large group of warriors from Jalakorodugu, Keleyadugu, Safe, Marakodugu, and Jitumu responded. The sovereign of Jalakorodugu, Jitumu, and Keleyadugu, Fotigi Samake, led the Jitumu.[24] In 1881, this confederation defeated the Fula, who had left Tajana to settle in Grinkunba. The united armies from the different *kafos*, made up predominantly of hunters carrying rifles, managed to defeat the garrison and bring back abundant booty, composed primarily of horses and captives.

Samori Direct Rule

Victory over the Fula was quickly followed by the Samori conquest. In July of 1882, Keme Brema, the youngest brother of Samori, settled in Faraba in the Cakadugu *kafo*. Fotigi Samake acknowledged

his authority and presented him with the many horses lost by the
Fula at Grinkunba.[25] Beginning in 1882 and continuing for a dozen
years, a politico-economico-military organization exercised absolute power over the entire region, in spite of several disruptive revolts. The task of this territorial army or military government was
to occupy the boundary separating Samori from the Fula of Segu
and from the French, who settled in Bamako in 1883. It was also to
control the commercial influx of horses from Sahel. Wolosebugu, in
Jitumu territory, was one of the principal markets in which horses
were exchanged for slaves. Moreover, the route Wolosebugu-
Ntentu-Sikaso was of crucial importance during the Samori siege of
the capital of Kenedugu in 1887.

The organization of the region by the Samori apparatus is well
known from the writings of Louis-Gustave Binger, who was stuck
for more than a month at Wolosebugu in 1887. Kali Sidibe, a
Moslem Fula originally from Wasolon who functioned as *keletigi*,
commanded the Samori apparatus. This military governor commanded a region of 20,000 square kilometers, with 100,000 inhabitants, and needed to meet the needs of a 5,000-man army.
Above these *keletigi* was a well-organized network of Samori representatives (*dugukunnasigi*) who were posted in most of the large villages. All these men, who were foreigners in the region, formed an
army, an administration, and a court. The Samori apparatus worked
to put the region's assets to good use, thus assuring its own upkeep
as well as supplying provisions to its fighting men. In Jitumu, this
mise en valeur (putting to good use) meant first of all the recruiting
of warriors into the Samori bands. Food provisions came from the
villages' collective fields (*almami forow*) and from pillaging the inhabitants' harvests. Transport of these provisions was carried out
by requisitioned peasants. Raids for captives within these same conquered regions supplied an additional source of revenue to the
state.

With the Samorian occupation, an absolutely original system of
exploitation was put in place that effected a complete restructuring
of the society. It was an administrative form that can be called "direct."[26] The chiefdoms, or confederations of chiefdoms that resulted
from wars, lost all their autonomy, and were replaced by military
governments whose power went beyond that of the former *kafos*.

The solidly implanted Samorian apparatus took over all military, political, economic, and religious functions of the chiefdoms. It also modified considerably the social structure of the conquered regions. The recruitment of warriors, the cultivation of collective fields, porterage, and raids drastically depleted the village community workforce and effectively dismantled agricultural production.

At the same time, the Samorian presence resulted, just as did Segu control, in a redistribution of social and political roles within the former chiefdoms. Thus, certain Jitumu warriors could make a career in the army and be given captives by Samori himself or by his generals. Jitumu thus saw a flood of slaves far beyond what existed in the preceding period. Had the Samorian domination continued, this influx would have no doubt deeply disrupted social relations.

The benefits of the Samorian wars did not prevent the Jitumu revolt in 1885, which included Banan and was directly motivated by the exploitative system. Villagers from these two *kafos* killed the *dugukunnasigi* of all the villages, then took refuge on a hill. Repressive action followed immediately: Fotigi Samake, the Jitumu chief, was executed, and part of the *kafo*'s population sought refuge on the Niger's left bank, then under French control.

The conquered regions' resistance to the new system corresponded to the empire's increasingly strict Islamization. In 1884, Samori, who was till then *faama*, took the title of Almami; in 1886 he turned the empire into a theocracy. At the local level, this transformation resulted in the banning of millet beer, the suppression of sacrifices, and the establishment of a Moslem justice system in accordance with the Sharia.[27] These measures extended far beyond the sphere of religion, because they ultimately destroyed the *kafo*'s ability to function.

In Jitumu, for example, sacrifices at the site of Jitumu Musa's disappearance constituted the cementing force of the chiefdom. When these sacrifices and their associated libations were suppressed, chiefs could no longer be enthroned nor could the hierarchy of the lineages be symbolically reaffirmed.

The institution of the Moslem state in the region thus meant the end of preexisting sociopolitical structures. In turn, the setting up of this religious framework no doubt provoked the revolt of 1889.

The Revolt of 1889

Binger described famine and epidemics that he witnessed during the rainy season in Wolosebugu in 1887 on his way to Sikaso, where he was to meet Samori.[28] He observed numerous ruins and a sizable decline in population. War took a great toll on the inhabitants, who appeared exhausted and suffered particularly from portage recruitment. Binger's perspective was no doubt biased, but it is certain that the population was ravaged by hunger, particularly during the period when the new state was establishing its power.

Two years later, Jitumu revolted against Samori. This revolt affected a large part of the empire and was due, structurally speaking, to the oppression and exploitation practiced by the conquerors. It coincided more circumstantially with the institution of theocracy and the requisitions occasioned by the siege of Sikaso. Other factors intervened—in particular, contacts between the Jitumu people and their relatives refuged on the left bank and, through them, with the French at Bamako. The inhabitants did not return to their lands until 1893, when the French, after the operation of Ntentu and the foundation of Bouguni, took possession of the Niger's right bank.

The transition from Segu to Samori domination, apart from the brief Fula interlude, was also marked by the transformation from a system of indirect rule to a system of direct rule. Contrary to general opinion, at least for this region, French colonial domination looked like a return to the indirect rule of the Segu period.

French Indirect Rule

After the Samake and their dependents returned to Jitumu, political life in the *kafo*, which had become a canton, is relatively well known thanks to the oral tradition collected by Riou in 1957[29] and the data that I collected myself. Around 1900, Jitumu became the largest and most powerful canton in the district of Bamako, rivaled only by Maramandugu. Its influence extended over all the other cantons of the Niger's right bank. Made up of lineages (Serimana, Fabunela, Furabala, Npiebala, Somala, Numuniziela, and Dogotu), Jitumu remained effectively without a chief, at least without a chief recognized by the new French administration. After restoration of

TABLE 2
List of Colonial and Postcolonial Chiefs

Source: Z.S.	Source: Riou
Duba Dansina	Dusuba Dansina
Dansina Bara	!
Furaba	!
Nielejoba	? (1914)
Falen	Falen (?-1929)
Shienu	Masiri Shienu (1929-34)
Monzon	Monzon-Z., coadjutor (1934-39)
Division within the Canton	
Cekurable	Cekura (1940-42)
Moroba	Moroba (1942-43)
Serimana	
Dantigi	Dantigi (1943-51)
Dansina, last *chef de canton*	Dansina (1954-59)
Kurseini, *kafotigi*	
Furaba, *kafotigi* in 1985	

the so-called traditional or customary authorities, the first chief to be accepted by the administration was the Fabunela Nielejoba, in 1914.[30] He was succeeded by another Fabunela, Falen, who was the first chief of the subdivision mentioned in the archives; he died in 1929. In a vote held the same year, the town notables elected his near relative, Masiri Shienu, who lived in Sanankoro, as the next canton chief.

In 1930 the district commander of Bamako wanted the canton chief to live in Wolosebugu, which was the canton's most important village because of its market and its location on the road linking Bamako to Bougouni. To facilitate this move, all the people of Jitumu took part in the construction of an enormous compound. That same year, Masiri Shienu made a triumphant entrance, which filled the Fabunela lineage with great pride.

According to Riou, the inhabitants of Wolosebugu were, as they are today, composed half of "Bambara farmers" and half "Dioulas, marabouts, and griots."[31] The last category was not slow in using flattery to influence the chief and curry favor with him. As a result, the canton chiefs became increasingly arrogant and abused their power.

Such abuses were the initial cause of the conflict in Jitumu. The

second was due to the nature of the colonial system, which was particularly harsh at this time. The colonial administrators ruled as absolute monarchs and saw the canton chiefs as extensions or even am-
plifications of their own power. Fearing their superiors, the chiefs
followed their instructions to the letter, but also took advantage of
indirect rule to conduct themselves as local potentates. In this period
of economic crisis, heads of families were hard put to pay their taxes.
Men found themselves forced to put their wives and children in service in the homes of more well-off peasants. Tension between chiefs
and subjects mounted. The tiniest spark could set off an explosion.

A Segmentary Revolt

There were basically no problems in the area until the death of
Masiri Shienu in 1934. His near relative, Monzon, succeeded him,
coming into power on December 1, 1934. But the district officer preferred a younger man and nominated as deputy his son Z., who was
still alive when I did my own research in the region. Z. lived in
Wolosebugu and his father in Sanankoro. Z. had attended primary
school and counted on his education to compensate for his youth.
He ruled despotically and all the elders of the lineage sided against
him. When the administrator asked him to supply men to work on
the Kuremale road on the Niger's left bank, he consented, and this
forced labor was one of the principal causes of the revolt.

It was plotted by a group of men from lineages opposed to the
Fabunela, all of whom laid claim to the chiefship. The Somala lineage complained of the exactions levied by Z. on the Serimana lineage and requested that all power be withdrawn from the Fabunela
lineage and given to the Serimana lineage. The Serimana lineage
declined and thereupon warned Fabunela to be on guard against the
Somala. This action amounted to treachery in the eyes of the Somala
and aggravated the conflict. Under the leadership of one of the Somala, a group went to Bamako, where they registered a complaint
with the district officer. He supported Z., but the firm resolution of
the lineage elders convinced him to imprison the principal leaders
of the revolt, certain of whom died in prison. When Monzon died in
1939, the conflict had still not been resolved.

The committee organized to designate his successor produced the following results: 3,248 votes for Solo Samake (Furabala), chief of Wolosebugu village; 3,166 votes for Serima Samake (Fabunela), near relative of Monzon; 286 votes for Zantigi Samake (Npiebala), chief of Dungurunan village. Since the Fabunela came in second, the administration did not accept the results of the vote.

Behind-the-scenes negotiations took place among the candidates and numerous mediators. Sanba Tarawele, canton chief of nearby Marakodugu, attracted a following among several lineage elders and campaigned for splitting the canton.

The idea for dividing this canton, composed of 49 villages, germinated for a few months and, at the beginning of 1940, 24 villages that supported Solo Samake asked to be annexed to Marakodugu. Colonial authorities hesitated at first and so did Sanba Tarawele, who would have to take on greater responsibilities. Before a solution could be reached, the Fabunela candidate, Seriman Samake, died without having taken power. The Fabunela who would have succeeded him was Cekura Samake. The administration reached its decision and on May 28, 1940, named him as chief of Jitumu canton and attached the 24 villages who supported Solo Samake to Marakodugu. Henceforth, Jitumu contained only 25 villages.

This segmentary revolt exercised a continuing influence on the canton's political life, since a Serimana, Moroba Samake, succeeded Cekura Samake, who died in 1942, and governed until his death in 1943. The next leader, also a Serimana, Dantigi Samake, ruled until 1951.[32]

At that point power returned to the Fabunela, with the official nomination on February 1, 1954, of Dansina Samake of Sanankoro. He was the canton chief when the chieftaincy as an institution was ended in 1959. Since that time, there have been no canton chiefs in Jitumu or in any other part of Mali. Only the *kafotigi* continue to exist, that is, the Fabunela lineage elders who succeed each other to the chiefship. Two elders have so far fulfilled this function: Kurseini of Serimanbugu and Furaba of Cenba, who was the *kafotigi* in 1985.

With independence and the setting up of the Malian state, these lineage elders lost all visible political power, though they retain considerable hidden influence. Many villagers consult them and everyone considers them descendants of Jitumu Musa, who remains an object of worship.

Even though the chieftaincy no longer exists officially, lineage distinctions remained in effect during the period following independence, particularly during the 1968 revolt. At that time, all the villages of Jitumu took part in the revolt except the Fabunela villages.[33] The Fabunela refrained because the leader of the revolt, a Kooroko businessman, had during the division in 1942 supported for the position of canton chief a man who also had the support of the colonial administration, the Serimana, Moroba Samake.

One of the characteristics of Jitumu's social structure, from its inception to the present day, is the permanence of what is called in Bambara *fadenkele* (conflict between brothers of the same father). Frequent throughout the history of the chiefdom, it becomes, furthermore, more and more comprehensive.

The first *fadenkele* laid the groundwork for all the others. It is the one that pitted Ngolo and Jitumu Musa against each other and resulted in victory for the junior lineage, the Fabunela, over the senior branch, the Serimana. The second and third *fadenkele* concerned Cesanatle and Semioba, both Jitumu *kafotigi* who were unseated by the people because of their despotism. The fourth episode occurred during colonization: the dispute caused by the exactions of Z., the educated son of a *chef de canton* and deputy chief of Jitumu.

Due to the recurrence of segmentary conflicts in the history of this *kafo*, we can hypothesize that in this type of society, combining political centralization with vertical cleavages, social protests necessarily take the form of a change in dynasty or secession. In his *Alur Society*, A. Southall defines the "segmentary State":

> The distribution of power in the segmentary state is characterized by the fact that, within any one segment, at any level of the pyramidal structure, there is at any one moment a certain degree of monopoly of political power, development of administrative staff and definition of territorial limits, whereas, within the system as a whole, the political relations of the various segments are determined by much the same factors as in the case of segmentary societies which have no political specialization at all.[34]

According to Southall, the segmentary state that characterized Alur society was an intermediate form between segmentary societies and state societies.

This political system possessed in embryonic form the attributes that Siegfried Nadel saw as characteristic of a state: territorial sovereignty, centralized government, specialized administrative personnel, and legitimate monopoly of the use of force.[35] Rather than adopting this typological and evolutionist perspective, we can see in Southall's model of a segmentary state (which was based on Alur society but could also be applied to Jitumu) what occurs when more powerful social forms dominate the peripheral political entities. In other words, lineage cleavages become more important when they are supported from a distance by the state, as was the case here with Segu beginning in the early eighteenth century.

The fact that Jitumu conserved a segmentary structure and that it never fully became a state is perhaps an indication that its genesis was the product, to a certain extent, of an exterior action. Thus we need to abandon the usual perspective and its dichotomies (stateless society/state society, noncentralized society/society with a centralized political power, etc.). Rather, we should see segmentary societies as the product of state societies and analyze the reproduction of the former as part of the latter. This effectively undoes the sharp distinction between these two systems. And if the state and the segmentary are merely two poles of the same hierarchized space, there is no longer any reason to endlessly debate the question of the state's genesis in segmentary societies.

7 White Paganism

Ethnology has always tried to "congeal" West African societies as far as religion was concerned, just as it does for race or ethnic matters. Following in the footsteps of Faidherbe, Gallieni was one of the very first administrators to formulate a *politique des races* (racial policy) and to develop an anti-Moslem political position. He based this position on the opposition between the Malinke and especially the Bambara–these anti-Moslem simpletons–and the Toucouleur of El Hadj Omar and Amadou, propagators of Islam. He counted on the Bambara to conquer the El Hadj Omar and Samori empires and to help extend French domination to the whole of Sudan.[1] After Gallieni, Binger, Coppolani, and Le Chatelier also pursued anti-Moslem policies.[2] As did Gallieni, Le Chatelier saw the spread of Islam among the black "fetishistic" peoples of West Africa as a successive advance through various races, beginning with the Berbers and then the Fulani.[3] It would be tedious to list all the colonial authors who, in one way or another, adhered to racial policies, since such policies more or less permeated all the anti-Moslem measures.[4] I will note only the main events in order to illustrate how directives regarding religious matters were reflected in the administration in general.

In his 1909 speech, the governor of western French Africa, William Ponty, explicitly linked what he called *politique des races* (racial policy) to the fight against Islam.[5] Like his predecessors, he attempted to eliminate the use of indigenous people for command positions in an effort to isolate the fetishistic natives from the power of the Moslem conquerors. To this end, he chose canton chiefs from among the animists and developed school instruction in French. An entire series of inquiries into the situation of Islam in different colonies grew out of this policy of direct rule, resulting in various publications, notably that of Ponty's great admirer P. Marty, who worked under his leadership at Dakar.

The link between racial policies and anti-Moslem efforts existed for many years during colonization and give rise to an attenuated form of Islam–Black Islam–and to a form of local mythico-ritualistic practice based on fetishism, animism, and naturism. The concept of "Black Islam" produced a series of "ethnic religions," such as the Bambara religion.

A quest for the degree zero of paganism, free from all external influence, can be detected in the racial-intellectual scheme characterizing colonial ethnology, whether it was practiced by colonial administrators or academic ethnologists. This is the route taken by Clozel,[6] Delafosse, and Brévié. In his preface to Brévié's *Islam contre naturisme au Soudan français*,[7] Delafosse criticized the notion of fetishism as inadequate to describe the local religions of West Africa. He proposed that the term "animism" be applied to "all the belief systems . . . of populations who . . . accept the existence of a personal and active soul in every being, whether living or dead, animate or inanimate from our viewpoint, and who . . . choose to be guided by the hidden action of these souls."[8] Delafosse considered animism, as he defined it, to be identical with Brévié's naturism, understood as "the type of civilization met with among Sudanese peoples, because they are still close to the natural state of primitives and also because, to them, man is the center of the natural world and sees it as being in relation only to him."[9]

Delafosse asserted that animism was the foundation of the black civilizations and that Islam, being of relatively recent importation, should play only a minor role on the African continent. According to him, the Moslem religion derives from the nomadic way of life and bears little relevance to the sedentary, agrarian way of life in Sudan.[10] Brévié's ideas regarding the relations between Islam and pa-

ganism are very near those of Delafosse. Like him, Brévié, drawing
on Lévy-Bruhl, considered that naturism, which is still practiced by
the majority of the Sudanese and which corresponds to the "anthropological stage," is the very foundation of African civilizations.
These national and ethnic religions should be impermeable to infil-
trations from foreign beliefs, particularly Islam, which is the religion par excellence of Semites. Therefore, there is no such thing as
an irremediable Islamization, especially if paganism is strengthened
by returning power to landowners, soothsayers, and religious teach-
ers while keeping it from the canton and village chiefs; if the most
common fetishistic customs are codified (Malinke, Bobo, Mossi,
etc.); and if one tries to keep Islam in check.

Brévié's entire enterprise thus consisted in keeping at bay the
menace that Islam supposedly represented, whether by evoking its
inevitable decline, which would be due to the decline of the Semitic
race itself,[11] or by aiding fetishism with "indirect rule"[12] and the
Africanization of education. Consistent efforts to identify a "Bambara religion" fall, then, within the context of the search for a pure
or originary fetishism.

The Unfindable Paganism

Though the first book on the subject, by the Abbot Henry, dates
from 1910, it was only with Tauxier's work of 1927 that the theme of
a Bambara religion really took shape.[13] But for both of them, and G.
Dieterlen as well, isolating a Bambara religion presupposes that
Bambara religious institutions be rid of all distorting foreign elements, in particular, the "Islamic alluvion" detected by Tauxier.[14]
Since the Bambara religion was originally and inevitably syncretic,
one would be surprised or even scornful of the "myths" that see
practices or institutions reputed to be pagan as deriving from the
Moslem world.

The Abbot Henry attributes "the ancient legend" of fetishes (boli)
coming from Mecca to the accommodating spirit of the animists in
an Islam-dominated milieu.[15] Commenting on this legend, Tauxier
evokes Bambara "puerility."[16] These legends are very widespread in
the region and to see them as just folktales, that is, to insist on their
inauthenticity, would be to misunderstand their true meaning.
When the Gwanan people declared, for example, that Maliki

brought back from Mecca fetishes and holy earth that would protect
his country, or when the fetishist priests (*somaw*), the Tarawele of
Keleyadugu, said that their ancestor came from Mecca or that he
made seven pilgrimages to that holy city, they were not presenting
these actions as literally true, nor were they trying to present these
acts as verifiable in the eyes of Islam. Rather, they meant that their
mythico-ritualistic practices were indissolubly linked to the religion
of the Prophet.

Applied to Africa, the term "syncretism" immediately evokes the
prophesies and the churches that originated with them (Matsua,
Kinbangu, Atcho, etc.).[17] But the very idea of syncretism supposes
the existence of an absolute referent corresponding, for example, to
a Bambara, Fulani, or Malinke religion. Moreover, religious phenomena do not obey principles different from those in effect in
other domains: it is valid to imagine a pre-Islamic period for these
groups of beliefs, or a pre-Christian period for other groups, but
nothing indicates that these aggregates were homogenous or
formed a coherent whole that was altered by the eruption of universalist religions. In this domain as in others, we need to suppose an
originary mixture that would contradict the idea that these mythico-
ritualistic practices formed a systematic whole.

Though we often hesitate to designate paganisms as religions, we
must not accept the expressions "system of thought" or "belief system" as more satisfactory.[18] Both concepts suggest the idea of clo-
sure, in opposition to the way these representations and practices
work. Paganisms, in fact, are characterized by their suppleness,
their pragmatism, and, as we will see, by their essentially political
dimension.[19] All these properties do not make paganisms into simple universalist religions in reverse, because a certain suppleness is
also at work in Islam and Christianity.

In the case of the "Bambara religion," it serves no purpose to
want to reconstitute a pre-Islamic situation that would alone be authentic. For today's ethnology, these representations and practices
are located first and foremost in the world of Islam, which constitutes their frame of reference. Nothing supports the idea that a
pagan-Islam mixture–a white paganism–differs in essence from a
previous mixture.

Since mythico-ritualistic practices include Moslem or Christian elements—and this has been true for the whole of Africa for many centuries—any effort to isolate pagan elements from their Islamic envelope becomes invalid. At the same time, it is no longer necessary to ask if these religions are "native" or of Islamic origin; one need only see them in terms of their relation to Islam. It is impossible in black Africa, just as it is in North Africa,[20] to sharply distinguish magic from religion; therefore, we cannot define the Islam of these regions as a "Black Islam."[21] There is no gap between Islam and paganism since this religion penetrated the sphere of paganism in successive waves as a function of different population movements. Moreover, the last wave always tended to define itself as a force for reform, and considered the previous wave as representatives of paganism. Thus what could appear to an observer as pure fetishism is often a disguised form of Islam. For this reason, in the domain of religion as in others (ethnic, political, etc.), identity is relative: one is pagan, a first settler, or Bambara in relation to Moslems or Malinke conquerors. The convergence with ethnic phenomena, then, is not arbitrary, since ethnic identity is often a function of political status and religious affiliation. From this perspective, to be Bambara is not so much to profess the Bambara religion—which would be the inverse of the Christian or Moslem religion—as to locate oneself within a network of forces that defines a person as being of the Bambara religion. Peasants from Wasolon and the surrounding regions can thus, today, be catalogued as Bambara by the townspeople, whereas they consider themselves Moslem. In this region, as elsewhere, he is Moslem who considers himself as such.[22]

It would be futile, in our study of this cultural sphere, to inventory all the institutions and practices influenced, "contaminated," or "perverted" by Islam. The Bambara-Malinke language contains a high percentage of Arabic terms. Though, as Caillié remarked in 1827, the people of Wasolon and surrounding areas were "idolatrous,"[23] they nevertheless felt great respect for the prophet and his religion. Thus, the youth of this region shaved their heads like the "Mohamedans" and most everyone wore cotton clothes. Such respect for Islam was no doubt linked to the proximity of important Moslem centers. At Garalo in Cemala, at Manfara in Manden, at Kankeri in Baya, at Sanbatigila, Wojene, and Kankan, religious men (*mori, karamoko, alkali,* etc.) who lived around the mosques (*misiri*) displayed great erudition in Moslem thought and texts. At Garalo, for example, the site of a very old mosque, the Kane coming from Wagadu in the eighteenth century wrote the *tarikh*, in which they recorded the genealogies of the region's principal dynasties. The Kane of Garalo, the Saganogo of Sanbatigila, the clerics of Ntentu or Kankan recorded so many ancient Islamic settlements that it is difficult to reduce their presence to isolated pockets of "restricted literacy," to use Goody's phrase.[24]

In fact, even in zones supposedly the most pagan (Banmana), in the heart of rural areas, Jitumu or Keleyadugu, for example, certain "first settlers" or landowners (*dugukolotigiw*) were marabouts (*mori*) or claimed to possess knowledge (*somaya*) acquired at Mecca. In other *kafos*, certain chiefs had Moslem advisors who used their magical talents in the service of political power. In general, the marabouts were welcome and enjoyed an immunity comparable to that of the privileged elite. Moreover, Wasolon and the surrounding regions constituted a Banmana zone before colonization, that is, a zone of low political pressure, where an entire series of groups came seeking refuge. They took their place as dominators or dominated, either by creating chiefdoms or by becoming dependents of powerful lineages. Among these groups were Moslems, such as the Jawara of Kingi who, in Kurulamini, became Kooroko, or the Fula of Wasolon who fled the theocratic revolution of Futa Jalon. Some of these groups were led by marabouts, such as the Bagayogo of Timbuktu, who founded the chiefdoms of Keleyadugu, Danu, and Bolon.[25] Most often these Moslems returned to paganism, but traces of Islamic thought remained that could subsequently germinate into a re-Islamization. Thus, when Nfamusa Bagayogo was forced to flee his kinsmen in Keleyadugu who had returned to the *banmanaya*, he threw his books into a wood (*mantu*) where there was a sacred well. The *mantu* became a pagan sanctuary and the object of numerous sacrifices. The cult of Benba at Dankasa in the Kuruba Gwanan possessed the same characteristics: there too, it was a case of adoration of a Koran belonging to a marabout who had long before disappeared and who became, in the pagan context of the region, a fetish (*boli*).

Such residue of Islam among Moslems who returned to paganism is particularly visible in conceptions of power, itself closely linked to divination. Geomancy, in fact, which plays such a central role in the exercise of power, is of Arabic origin.[26] As we have already seen, Jitumu Musa made use of geomancy to vanquish the secret society of the *komo*, whose adepts figured among the "first settlers" of Jitumu. Today, in Mali, pious Moslems, in particular Wahabis, consider geomancy a typically fetishistic practice.

These different phases of Islamization provoked polytheistic reactions, of course, but they could in no way be considered a resurgence of a primary paganism. Armed resistance against neighboring Moslem states—such as the "war of the sons of the dream" led by "possessed" Fulani of Wasolon against Kankan and Kabadugu—were just as much an expression of "savage mind" impregnated by Islam as a return to fetishism.

This pale paganism or latent Islam was the leaven for further re-Islamizations. Under pressure from the neighboring kingdom of Kabadug, Jakite Saabashi made permanent efforts to reconstruct the state in Gwanan. Around 1870, Farabalay converted to Islam, studied the Koran with the Ture in Sanbatigila, became a marabout, and subsequently converted part of Wasolon.[27] Farabalay also became, for a while, the representative of Kabadugu in Wasolon, and then allied himself with Samori, who conquered the entire area.

Samori changed Islam's mode of diffusion in the region. Belonging to a lineage of Konyan Moslems who returned to paganism, then reconverted to Islam,[28] Samori linked Islam very closely to his practice of direct rule. Even though he is not known as a reformer of the same scope as Al Hajj Umar, for example, Almami conquests overturned the structure of the *kafos* and *jamanas*.

Several means were used to reach this goal. First of all, a tight network of Koranic schools was implemented in Wasolon and the neighboring regions. This implementation had the support of the local Moslem chiefs, such as Farabalay, who joined with Samori and became his representative in the region. The epic of the Jakite Saabashi of Gwanan mentions that four Koranic schools were created at Yorobugula in Gwanan, Ntentu in Kurulamini, Buguni in Banimonoce, and Garalo, the old Moslem center of Cemala referred to previously.

These schools, directed by marabouts, supposedly each had several hundred students fed and housed by the Samorian state.[29] Under this apparent generosity, however, was hidden the fact that these schools were in reality very much like the "hostage schools" or "sons of the chief schools" set up by Faidherbe in Senegal. The *kafotigi* and the *jamanatigi* were, in fact, required to send contingents of students which included members of their own families. Such a form of education, doubling as political control over local sovereigns through their sons or brothers, was reinforced by prohibitions concerning the consumption of millet beer and the practice of sacrifices. Just as was Koranic instruction, these measures were directed at eliminating all the rituals (enthronements, funerals of chiefs, and so on) forming the basis for the semiautonomous functioning of the *kafos* and *jamanas*. Most significantly, a justice system conforming to the Sharia supplanted the former jurisdictions exercised by the *kafotigi* and their courts. During his stay in Wolosebugu in 1887, Binger remarked that the hands of thieves were cut off in conformity with Islamic principles. As we have seen, this radical Islamization did not fail to provoke violent reactions in the *kafos*. When the people of Wasolon and the adjoining regions revolted after the siege of Sikaso, they rose up against the propagation of a new ideology, no doubt, but also, and especially, against centralization and the system of exploitation put in place by Samori, which were indissolubly linked to his religious political practice.

Colonization and the
Attraction-Repulsion Toward Islam

After eradicating this "vector" of the Moslem "epidemic" represented by Samori, the Bougouni district officers adopted a very ambiguous attitude toward Islam, going from one extreme to another, sometimes seeing Islam everywhere, sometimes nowhere.

Initially, the district officers sought reassurance in what they observed as the slight influence of Islam in the region. The *Rapports politiques* from the beginning of the colonial period adamantly insisted on Islam's weakness, the few Koranic schools, and the crushing domination of fetishism.[30] From the perspective of racial theory, Islam was linked essentially to trade, which displaced "foreign hegemony" as the principal factor in the spread of this religion. In the Bougouni district, the minority and marginal *dioulas*–the Kooroko and the Marka of Garalo–were the primary recipients of Islam, with the great majority of the population, composed of Bambara and Ouassoulounke peasants, remaining faithful to animism. Yet, in certain cantons, difficulties experienced by the authorities were attributed to Islam: either that the *dioulas* maintained a pernicious influence on the chiefs (Jitumu) or that the Moslem lineages excluded from the chiefship actually possessed a very real prestige (Gwanan). In any case, this Islam had a purely local character and maintained practically no links with the exterior.[31]

Already in 1899, Le Chatelier referred to the calm of the district officers in noting that "in the Mande area covering both banks of the river extending to Kenedougou, the majority of the Malinke are fetishists . . . even though they were . . . officially converted during the time of Samory."[32] Echoing Le Chatelier 24 years later, Brévié wrote:

> The traveler who visits Ouassoulou today would be very surprised if he were told that this country was Islamized less than a century ago. . . . In 1885 there were still from 800 to 900 young men of Ouassoulounke receiving education from the *tolbas*. How many were there ten years later? There had been a complete regression: the fetishist tradition dominated once again, mosques had fallen into ruin, schools were closed and their student body reduced to only 64 in 1908. And these were sons and relatives of the few marabouts remaining in the area.[33]

After this brief wave of Islamization, the Bougouni district returned to fetishism or an inferior form of Islam. For thirty years the district officers merely reiterated this fact. Only in 1955 did officials record a rise in Islam,[34] which occurred most noticeably in the central area of the district, around the city of Bougouni. "A few years ago," declared the district officer, "the majority of the cantons were animist," but today "everyone is Moslem and does 'salam.'" As was the previous Islamization, this one was due to the *dioulas*, but there were two other notable factors as well: the *navétanes*, or migrants, and the former soldiers. In this part of the district, there were as many Tidjanias as Quadriyas among those who received the *ourdou* (*wird*) of a brotherhood, but most of those Islamized had no real affiliation. Nevertheless, Fanta Madi Toure, sharif of Kankan and an important religious personage, had considerable influence over the entire region through his disciple, Cheikh Mamadou, who lived at Koloni in Bolon canton. On the whole, the religious situation in the central portion of Bougouni district was rather varied. Though the largest percentage of the population could be considered Islamized, with fifty official Koranic schools in 1954, animism survived, especially among the elders.

In contrast, animism was dominant in the Yanfolila subdivision, which included all of Wasolon, even though "the general tendency was to identify oneself as Moslem." Animism took the form of worship of political ancestors, on whose graves the Wasolon people swore oaths of loyalty. One of the subdivision's cantons, Baya, remained completely resistant to Islam, which the district officer attributed to the Malinke component in its population. The only thing lacking in this picture is the reformist touch that inevitably accompanied every colonialist chronicle on the Sudan of the period. This element is supplied by El Hadj Moussa Diallo, former student at the University Al Azhar in Cairo who was repatriated for lack of money, arriving in Bougouni in 1955. The colonial administration found his presence particularly disquieting, seeing in him a Wahabi completely given over to oriental pan-Islamism. The administration refused him permission to teach.

As we can see, colonial literature is of limited interest regarding the identification of religious phenomena in this region. Being contaminated by Islam, the mythico-ritualistic practices of Wasolon and its environs could only be described in a fantasy-laden interpretation that continually vacillated to serve the needs of the administration: either every one is Moslem, or no one is.

There too, a problematic of purity is at issue. It was thought that by extracting animism from its Moslem gangue, one could find the key to understanding religious phenomena on the banks of the Niger. This colonial problematic regarding Islam continues to shape ideas of religion in the Mali of today (fetishism, animism, etc.) and it still serves as the foundation for ethnological analysis. For this reason, we need to examine this problematic closely, even if only to invert the terms. In other words, we need to measure how extensively Islamic traces remain in the Bambara region and, additionally, to shed light on the political cults that are the essential factor in what we have called pale paganism. Rather than postulate the existence of an originary paganism and then examine the ways it adheres to Islam, it is more pertinent to begin with racial theory and the colonial vision of Islam and then move to the principal element in religion in the *kafos* and *jamanas* of southern Mali–namely, politics.

The Cult of Political Ancestors

If, as M. Augé has written,[35] every organization is simultaneously a representation of itself, and if, consequently, a homology exists between political structure and religious structure, then an inventory of the successive political forms that existed in the region will yield a definition of the corresponding mythico-ritualistic practices. We will begin with the most encompassing organization, that of Segu, and then look at smaller and smaller groupings: the *kafos* and *jamanas*, villages, and the individual.

While our knowledge of Segu's domination of regions to its south is fairly complete in the areas of economy and politics, many gaps remain in the information we possess on its culture and religion. Studying the system of "indirect rule" set up by Segu in the peripheral sections of its sphere of influence, one has the impression that, just as the economy was based on open access to slave reservoirs, there existed a religious organization that integrated the periphery into the heart of the kingdom.

We know that the royal fetishes (*boli*) of Segu were named Nangoloko and Makungoba, and that they were kept in important central villages of the kingdom.[36] But it is less well known that these fetishes or their offshoots were also located in peripheral provinces, areas only slightly subservient to Segu. In Jitumu, for example, the *kafo*'s fetishes were also called Nangoloko and Makungoba, and one can therefore imagine that, since Segu played a central role in founding this chiefdom, offshoot fetishes had been transported from the central zone to the kingdom's periphery to support the *faama*'s delegation of power to their representatives in the vassal provinces.[37]

The existence of this hierarchized religious network reinforces the hypothesis that the empire's central zone and its periphery were not simply juxtaposed, but were quite integrated into a whole. The fact that fetishes originally from the heart of the kingdom were transplanted to Jitumu, as they no doubt were to other chiefdoms, insured a relative cultural and religious homogeneity throughout the entire political entity. If a "Bambara religion" existed at this period, it rested atop a political armature; it was a function of the power relations exercised by the state on the area it controlled.

Both before and after Segu's takeover of this region, the founders of the chiefdom or the "first settlers," those who were able to establish a lasting authority in a *kafo* or *jamana*, were and continue to be the object of cult worship. Each chiefdom, then, has its prestigious founding ancestor on whose grave people go to swear oaths and to request aid and protection.

To describe precisely the cult of political ancestors, let us take an example of the sacrifices carried out on the "grave" of Jitumu Musa in the *kafo* of Jitumu, which I witnessed in 1976. Both weekly sacrifices and annual ones were made to this personage.

Weekly sacrifices took place near a village called Janinkoro, on the road leading to Jitumu Musa's "grave" or, in other words, the spot where he disappeared leaving behind his spear and scrip. Each Sunday, people rush there to offer kola nuts, chickens, and goats, with the aid of the priest affiliated with this cult. The position of sacrificer (*murukalatigi*) is handed down from generation to generation within a family from Janinkoro, the Samake of *babon* Fajalala, who is himself of the dominant Fabunela patrilineage from which came the *kafotigi*. The sacrificer is the only person who knows the prayers necessary to obtain Jitumu Musa's blessing and his help in various requests (to have a child, recover a stolen object, etc.).

Previously, large sacrifices took place every seven years on the "grave" itself in the presence of the entire canton. The *kafo*'s three principal lineages–Fabunela, Sirimana, and Somala–were present or represented. For the last ten years or so, sacrifices occurred every year at the beginning of winter. The goal of this ceremony was to obtain the ancestor's benevolence toward his descendants, to protect them, and to strengthen cohesiveness within the *kafo*.

Jitumu Musa's "grave" is located out in the bush, in the hamlet of Nfamusala about three kilometers from Janinkoro. Here the people of the *kafo* gather to honor their glorious ancestor. A tree has grown on his "grave."[38] Stones have been placed nearby and, in order to set it off from the surroundings, a low wall has been built. The sanctuary (*fogo*) thus looks like a sort of rectangular courtyard with a tree in the middle.

On the morning of the ceremony, the people–men and women of all ages and from all the villages of Jitumu and even Bamako–wait beneath the trees. The delegations from the Fabunela, Sirimana, and Somala lineages keep apart from the others and discuss matters regarding life in the *kafo* with the village chiefs or their representatives. The chickens, goats, sheep, and bull calves are tied. Drummers of the *ton dunu* (war drums), who play only on the most important occasions, play their instruments. The sacrificer arrives alone with his saber and knives. He hangs his saber from a branch far from the crowd and joins the notables beneath a tree. After greeting them, he sits near the sanctuary. At that moment he offers his vows and blessings to all present.

The Sirimana lineage presents its offerings (*jansa*): a bull calf and two chickens, to which are added the cocks brought by the lineage's village chiefs. The Somala and Fabunela lineages do the same. But the other offerings are not presented to the public: these are the chickens and goats brought by people wishing to thank Jitumu Musa for help they received from him.

The sacrificer then enters the sanctuary, spreads millet flour mixed with water (*jalan*) over the stones, slits the throat of a chicken, and throws a white kola nut and a red one. The *ton dunu* players begin drumming again and continue until the end of the sacrifices. The sacrificer cuts the throats of the bull calves and pours the blood on the stones. When the obligatory ritual offerings have been completed, those who have brought something go before the priest. Each one explains the reason for his gift and the priest, while immolating the animal or throwing kolas, intercedes with Jitumu Musa on behalf of the donor.

When the offerings have been completed, the sacrificer sits on the low wall and blesses the entire *kafo*. In return, he receives the good wishes and thanks of the patriarchs speaking for all present. Each lineage sends representatives to carve up the sacrificed animals, after which the priest invites the oldest representatives into the sanctuary. Preceded by the war drums and the sacrificer, they walk around the sanctuary three times. The *ton dunu* is then played for those Samake present who are thought to have the power to transform into elephants.[39] Next, two women appear and begin to dance. Money is thrown, which the sacrificer picks up to give to the dancers. The war drum returns to its normal rhythm while the older men dance a war dance, their sabers in hand.

All the others are then invited to eat the food and drink the millet beer brought by the women. The remaining animals are carved up and a Samake from the Fajalala area is asked to divide the meat among all the villages. Affines receive their share. The chickens are distributed among the *kafo* notables. Offerings of money and kolas are in principle destined for the sacrificer, but he redistributes a part to the elders and, particularly, to the *kafo* chief. On this note, the ceremony ends. Weekly or annual sacrifices on Jitumu Musa's grave clearly constitute a sort of national cult whose purpose is to symbolically reaffirm the lineage hierarchy, the cohesion of the *kafo*, and the warlike nature of its organization. During this ceremony, the entire political unit of the chiefdom is reactualized. From this perspective, the adoration of Jitumu Musa appears as directly political: in his person, the founding ancestor of the royal lineage is deified.

Village-Level Political Cults

The intricate connections between Islam and paganism that I have called "pale paganism" result from the formal domination exercised by this religion on the polytheistic belief systems. In opposition to the theory of "Black Islam," which insists on animism's corrupting influence on Islam, we must no doubt in many cases see paganism as a product determined in the final analysis by Islam.[40] For example, the periodicity of ceremonies could have been influenced by Islam. This link with the Moslem world, visible in the cult of political ancestors, is also apparent in religious manifestations in the villages or those related to various secret societies in that they took place every seven years. We know that the number seven plays an important role in the magic and religion of North Africa as well as in the Old Testament.[41] Thus, to see in the number seven, as do certain ethnologists, one of the essential characteristics of Bambara metaphysics and cosmogony amounts to an arbitrary isolation of that region from its sociohistorical environment.[42]

The symbolism of the number seven occurs in all of western Sudan: just as do the sacrifices to Jitumu Musa, the ceremonies of the *kamablon* of Kaba[43] took place or take place every seven years. The same goes for rites practiced by the initiatory societies of the *komo*,[44] the *jo*,[45] the *kote*,[46] or those whose purpose is to purify the Minyanka village.[47] This symbolism also exists outside the area of our concern, since it can be found among the Hausa[48] and no doubt in many other areas of West Africa. It is tempting to see in this recurrence the sign of a common structure informing West African thought. But that would be to forget that in the Mande cultural sphere in its broadest sense, just as in the entire subcontinent, Islam is deeply rooted in social and religious life, and that Islam impregnates with its influence even those cosmogonies and rites that seem to be the most resistant to it.

Thus, geomancy plays a central role in the *komo*[49] and the *jo*,[50] informing the repesentation of the world for religious leaders and initiates alike. Moreover, it is unthinkable that this divinatory technique, given its implications for the individuals who use it, has not affected the whole of the intellectual schema understood in the present day as the "Bambara religion."

Some will object that the adepts of the *komo* consider their membership in the secret society as strictly antinomic to adherence to Islam; abandoning one for the other was even considered treason.[51] Rather than seeing a gap between paganism and Islam, is it not more accurate to see a simple gradation, analogous to that which opposes the different forms of Islam (Kadirriya, Tijaniya, Wahabiya, etc.)? For the Samake-Ture, who founded Jitumu in the eighteenth century and who could not have been fervent Moslems, it was their mastery of geomancy that enabled them to dominate the first settlers, who possessed the *komo*.[52] What today might appear as a slight difference between the two institutions must have at the time represented high stakes indeed for those involved in the conflict.

An entire series of stages exists within paganism. One passes imperceptibly from a pagan condition to a Moslem condition, which itself is no less composed of a series of stages.[53] As with an ethnic group, a person is more pagan than Moslem in certain cases, more Moslem than pagan in others. What we need to understand is the logic of this phenomenon of oscillation.[54]

This is where an analysis of the bonds between state power and religion becomes necessary. While it is tempting to oppose centralized, Moslem forms of power to segmentary, pagan forms, in reality the matter is not so simple, since numerous pagan kingdoms existed in Africa. One would need to distinguish, for example, several forms of paganism and explain how it was that state powers or phases of state power established and reorganized pagan practices.

The problematic of power does not allow us to be content with the usual analyses of the different secret societies: *komo*, *jo*, *kore*, *ndomo*, and so on. Given that these societies extended beyond what was generally recognized as their ethnic limits, and that they functioned in an essentially local context, it is not surprising that those who have studied them thought in terms of diffusion and considered these institutions as operating strictly within a single village.[55] Yet it is difficult to think that these societies, whose function was to maintain order within peasant collectivities, were shielded from intervention by the political forces that dominated the region. G. Dieterlen and Y. Cissé, for example, establish a link between the extension of the *komo* and the Malian empire, seeing in the structure used by this secret society a replica of the *kamablon* of Kaba. But in the absence of a systematic study of the ways in which these sanctuaries and their associated religions disperse, no conclusions can be drawn.[56] In Griaule's school of thought, history sins either by excess or default: either too large a grouping is studied–that is, West Africa–or researchers totally neglect the historical approach for a hermeneutic and gnostic analysis.

Today it is extremely difficult to retrace the steps taken by different secret societies within what can be appropriately called the Mande cultural area. But to the extent that we recognize these institutions as having a transethnic base, present-day anthropology should more systematically relate the large political forms with the implantation of these cults. At least that would have the advantage of avoiding the simplistic opposition between an Islam of the royal court and a paganism of the countryside, as far as the important empires of Ghana, Mali, and Sonrai are concerned.

The secret societies of this region developed a cosmogony and a metaphysics that, in reality, define the major components of the person. It is the notion of the person, then, that we shall look at next, in the framework of a problematic of identity negotiation.

Politics of the Notion of the Person

Whether it concerns the functionalist current or Griaule's school, the notion of the person has always been envisioned from an internal and static point of view, without being placed in an all-embracing framework. Of course, efforts have been made to distinguish several types of personalities within a specific society with regard to the range of social categories. In addition, some scholars have begun to analyze the notion of the person as the result of a relationship of both internal and external forces, but much remains to be done in this domain.[57] This lacuna results from the problematic of ethnic groups being the main concern in the study of African religions. I do not intend to propose a new theory of the person in the Mande cultural area, but simply to propose a few epistemological reference points. First, it does not seem possible to isolate the notion of the person as it appears in this zone from the larger environment in which it is integrated. As is true of the initiatory knowledge of the *komo*, the notion of the person among the Bambara and the Malinke is inseparable from geomancy, which is of Arabic origin.[58] It would thus seem futile, in this area as in others, to try to locate a pagan substrate free from all Moslem influence. Saaba Jakite, founder of the Gwanan chiefdom, whom the griots (*jeli*) present as a completely pagan being, is nonetheless defined as one who possesses *barka* (*barka tigi*), meaning, in the context of the period and region, that he was a magician, even though the Arabic term is the one used. Of course, the use of an Arabic concept does not necessarily define a particular phenomenon as Arabic. But one could just as well think that in the current context of Mali, where Islam is omnipresent, the griots purposely denigrate Saaba Jakite in order to better distinguish him from Farabalay, the principal architect of Islamization in the region.

Another rarely considered determining factor for the person is the political element: rather than abstractly isolate the person from his context, it would be more appropriate to begin from an all-encompassing perspective, which in this region amounts to the "nation."

Thus, both the notion of person and that of identity, since they are synonymous here, have a "national" political body—the *kafo* or the *jamana*—as a record-keeping matrix. By means of a network of neighboring "nations," personal identities are distributed that result in a definition that is both internal and external. In effect, the "nation" is not only a political unit but also the source of the praise name (*jamu*), the ban (*tana*), the personal double (*yelema*), and its accompanying interlineage pacts (*senankuya*). In Jitumu, the praise name Samake (literally male elephant) is simultaneously the praise name, the ban, and the double. The elephant is thus a sort of banner or sacred "onomastic emblem"[59] into which certain persons can supposedly transform themselves. Only members of the dominant lineages and their associated or dependent lineages can take this *jamu*, but in a certain sense all the subjects of a chief can be greeted either by their patronymic (Dunbiya, Kulubali, etc.) or by the praise name Samake. The praise name thus defines a dominant identity, an identity by which other identities are defined. In this sense, there is no ideology common to the whole social body, a fact that reveals these organizations to be both statelike and segmentary.

In identity negotiation, the notion of person or identity is at stake: I can change identity according to the context in which I find myself, which is true not only for the praise name, but also for a first name (*togo*).[60] The founder of the Gwanan chiefdom had Tonkere as a first name, the *jamu* Konate or Jara, and as ban (*tana*) the lion. Upon arriving in Gwanan, he changed his praise name to Jakite and his given name to Saaba (large snake), which also became his person double (*yelema*).

These identity changes, which are also changes in the conception of the person, since Senufo thereby become Fulani, occur very frequently and are well documented for the region we are looking at here, and more generally so for West Africa and even all of Africa. There is thus an international network or a chain of societies that determines in the final analysis the identity of each actor. This does not mean, however, that when a person or group changes identity, memory of characteristics from the preceding social situation is not retained. This explains, for example, how certain persons possess several *tana* or several *senankuya*, with some of these bans or pacts being linked to a previous *jamu*. Inversely, certain categories of dependents can be denied access to a new identity. When the Bagayogo of Bolon changed their *jamu* to Sangare, they forbade their slaves to do likewise, a fact that identifies to this day all the people in Bolon named Bagayogo as descendants of slaves.[61]

The notion of the person or identity is thus not written in an immutable cosmogony or metaphysics, as Griaule's school would have it. The notion of the person is constantly renegotiated and is at stake between groups situated within the same political entity as well as between neighboring political entities. With the advent of the district register and the resulting written registration of identity, the notion of person acquired a greater fixity. It became much more difficult to change identity or even to modify the spelling of one's first or last name. Since it could no longer affect the components of the person, the negotiation of identity shifted, as is the case in the West, onto other sectors of social and individual life.

The Bambara religion conceived as a paganism could well be a barbarous idea. To the extent that a Bambara cosmogony and metaphysics can be isolated, it seems that they can be situated on an axis whose two poles are the civilized Moslems of the cities (Timbuktu, Djenne, Kankan, etc.) and the pagan "savages" of the countryside (Minyanka, Senufo, etc.). Between these two poles are found the Bambara, that is, pagan warrior-peasants whose system of thought is "barbarous" in the sense that it combines paganism with Islam. Given this, we need to examine the entire series of institutions (of kinship and so on) categorized as Bambara and distinguish these people from others, such as the Senufo.

8   Cultural Identities and Cultural Models

Anthropologists have only recently begun to investigate the field of "development," which has been studied from essentially two perspectives: the epistemological analysis of how practices of development and concepts of anthropology are linked; and the economic and social history of different regions of Africa. The first perspective avoids the "history of ideas" and the second has made it possible to relativize current, supposedly unprecedented, "development schemes."[1] Cotton culture in southern Mali and northern Ivory Coast provides a good example of the link between anthropology and development. Since its inception, the colonial period set up a policy of homogenous development of cotton production in this entire zone, with varying results among the ethnic groups. On both sides of the border separating Mali from the Ivory Coast strongly similar groups live, with the Fulani, Malinke, and Bambara living to the west and the Minyanka and Senufo to the east. This east/west opposition partly conforms to the opposition between successful and unsuccessful cotton-growing areas. From the beginning of colonization, these opposing results have been interpreted in ethnic terms: the Minyanka's tenacity in the fields was constantly opposed to the laziness of the Fulani in Wasolon. Both ethnologists and developers have absorbed these stereotypes and, on the whole, relied on this explanation when they did not attribute the failure of cotton cultivation to colonial domination.[2] But neither of these explanations is valid. Since colonial domination was uniformly applied, it could not explain a difference in evolution of two groups under its sway. The ethnic explanation is equally inadequate, since it takes the effect for the cause. In order to understand the phenomenon of unequal development and the concomitant adoption of ethnic stereotypes, the history of cotton production in this entire region needs to be analyzed.

The Precolonial Period

Cotton has been cultivated in West Africa for centuries and we know that the expansion of its cultivation was closely linked to the spread of Islam.[3] Unlike C. Monteil, we cannot automatically associate the simple fact of being clothed with the quality of being Moslem, but the wearing of clothes made of bands of cotton must be placed in the context of Islamic expansion. As Caillié noted in 1827, the inhabitants of Ouassoulo lived near major Moslem centers and, though "idolaters," they felt great respect for the prophet's religion.[4] The region's young men shaved their head like the "Mohamedans" and the whole of the population wore locally produced cotton clothing.[5] This local crafting of clothing was based on an agricultural system that considered cotton production very important, and grew two crops of it a year, along with corn. The seed was broadcast, but Caillié considered the cotton plants too close together and felt that the plants were not well tended.[6] The harvests at this period have been estimated at a hundred kilograms per hectare.

Craftsmen produced cotton to clothe the inhabitants of Ouassoulo as well as for export. Once harvested, the cotton was spun by the women and woven by the men. Merchants purchased the five-inch-wide strips of cotton and resold them in Kankan.[7]

Throughout Caillié's expedition of 1827–28, which took him from Kankan to Jenne, passing by Sambatikila, Time, Tengrela, Kenedugu, Minyanka, Bendugu, and the Bwa area, he was continually struck by the importance of cotton cultivation. As in Ouassoulo, it was sown among cereal crops.[8] At the time, cotton constituted the basis of a profitable "Bambara" agriculture (Senufo, Minyanka) that supplied material to craftsmen and supported a Mande-Dioula trade based probably to a large extent on slave labor. Cotton strips and cloth comprised an integral part of an international division of labor based on long-distance trade for kola, rock salt, and slaves.

Sixty years later, on his way to Sikasso and Kong, Binger traversed a wartorn region but also witnessed the dynamism of cotton cultivation and the trade in cotton fabrics. Like Caillié, he observed that the cotton produced by the Senufo and Gouin peasants was bought and processed by the Mande-Dioula, but he specified that slaves did the weaving.[9] At the beginning of colonization, there was no fundamental difference between the Wasolon and its surrounding area on one hand, and the Senufo and Minyanka on the other: both regions produced cotton to clothe themselves and to supply other areas deficient in that material.

In the nineteenth century, the Fulani of Wasolon, the Bambara, and the Malinke were as energetic in growing cotton as the Senufo and the Minyanka. Only with colonialism did racial and psychological stereotypes define the Wasolon Fulani as mediocre cultivators and the Minyanka as model peasants. What is the origin of such a distinction?

Caillié created an idyllic vision of Fulani life in Ouassoulo because, at the time of his visit, it had not yet been devastated by wars.[10] It is true that at the end of the eighteenth century and in the first half of the nineteenth century, Ouassoulo was already a hunting ground for slaves: Mungo Park, for example, noted on his return from Gambia that several captives in his caravan came from an expedition to Vassela led by Monzon, king of Segu.[11] But only after the 1850s, as Gallieni and Binger pointed out, following the "war of the sons of the dream," the war of Kaba Ture of Wojene, the incursions of Denba and Torokoromari, kings of Segu, and the Samorian conquest did Wasolon really become the slave reservoir of Sudan.[12] A dense population most certainly explains how this region could have been one of the principal sources of captives in West Africa for a good part of the nineteenth century.[13] Until the middle of the nineteenth century, this large population was an essential factor in economic prosperity: rich in slaves, the Wasolon Fulani were able to exploit their multiple natural ressources,[14] exporting captives, ivory, rubber, and cotton cloth.[15] With an effective agricultural system based largely on slave labor, the Fulani were far from limiting themselves to the sedentary life of raising livestock that colonial and postcolonial stereotypes later attributed to them. They also devoted themselves to warfare, the favorite occupation of aristocrats.

Segmentary wars (*badenkele* or *fadenkele*) undertaken by various villages, lineages, and *kafos*, combined with incursions by outside states, produced so many slaves that Wasolon and the neighboring Bambara and Malinke areas began to deteriorate.[16] This "permanent state of war," as Gallieni called it, or this "war of all against all," in Hobbes's formulation, accelerated a process that nearly decimated Wasolon.[17]

Paradoxically, the peace brought about by colonialism also weakened the foundations of the region's agricultural economy. With the cessation of wars and the subsequent liberation of slaves, the reigning dynasties that prior to the French conquest had been able to keep their captives and even increase their number were themselves forced to work in the fields.[18] Fierce warriors that they were, the Wasolon Fulani suddenly became reluctant farmers. More than any factor such as the raising of livestock, hunting, or migration, peace seems to be the origin of the contrast between the region's economic potential and its current underdevelopment. What effect did the *pax gallica* have in what became Mali's cotton belt?

The Fulani, Bambara, and Malinke societies can be qualified as "historical" because they formulated a discourse that refers to the past, even if it does not expressly talk about it. The Senufo and Minyanka societies, however, can be defined as "societies without history." Only mildly centralized, endowed with genealogies that do not go very far back into the past, and encapsulated within states, the Senufo and Minyanka societies were more the subject of a history that surpassed them than actors in their own historicity. In addition, the states of Segu and Sikaso utilized Minyanka and Senufo as slave reservoirs, since they contained highly structured village communities of farmers. But this predation never had the weakening and depopulating effect that occurred in Wasolon at the beginning of colonization.[19]

Colonial Efforts to Develop
Cotton Production (1903–45)

From 1898, when the French took control of southern Sudan and northern Ivory Coast, the peasants in these regions once again began tapping rubber. They sold the rubber to trading houses to meet their needs for cash and to obtain money to pay their taxes. But the rubber boom was cut short in 1911 as the Asian rubber plantations came into production.[20] With the subsequent collapse of their own rubber production, the peasants had to resume the commercial production of cotton, which for several years the colonial administration had been encouraging.

In 1903, the Colonial Cotton Association (A.C.C.) was established, with the mission to supply the French market, which was considered too dependent on the United States. From 1903 to 1910, the A.C.C. attempted to introduce American cotton into the districts of Bamako, Segou, San, Djenne, and Koutiala, because that variety suited the French textile industry better than did the indigenous cotton.[21] This was a failure, however. The fragility of the plants coupled with the peasants' distrust of what they saw as the "white man's cotton," forced the A.C.C. to go back to the indigenous variety. Seeds were selected in the Segou, San, and Koutiala districts, but they did not produce cotton of sufficient quality to satisfy the requirements of French industry. Around 1910, the Koutiala district alone supplied three-fourths of the cotton exported.[22]

In 1906, the A.C.C. made cotton cultivation compulsory in the Sikasso district. A collective field was maintained in each village for the chief's profit. As of 1920, the rubber crisis provoked the A.C.C. to once again require each village to maintain a collective field for cotton. It also required the peasants to grow this plant in individual fields and to provide ten kilograms of raw cotton each year. In 1926, however, collective fields were abandoned. Administrators attributed this failure to the fact that the Senufo did not work the land sufficiently, refused to use fertilizer, continued to sow by broadcasting, and did not hoe or weed correctly.

In reality, the peasants thought it more advantageous to weave the cotton into bands that could be used locally for loincloths and blankets rather than supplying low-cost cotton to the European markets. To restrict the weaving of cloth and local trade in the product and to force the growers to deliver raw cotton to the A.C.C., the administration imposed a tax on cotton strips.[23]

In the Bougouni district, which includes Wasolon and the neighboring regions, the same phenomenon occurred. In 1904, when the area had just begun to increase its population and recover from its devastation, cotton was the third crop in importance after cereals.[24]

Only in 1920 did cotton move to the forefront of the colonial administration's preoccupations. Until then, rubber was the major cash crop and local officials devoted their attention solely to that. Following the collapse of the rubber market and the drought of 1913, the trade houses left Bougouni district. Growers were thus free to return to their own system of production and trade. Growing and weaving cotton remained very important for the rural economy. Strips were exported by the "Dioulas" (Kooroko) in Guinea and in Ivory Coast, where they were exchanged for kola nuts and other products reintroduced into the district.[25]

Generally, however, administrators felt that the district's population, made up principally of Fulani, was little inclined to agriculture.[26] It quickly became obvious that propaganda supporting cotton cultivation, begun in the 1920s, had failed in spite of a Cotton Association factory set up in Bougouni in 1927.[27] Only the district chiefs' collective fields had some success. Consequently, efforts to export cotton were progressively abandoned from the end of the 1920s to the beginning of the 1930s. In fact, in Bougouni district, just as in Sikasso district mentioned above, the real reason for the failure of organized cotton production lay in the colonial system's inability to capture the interest of local producers, who found greater returns in weaving cloth for African markets.[28] In northern Ivory Coast, the policy of cotton development was largely identical to the one implemented in southern Sudan.[29]

In both of these areas, the cotton policies implemented from 1903 to 1930 failed because of the inadequacy of American varieties and the administration's inability to offer a purchase price higher than what producers received from the local markets. Until the 1960s, when revenues and the size of land cultivated increased significantly, African traders successfully countered all efforts to develop a cotton production destined exclusively for Europe. As of 1925, Bélime, founder of the Niger Office, spoke of this situation so inconvenient for European trade:

> Take, for example, cotton, which has domestic (trade in strips) and foreign (exportation to Europe) markets. The part of the harvest sold to Europe is used only to acquire francs in order to pay taxes and to

purchase certain goods from abroad. We have just seen how the
Blacks obtain money thanks to a particularly advantageous cowry exchange rate. To obtain it, the inhabitant of Koutiala sells much less
cotton than before. What he keeps from his harvest, he profitably
transforms for local sale. With his woven bands, he buys kola nuts
and livestock. He buys more than before, because cotton is one of the
few products that, in terms of cowries, has considerably risen in
price. In Koutiala, the price of raw cotton rose from one hundred and
fifty cowries before the war to three hundred cowries per kilogram in
1924. Since cotton bands have such a large exchange value, natives
try to sell most of their production in this form.[30]

In another text, Bélime wrote that it was indispensable to crush
the local economy, which was, according to him, based on the principles of "communism."[31] The system of production was not the
only thing Bélime threatened, in fact, since he had every intention
of disrupting the chain connecting the different West African societies, in which long-distance trade was the principal link. Since the
colonizers were not willing to do that by paying a higher price to the
producers and, besides, the quality of cotton from the dry regions
did not meet the demands of French industry, the colonists installed
an irrigation system. Bélime established the Niger Office in 1932 in
an effort to dismantle "Sudanese communism" and create an economy based on modern agricultural methods.[32] But it rapidly became
apparent to the Niger Office that the cultivation of cotton was a failure. Instead of the planned one hundred thousand tons, production
never surpassed six thousand.[33] This failure led the directors of the
Office, in 1970, to definitively abandon such speculation.

Efforts to develop the use of irrigation for cotton production by
the Niger Office were corollary with the end of forced production in
the dry areas of southern Sudan and northern Ivory Coast. During
the 1930s in the Sikasso district of Sudan, cotton cultivation was
progressively abandoned, until 1941, when it was reestablished by
mandatory production. In 1945, production recovered its 1931 levels. But in 1947, following the end of forced labor, production
dropped off again and only with the arrival of the French Textile
Company (C.F.D.T.) through the years 1948–50 did the peasants
once again resume production for export.[34]

In the Bougouni district, as we have seen, cotton production was neglected at the end of the 1920s and the early 1930s. It was resumed in 1935 with the introduction of the Karangani variety, but the results did not meet the expectations of the colonial administration.[35] The purchase price was too low, the local weaving, as before, competed with exportation and, in 1945, all policies aimed at promoting cotton cultivation in the Bougouni district were dropped. In the north of Ivory Coast, after a peak in 1930 and despite the distribution of the Karangani variety beginning in 1935, commercial production fell for the same reasons as it did in Sudan.[36]

Until the end of World War II, attempts in southern Sudan and northern Ivory Coast to produce cotton for export were met, as in the preceding period, with total failure. The reasons were many, but they all stemmed from a single phenomenon: producers received too little money for their goods. In fact, the purchase price agreed upon by European buyers was not only less than what producers could receive on the African market, which had significantly increased, but also less than the price of peanuts and other food crops, which had higher yields.[37]

C.F.D.T. Policy in Northern Ivory Coast and Southern Mali

Only in 1951, with the C.F.D.T.'s distribution of the Mono variety of cotton in northern Ivory Coast, did cotton yields show a significant increase. After 1960, the Institute for Research on Cotton and Textiles (I.R.C.T.) and the C.F.D.T. embarked on a new phase of production intensification with a "technological package" that included the Allen variety of cotton, the use of pesticides and fertilizer, and close adherence to a farming calendar. Consequently, northern Ivory Coast became a model site for cotton monoculture.

This is the policy pursued from 1960–1970 by the Ivory Coast Textile Company (C.I.D.T.). Widespread use of draft animals and motorized equipment, an increase in the prices paid the producers, and subsidies for fertilizers and other amendments made Ivory Coast in the 1980s one of the top three producers in Africa, along with Chad and Mali.

Rather than taking the economist's more global approach, we observe that the volume of production was not uniform throughout northern Ivory Coast. The most productive areas were in fact those where the Senufo predominated, whereas the less productive areas were primarily Malinke or Dioula. Beyond the differences that might be explained by demography or soil conditions, there are sociohistorical factors that must be considered which also obtained in southern Mali.[38]

In the south of Mali, from 1945-50, the C.F.D.T. began to intervene; it was replaced in 1975 by the Malian Textile Company (C.M.D.T.). Different phases may be distinguished: start-up (1945-60), consolidation (1960-70), growth (1970-75), and boom (1975-80).[39]

During the start-up phase, after a few attempts in the Fana and San regions, progress spread rapidly with use of a "technological package" analogous to the one used in northern Ivory Coast.[40] In 1960, cultivated land neared 30,000 hectares, which led the C.F.D.T. to install cotton mills in San and Koutiala. Production remained weak, however (300 kilograms per hectare), and commercial production did not surpass 6,000 tons.

During the second phase, land areas doubled and the harvest attained 40,000 tons. Production concentrated around Koutiala in Minyanka country and included two secondary poles at San in Bobo country and Sikasso in Senufo country. Productivity also increased, but commercial yields did not exceed 600 kilograms per hectare on the average. In fact, during this entire period, the local market remained strong. At the end of the 1960s, it was estimated that more than 10,000 tons were not sold through official channels, but this amount continued to decrease.

In the third phase, the land cultivated diminished severely, to not more than 70,000 hectares, because of drought. Nevertheless, an increase in productivity compensated for this stagnation and about 900 kilograms per hectare were harvested.

The fourth period witnessed an increase in the amount of land cultivated. This number rose to 118,000 hectares. This was coupled with a boom in average yields–from 880 to more than 1,100 kilograms per hectare–and a concomitant increase in commercialized production to 150,000 tons in 1980. Of these 150,000 tons, more than half was produced in Minyanka country (Koutiala and Yorosso districts), and three-fourths if we include Senufo country (Sikasso and Kadiolo districts).

What is the reason for these geographical variations in cotton production in southern Mali and northern Ivory Coast, given that these regions both possessed the same general economic potential in the precolonial period? Explanations based on the colonial presence have no validity since it functioned uniformly in all the regions in question. There remains only the dynamism of the societies concerned that, along with other criteria, provides specialists as well as certain ethnologists and historians with a way to account for regional disparities.[41]

Rainfall is the most significant of these other criteria. Mali's cotton belt covers a vast land surface that receives varying amounts of rain depending on latitude, with the two extremes being the regions of San and Bougouni. Cotton is considered to grow best in between these two areas. Other factors that affected the success of cotton production include soil condition and average population density.

Certain other factors can hinder cotton production. Endemic sicknesses or the lack of roads for transporting the cotton have been named as reasons for the failure of cotton policy in specific regions. The last criterion has to do with the production system itself. Inasmuch as production varies according to cultural identity, developers will sketch out an ethnic portrait of the Fulani, Bambara, Malinke, Senufo, and Minyanka. To this portrait will be added complementary information, such as the average number of persons per farm, the impact of migrations, the role of cereals production relative to export products, social differentiation in the farms, the extent of equipment supplied and supervision, and so on. In fact, none of these criteria satisfactorily accounts for the variation in cotton production in southern Mali and northern Ivory Coast.

The first three criteria, rainfall, soil condition and use, and impediments to production, explain why cotton production has not been successful in certain areas, but they cannot account for its successful cultivation elsewhere. Developers and ethnologists consider the fourth criterion, the type of production system or ethnic affiliation, to be the most important one. For them, production volumes in each region are linked to a specific ethnic group. But this ethnic difference is itself the consequence of a rupture in the chain of societies that existed before colonialism. The colonial syntagma Fulani-Bambara-Malinke-Senufo-Minyanka is a system of transformations whose rules have been forgotten. In order for this ethnic leveling to take, identity changes, which were extremely frequent before colonization, had to be overlooked. Therefore, an explanation based on ethnicity could not be valid since it takes the result to be the cause.

Henceforth we can no longer associate the success of cotton with the Minyanka or its failure with the Fulani. It now remains to be shown just why the Minyanka or Fulani identity is indissolubly linked to hard work in one case and to nomadism and laziness in the other. To shed light on how the ethnic stereotypes that justified unequal development in the cotton belt came about, I will examine two identity groups. The first includes the Fulani, Bambara, and Malinke populations of southwest Mali and northwest Ivory Coast; the second includes the Minyanka and Senufo of southeast Mali and northeast Ivory Coast. These two groups, located at the poles of a single axis, represent the two extremes found in this region.

The Fulani-Bambara-Malinke Model

The Fulani, Bambara, and Malinke chiefdoms of Wasolon and surrounding areas functioned in terms of warriors and slaves. They drew from Islam support for a worldview that allowed them to claim that they were "historical" societies in contrast to the "ahistorical" Senufo and Minyanka societies. With the *pax gallica* of 1898 and the suppression of slavery in 1905, the warrior and slaveholding aristocrats lost their principal means of social reproduction and unwillingly became farmers.[42] Given their disdain for agricultural work, what strategies did these societies employ to most advantageously integrate into the colonial system? They based their strategies on the new conjunction opened by colonization, the Islamic-trading model.

At the time of the French conquest, Wasolon and its surroundings were a wasteland. Bled dry by the wars of the second half of the nineteenth century, the region rebuilt its population very slowly.[43] Initially, the Fulani, Bambara, and Malinke concentrated their efforts on tapping rubber, raising livestock, and growing food. After the rubber crisis, they turned to peanut production, gold mining, and especially migration.[44]

The numbers of those migrating swelled considerably. At first the migrants fled the burdens imposed upon them by the colonial administration (forced labor, military recruitment, etc.), but these were by no means the only reasons for movement. Many peasants left for positive reasons as well. They left their homes to cultivate peanuts in Senegal or cocoa in Ivory Coast or the Gold Coast, where they could earn money in the agriculturally developing coastal countries.[45] With the new situation created by colonization, migration for the purpose of earning money offered the best compensation for the loss of war and slavery.

As a result, by the end of the 1920s, colonial administrators continually complained of these massive departures, which they attributed to the Wasolon Fulani's nomadic nature:

> The Fulani-Bambara inherited the bad habit of nomadism from their ancestors. For no reason at all, they will leave the district and travel to Bamako, Guinea, Ivory Coast, or Senegal. The regions we visited need as much manpower as possible, but their productive capacity is diminished since they cannot benefit from the work of their inhabitants, who are true nomads and who sometimes leave for three or four years. In the villages, it is not rare to find 50 percent of the population gone.[46]

This stereotype endured throughout the entire colonial period and even after independence. It gave the cotton company and the Malian administration a reason for believing that this area, despite its excellent soil and good rainfall, could not be developed.[47]

This cliché was also adopted by the small group of Wasolon students living in Bamako, who explained the massive exodus from the region by reference to the Fulani vocation for raising livestock. But curiously, the Gwanan village of Tabako, chosen by one of these students as his fieldwork location for a study of migrations, was composed mainly of Jakite Saabashi, that is, "fake Fulani."[48] Fulani identity imputed to people from a Senufo background supposedly explained the Wasolon penchant for raising livestock and the accompanying repugnance for agriculture.

The behavior of the Fulani in this region seems rather to be closely linked to the Islamic-trading model, which replaced the former warrior-slaveholder model. The Islamic-trading or Mandean schema can, in fact, explain past and present behavior of Fulani from Wasolon as well as that of the Bambara and Malinke from that area. This model allowed the peasants of southwest Mali and northwest Ivory Coast to seize every possible occasion for monetary gain since the French conquest. These opportunities shaped their production systems in characteristic ways.[49] Inasmuch as this model spread throughout the entire country, it also distinguished the behavior of Malian immigrants in Ivory Coast from those coming from other countries of the savannah, such as Burkino Faso. Though immigrants from Burkina Faso, who made up a large part of the foreign population living in Ivory Coast, predominated in rural areas, the Malians, even if they had begun to work on plantations, abandoned agriculture as soon as they saw the chance to become craftsmen or traders.[50]

The Senufo-Minyanka Model

The economic characteristics of the Senufo and Minyanka model during the colonial period can be situated on an axis with the Fulani, Bambara, and Malinke at one end and the immigrants from Burkina Faso at the other.[51] These peasant societies, in particular the Minyanka, were much less affected than Wasolon and its surrounding areas by the devastating wars of the second half of the nineteenth century. Similarly, the colonial system did not affect equally the two regions under consideration here. Of course, some factors were in effect everywhere, such as forced labor, military recruitment, and mandatory plantings, as well as their consequences (migrations, etc.), but the Senufo and Minyanka societies were much less disrupted than the Fulani, Bambara, and Malinke by the cessation of wars and the end of slavery. Since they possessed few captives, the populations in southwest Mali and northwest Ivory Coast were able from the beginning of colonialism to reaffirm their agricultural vocation and the Minyanka very quickly took the lead in cotton production. This agricultural dynamism was without a doubt due largely to the role played by women in the production system but also to the fact that relatively few people migrated. While women did not work in the fields alongside men in the Islamized regions of Bougouni and Bamako, the women of Koutiala and Sikasso were fully dominated by the men and worked with them in the fields.[52] Similarly, in Senufo as in Wasolon, movement toward Ivory Coast began very early under colonization and quickly became a veritable institution, whereas in Minyanka, the rural exodus, after an initial success in the colonial period, gradually halted in the 1970s just when cotton production began to expand.

One can use ethnic terms to analyze differences between the Senufo and Minyanka, on one hand, and the Fulani, Bambara, and Malinke on the other; specialists have done so. However, rather than reducing the range of production systems in southern Mali and northern Ivory Coast to ethnic factors, it seems to me preferable to link this range to a selected group of elements located in a single sociocultural continuum. Without necessarily postulating a common substrate from which the Senufo, Minyanka, Fulani, Bambara, and Malinke societies diverged, one can legitimately suppose that these entities composed a single system of transformations whose agents were Islam and commerce. Thus instead of juxtaposing societies, as ethnologists and economists have done, we can envision a dynamic system in which the only difference between the Minyanka and the Fulani, for example, would be a greater or lesser Islamization and a more or less developed mercantilism. The more pagan and peasant-like societies would constitute one of the poles, the more Moslem and merchantlike societies would constitute the other.

This hypothesis seems confirmed by the identity conversions so visible today in southern Mali and northern Ivory Coast. In these areas, in fact, a Senufo who embraces Islam and works as a merchant becomes a Dioula and consequently integrates into the Mande world.[53] Ethnic oppositions could thus be replaced by religious and professional differences, whereas the evolutionist paradigm primitive-barbarian-civilized gives way to a system of social, synchronic, and spatial transformations.

As has already been noted elsewhere, the process that produces ethnonyms and their accompanying stereotypes is contemporaneous with the break-up, under colonization, of the chain of relations that united West African social formations.[54] Colonial authorities could thus formulate in substantialist and psychological terms the differences between Senufo, Minyanka, Fulani, Bambara, and Malinke. At the end of the eighteenth and beginning of the nineteenth centuries, the conditions for formulating a science of ethnic groups had not come about; travelers were aware of an international division of labor in West Africa and the recurrence of identical cultural patterns in societies that maintained all types of links with each other (war, trade, slavery).[55] Only when each society turned more toward the world market than toward its neighbors did it take on and had to take on the appearance of an ethnic group. In order for the colonial science of ethnic groups to take shape, the bonds linking precolonial societies had to be destroyed and repressed.

The two principal traditional explanations put forth by sociology to explain the transformations taking place in Africa at the time—colonial domination and social or ethnic dynamism—are both inadequate. The sociology of the years 1960-70 regarding colonial or imperialist domination was too general to grasp local peculiarities: because of its past and its culture, a given society did not react the same as its neighbor to the colonial situation, which, on the whole, was the same everywhere. The excesses of the sociology of domination provoked a return, in the 1980s, to an emphasis on the specificities of African societies.[56] While this approach corrected previous excesses, it seems no more satisfactory than its predecessor. It hypostasizes these different societies, elevating them as timeless essences placed within an identical global context. Such a substantialist conception of society or an ethnic group does not correspond, as we have seen, to the labile character of former African "nations." Each ethnic group now existing is itself the product of the disintegration of the precolonial world economy. Therefore, a problematic of these societies as local entities, which makes these transformations into theory, participates integrally in colonial ideology and its underlying racial theory.

9 Understand in Order to Act: Mestizo Logics

The eye that sees is the eye of tradition.
–Franz Boas

Anthropologists typically situate knowledge/power relations in the colonial context, where they have to do with the idea that anthropology and imperialism are related.[1] But this problematic seems too limited because it makes an abstraction of an agent prior even to colonization: the state. The state and its privileged instrument of registration, writing, supply an indispensable analytical framework for these relations.

Those who postulate a link between knowledge and power most often bring out the distortions of meaning that would result from placing the act of knowing in the sphere of action. Throughout my analysis here, I have tried to show that the implication of anthropologists and administrators in the colonial system resulted, in many cases, from a misunderstanding.

Since it is difficult to imagine an anthropology not rooted in a particular time and place, however, it would be incorrect to discount the entirety of colonial wisdom because of this rootedness. "Knowledge in spite of everything," said F. Pouillon about the work of colonial administrators in southern Tunisia.[2] In effect, the anthropologist finds his information where he can; and the projection of his own problematic onto those of the past is the deciding factor in each case on how much credibility to give various accounts.

Wasolon and the surrounding regions that contained the "shrunk states" and "dominated segmentary states" were subjected for long periods to the hegemony of different kingdoms and empires. These large state formations set up specific techniques for managing local societies, depending on whether they practiced "direct" or "indirect" types of administration. While we lack the information for a good understanding of organization within autonomous *kafos* and *jamanas*, it is possible to reconstruct with some precision the ways populations were registered when these same chiefdoms fell under the rule of Segu. Of course, the oral tradition sometimes refers to methods used to calculate the duration of a local chief's reign (stacking stones, for example) or other information.[3] But it is only with the extension of Segu's domination to the whole of the region that the necessity arose for a numbered system for recording population. Such quantifiable record keeping was, of course, indissociable from taxation.

The nature of the tribute required by Segu from the vassal provinces was not fixed; it was simply a matter of the subjects from the kingdom's periphery assuring themselves of the sovereign's benevolence by sending him gifts.[4] On the other hand, at the local level of each chiefdom, the collection of tribute from the individual *kafos* or their subdivisions was determined by very strict rules and subjected to scrupulous accounting procedures. In Basidibe, for example, the province chief customarily collected a measure of millet per person; in Jalonfula, each village chief was required to furnish one *talikise* of gold per person to the local *mansa*, who theoretically had to turn over the entire amount to the king of Segu as a sign of his obedience.[5] One can easily imagine the multiple exactions allowed by this method of indirect collection; on the pretext of providing tribute to the sovereign, the *kafotigi* increased fiscal pressure to inflate their personal fortune.

The Samori system of "direct rule" worked differently in the conquered regions. In principle, the tribute had to be given in its entirety to the army and the court. The empire's central administration required a precisely fixed amount: Juma sent a *jaka* of one thousand loads of rice, Bure eight hundred lots of gold, and so on. Likewise, fields cultivated collectively for Almami corresponded to one-tenth of the harvest. In Wasolon, moreover, each village had to send a fixed number of students to the Koranic schools.[6] Generally speaking, it is likely that the Samori empire's Islamic foundations favored the use of writing in order to keep accounts of the goods stored in royal warehouses.

When the French established the Bougouni district in 1893, they knew they were taking possession of a region devastated by Samori, devoid of inhabitants or almost so. Since the French administration ordered an end to slavery, in 1894 the governor of French West Africa asked all the district commanders to fill out a questionnaire regarding captivity. The census taken in different areas of the district revealed only a few captives, a lot less at least than in the zones that functioned as slave markets for Wasolon during the second half of the nineteenth century.[7] The survey contained the general headings of a questionnaire, without any unusual notations. The district officer did, however, observe that if slave trade was not to be tolerated, at least "household" captivity had to be, or else agricultural production would come to a halt.[8]

In reality, the colonizers were first and foremost occupied with the necessities of indirect rule, and these were the reasons for successive surveys made by Louis-Edgar de Trentinian, Ernest Roume, Martial-Henry Merlin, and Marie-François Clozel.

In 1897, the lieutenant governor of Sudan, Trentinian, sent all the commanders of regions, districts, and posts a questionnaire from the Berlin Union of Law and Political Economy concerning the "customary law of Sudanese natives." In a note, he draws the commanders' attention to the scientific as well as the practical interest of this work.[9] C. Monteil produced his monograph of the Khassonke with information drawn from this inquiry.[10]

In 1904, Merlin, the interim governor of French West Africa (A.O.F.), ordered each district of the Upper Senegal–Niger to produce a monograph.[11] The Bougouni district monograph contains historical, ethnographic, economic, and demographic information and a list of all the cantons with the names of their respective chiefs.[12] Five years later, the governor of Upper Senegal–Niger, Clozel, decided to update these monographs and at the same time to undertake a study on indigenous common law, along the same lines as what he had already done in 1901 in Ivory Coast. This study's questionnaire, modeled directly on the French civil and penal codes, was designed to collect local customs that, once codified, would al-

low the indigenous justice system to function in accordance with
natural law.[13] Successive studies, invariably following the same
logic as their predecessors, provided the information for M. Delafosse's *Haut-Sénégal-Niger*, a masterpiece of colonial ethnology
which, for several decades, was the bible for scholars.[14]

By organizing the collection and codification of indigenous customs and by applying them, the colonial administration showed its
respect for ethnic and cultural differences rather than a desire for
assimilation of the local populations, a fact that runs counter to the
idea people often have of French politics in Africa. Such a close link
between ethnographic studies and the administration allowed the
district officers to understand how the Sudanese societies functioned and to effectively take possession of the conquered territories. By applying the territorial model of the canton, based on the
French division into departments and imbued with the ethnological and racial approach that had developed throughout the nineteenth century, the French authorities drew the boundaries for districts and cantons so as to create administrative entities easy to govern, and they delegated power by installing as chiefs only men of
incontestable lineage. Thus, from the very first years of colonization, a system of indirect rule was set up that lasted until independence, even if officially, from 1909 to 1917, it was replaced by a system of direct rule in response to the "racial policies" of Ponty.[15]

The shortage of French personnel required the district commanders to rely on the goodwill of the village and canton chiefs, the only
ones capable of maintaining order, dispensing justice, keeping track
of population numbers, and collecting taxes.[16] But in practice, drawing district and canton boundaries turned out to be an extremely
delicate matter: different groups overlapped and the French territorial model as a form only partly corresponded to the segmentary
and war-based nature of the *kafos* and *jamanas* that emerged once
they had rid themselves of Samorian control.[17] To mitigate these difficulties, the district officers increased their rounds, which allowed
more frequent census-taking and furnished material for smaller-
scale monographs on the various canton groups.

They hoped in this way to identify members of the "chiefs of noble
race," whose legitimacy would be incontestable and who might,
moreover, be educated and thus able to govern effectively. It was not

enough, however, for a man to possess these qualities; in addition, neither he nor his family could have collaborated with Samori. If he or they had, a chief would have to be chosen from a rival lineage. It also happened on occasion that the choice proved inadequate and that the administration had to reestablish a lineage not previously considered a source of chiefs. Whether the chief was recruited from a recognized lineage or chosen from an illegitimate family, an effective management of the chiefdom ultimately depended on the canton chief's nobility and lack of servile origins.

Difficulties experienced by the leadership appeared, for example, in the Van Vollenhoven circular of 1917, which cast doubt on Ponty's "direct contact," as well as in Labouret's observations on the necessity of choosing legitimate village and canton chiefs.[18] For the canton chiefship, considered the successor of the precolonial *kafo*, Labouret developed a genealogical and racial analysis that has repercussions for anthropology even today.[19]

In 1931, these same difficulties led Brévié, then governor general, to undertake a new survey in all the A.O.F. districts for the purpose of gathering and codifying the different common law. Overall, this survey followed the form used by Clozel in 1901 and 1909 and resulted in a report, dated 1932, on Bambara customs in Bougouni district.[20] Even though this collection, written by Aubert, is one of the most complete—it includes sections on precolonial canton organization and the functions of the chief—it remains somewhat obscure on several points. Aubert did not see the canton as essentially anything more than a unit controlled by a dynastic or lineage principle. He thus effectively ignored all state domination of the region. What is more, he alluded only once to the influence of Islam.[21] The narrow legalism and even the essentialism of this type of document obviously favored a frozen vision of the precolonial chieftaincy that directly supported the interests of the local notables, the principal informants for Aubert's report.[22]

It was not enough, however, to find chiefs of noble lineage. They also had to be skilled and educated as well as docile. In other words, they had to bring in the taxes, deliver men for forced labor, and serve as an example in providing mandatory crops. The administration thus found itself caught between two contradictory possibilities; they could choose either a chief who was legitimate but uneducated, or one who was educated but of nonnoble heritage. One way of resolving this dilemma was to appoint as deputy a son or distant relative who had received some education, who would ostensibly assist the official village or canton chief, but who in reality would wield power.[23]

Consequently, the colonial administration contained an inherent contradiction, but this must be equally attributed to the election system by which village and canton chiefs were chosen.[24] This system apparently allowed all kinds of manipulations, with district officers not hesitating to exert pressure in favor of their candidate of choice. Nevertheless, the electoral procedure tempered the arbitrary nature of administrative decisions and allowed the electoral college to have a voice.

In reality, the juridical form of the canton provided the Sudanese populations, as well as all French African colonies, with an institutional framework that they appropriated to pursue their own aspirations. Something like a "working misunderstanding" allowed a certain form of political life to evolve.[25] The entire sixty-year period of French occupation was very calm, marked by no uprising or revolt, unlike other Sudanese regions (such as the Beledugu, Bwa, and Dogon areas). Nevertheless, an active political "work" occurred, evident through relatively discrete events, such as redesigning the cantons or replacing chiefs. A decrease in the number of cantons, the modification of their configuration, or the recruitment of authority figures in the different lineages were in fact an expression of peasant discontent.

In response to all these modifications, the local notables negotiated among themselves and intervened with the colonial administration. In particular, they addressed auxiliary figures (interpreters, etc.) from whom they obtained written documents permitting, for example, a family that had previously acceded to the chiefship to reclaim that right.[26] The proliferation of administrative literature reinforced the idea of a quasi-structural form of political life in the cantons. The pre-Samorian *kafos* and *jamanas* functioned according to a warlike and segmentary principle because they functioned so intimately in conjunction with the strength of neighboring kingdoms. But in the colonial perspective, the cantons were fixed organisms in which access to power was conceived only in terms of a set alternation among several lineages or between senior and junior branches of a single lineage.

This view is most clear in the *Monographies du cercle de Bougouni*. They were written after World War II, when what the Malians call "politics" was in effect, that is, a peaceful competition among factions or political parties that operated by means of manipulation or ruses (*kekuya*) and opposed brute force (*fanga*).[27] The conflict between the P.S.P. and the R.D.A. became entangled with intralineage or interlineage conflicts (*fadenkele*).[28] In this way, the colonial politics of segmentation revived a tradition practiced by Segu, which dominated the region by stirring up lineages, villages, and chiefdoms against each other. The actors were strongly aware of this historical continuity, as the words of this Keleyadugu peasant reveal: "Manipulation was the way Segu dominated Keleyadugu. We know that the whites used the same system, at least, in Keleyadugu." He also told the interpreter: "Right now you are using the manipulation method with us. Politics has existed forever and that is what runs the world."[29] Beginning in 1946, "political politics" sharpened tensions within chiefdoms and led the administration to increase "palavers" and census-taking. This direct contact with the back country, reviving Ponty's "racial politics," allowed the gathering of data and the preparation of pamphlets on the history and political organization of the cantons. The undertaking began in 1953–54 with the writing of the *Monographies du cercle de Bougouni*, documents containing precisely organized information gathered during the rounds made by Touze or his assistants. They contain a file for each village with demographic, fiscal, economic, ethnologic, and religious information compiled and synthesized for each canton. Aside from the synthesis of data for each village, each document also contains data on the history and ethnology of the canton, principally regarding the chiefdom.

The *Monographies* gave the district commanders a rather precise understanding of the social factors provoking most of the disruptive conflicts within the cantons. One of them contains the following: "To command, one must at least be able to know,"[30] and to know, according to administrative logic, one must first learn the history of each canton and, consequently, the history of the groups living in it.

The resurgence of "politics" as the Malians understood it gave rise to studies and the elaboration of a specific colonial knowledge that augmented the effect of segmentarity. What form did this knowledge founded on an ethnographical approach take in the aca-

demic anthropology of the period? What use can we make of it today? Even if they are fundamentally tributary to racial theory, these
writings adopted indigenous theories and principally because of this
they reflect a colonial vision. On the other hand, these writings reveal a perceptive observation of local dynamics. For example, they
allow us to know for how long people have been changing their ethnic identity. Informants now are often unable to supply such information, even if it is only because a unanimist veil ("We are all the
same") generally shrouds local political history. A meaningful understanding of such data is possible only after close scrutiny, for
such information is only of marginal significance in the larger body
of this enormous administrative work. This is true because colonial
administrators were more often than not at the mercy of interpreters, the true possessors of local political power, as A. Hampate
Bâ has admirably shown in *L'étrange destin de Wangrin*.[31] They often allied with the notables to make up a history and sociology to
serve their own purposes. In fact, the district commanders had to
develop a "middle" tradition themselves that would legitimize the
authority of their subordinates (canton and village chiefs) while in-
suring peace.

Despite its weaknesses, the ethnology of colonial administrators
easily supports comparison with professional ethnologists working
concurrently in the region. Postwar administrators were much better informed than their predecessors and possessed a more sympa-
thetic attitude toward the Africans. Moreover, in contrast to ethnologists in the Griaule school who made up myths and cosmogonies
agglomerating decontextualized cultural elements, the district officers were directly confronted with political problems and thus
were forced to acquire a more accurate knowledge of the history and
social organization of the societies under their supervision.[32]

In the 1950s, a certain number of conditions coincided that allowed the conception of an ethnological knowledge relatively de-
tached from the constraints of the colonial system: forced labor and
the *indigénat* were ended, certain social projects were realized
thanks to F.I.D.E.S. (Investment Funds for Economic and Social Development), and administrative pressure on the peasants was re-
laxed.[33] Generally speaking, the command personnel felt doubt about
the future of France's presence in West Africa and began merely ac-

companying the movement toward independence, especially after the *loi cadre* of 1956. It was at this time that the surveys mentioned above were undertaken. In addition, some enlightened administrators undertook research that led to several doctoral theses.[34]

As a whole, this accumulation of administrative or academic writings was appropriated by the local actors. Canton and village chiefs utilized the written documents to confirm their legitimacy. In general, the whole of the population used written administrative documents to support and realize various claims. Upon independence, moreover, this ethnology and history were not rejected as one of the props of colonialism. Since 1960, they in fact allow Malian civil servants posted in the Bougouni and Yanfolila districts, as well as people who originally came from these districts, to confirm their identity.

The Malian administration and the C.M.D.T. have retained in part the political system and colonial ideology, even institutionalizing such a continuity in the realm of politics. Even though the canton chiefs were replaced by *chefs d'arrondissement*, civil servants having "direct contact"[35] with the local people, the district officers have remained in place. On the ideological level, administrative personnel and cotton agriculture agents alike reflect the colonial stereotype by attributing the failure of cotton farming to the laziness of the Wasolon Fulani.

As a result, the people of Wasolon, whether in their region of origin or in Bamako, have developed a counteridentity based on exaggerating minute differences between the Fulani and the Bambara. In this way, they emphasize an identity founded on the practice of raising livestock, a definition taken, as whole cloth, from the works of Péroz and Person.[36] Of course, in the framework of the construction of the state and the constitution of a ruling class, the identity claim is also a means for the Wasolon Fulani to position themselves advantageously in the various client networks that structure the entirety of Malian society and that function by the logic of predation and redistribution taking place there.

Similarly, in the political arena, intellectuals from the Bougouni region have used analyses by Labouret and Aubert on the kinship nature of relations in the *kafo* to call for a recentering of Mali's history around the smaller political entities and a turning away from what for them was too great a focus on the large empires of the past. The anthropologist must be wary of the feedback-like phenomenon seen here, especially since not much has been written about the region under study. Throughout our work on the history of *kafos* and *jamanas*, in fact, our questions were often answered with fragments from the *Monographies du cercle de Bougouni*. Often, we were directed to the former district interpreter, who was the initial collector of the information used in producing the *Monographies* and was thus the preferred informant of Malian and foreign scholars. In fact, and particularly at the beginning of our study (1967–69), our presence was perceived as the forerunner of the "return of the whites" and its corollary, the reestablishment of the canton chieftaincy. Consequently, as one can imagine, informant responses regarding the area's population history took on a particular slant.

This feedback phenomenon shows us that the question of our relation to colonial ethnology is grounded in the more general question of our relation as ethnologists to written documents. The administrator's or the anthropologist's approach, to the extent that it arbitrarily selects certain indigenous theories and legitimizes them by writing them down, privileges certain versions to the detriment of others.[37] This, among other things, explains the apparently bizarre conjunction of nineteenth-century European racial theory with the history of a local population.

The societies that anthropologists analyze and characterize by "tradition" or "orality" could, more often than one would think, bear the mark of societies with a closely related scriptural transmission. Colonial knowledge represents one of these major influences, but it is patent, as has been observed regarding the "Bambara religion," that the Arab and Moslem civilizations, and no doubt others before, have also affected "oral" societies.

Rather than define these societies as the exact opposite of societies with writing or as oceans of orality dotted with islands of literacy, it would perhaps be preferable to see them as places where the written is reproduced in the oral. In this sense, the idea of an oral tradition would indicate a form of judgment that makes imputations because of a "graphic" way of thinking. Such an idea effectively denies primitive societies the right to a historicity by refraining from looking in their oral productions for an influence of writing, which one can never exclude to begin with. If anthropologists are inclined to use the notion of "oral literature" and if they have so much trouble finding other terms to designate this type of material, it is perhaps because the oral epics of West Africa, for example, as Goody has shown, themselves contain traces of Moslem written works.[38]

Just as we have observed the presence of the state in the segmentary and that of Islam in paganism, we must detect the written in the oral. We would then renounce ethnological reason, that is, an action that consists in decontextualizing certain data so as to define types, and see instead a problematic of the reproduction of the Same in the Other. From the idea that societies are intrinsically oral, pagan, or segmentary, anthropologists shift too easily to the certainty that these societies *refuse* the written, Islam, or the state. Yet, in Sudano-Sahelian West Africa, as no doubt in other parts of the world, it is difficult to imagine that societies could define themselves independently of the literate Moslem states surrounding them.

This is why diffusionist theories that *measure* the influence of the written on the oral, of Islam on paganism, or the state on the segmentary are themselves inadequate. If one or another society "accepts" the written, Islam, or the state, it is not because of tendencies to do so, but because that society bears within itself the imprint of these institutions. In other words, to think about oral, pagan, and segmentary societies in a region of the world where the written, Islam, and the state have existed for centuries would be quite a challenge, for one could do this only by arbitrarily isolating microelements at the center of a sociohistorical continuum.

If the ethnic group or the canton chieftaincy, as colonial creations, "take" so easily in the consciousness of the actors, it is no doubt because they constitute forms derived from a distant statelike past, because they are in a certain way "already there." Far be it from us to invert the problematic and posit a necessary anteriority of the state, of Islam, or of the written. On the contrary, the analysis in terms of "mestizo logics" allows one to escape the question of origin and to hypothesize an infinite regression. It is no longer a question of asking which came first, the segmentary or the state, paganism or Islam, the oral or the written, but to postulate an originary syncretism, a mixture whose parts remain indissociable.

Reference Matter

Notes

Introduction

1. R. Thornton, "Culture," 20.
2. J. Clifford and G.-E. Marcus, *Writing Culture*.
3. "The classification of a population according to race will remain in place. Besides, we do not speak of races anymore, but of groups. Political rights will be conceded as a function of 'cultural identity,' that is, as a matter of ethnic identity." "South Africa: The National Party Congress," *Le Monde*, June 30, 1989.
4. Interview with M. Arkoun, *Le Monde*, Mar. 15, 1989.
5. Hume, 1753-54. Kant, 1968 (1764). Regarding the Enlightenment influence on Herder, see E. Cassirer, *Philosophie des Lumières*, 303.
6. "Prejudice is good in its time, because it makes one happy." J.-G. Herder, *Another Philosophy*, 185.
7. "The organization of justice in New Caledonia, Melanesian common law will be taken into account more often." *Le Monde*, Apr. 6, 1989.

Chapter 1

1. E. Benveniste, *Le Vocabulaire*, 1: 360; Meillassoux, *Anthropologie*, 1: 106.
2. J.-L. Amselle in Amselle and M'Bokolo, *Au coeur de l'ethnie*, 11-48.
3. E. Benveniste, *Le Vocabulaire*, 1: 368.

4. Ibid., 2: 9.

5. E. Will, *Doriens*, 14.

6. Aristotle, *Politics*, 1261a, 1276a.

7. V. Ehrenberg, *L'Etat grec*, p. 53; A. Southall, *Alur Society*.

8. Gaffiot, "*ethnicus*"; Littré, "*ethnique*."

9. M. Mauss, *Oeuvres*, 3: 580.

10. From the Latin *natio*: birth.

11. S. Sala-Molins, *Le Code noir*.

12. W. Rodney, *A History*, 33.

13. J.-G. Herder, *Another Philosophy*.

14. "The principal States of modern Europe have today reached a high degree of territorial unity; and the custom of living under the same government and in the heart of the same civilization seems to have produced among the inhabitants of each State an entire community of mores, language, and patriotism. However, not a single one of these States presents living traces of the diversity of races that, over time, gathered on its territory." A. Thierry, *Histoire*, 1: 3. "Race, milieu, and the moment—with this information, one can reconstitute a complete, real history." Cited by F. Léger, "L'Idée de race chez Taine," 89.

15. E. Gellner, *Nations*.

16. J.-A. Gobineau, *Essai*.

17. Vacher de Lapouge, *Les Sélections sociales*.

18. E. Renan, "Qu'est-ce qu'une nation?" On Renan's ambivalent attitude toward the notion of "race," see M. Olender, *Les Langues du Paradis*, 82–89.

19. E. Will, *Doriens*, 102.

20. Fustel de Coulanges, *Histoire*. On Fustel de Coulanges, see F. Hartog.

21. C. Lévi-Strauss, "Race," 25–26.

22. "I was not content to know the character of the Savages and to investigate their customs and practices, I sought in these practices and customs vestiges of the most ancient Antiquity." *Moeurs des Sauvages Ameriquains*, P. Lafitau, 1: 5.

23. "In Aristotle's *Politics* (the word *ethnos*) designates peoples not living in cities, whether barbarians (no barbarians live in the city) or Greeks (some Greeks live in cities, others not). The connection made (in Aristotle's text) between family and villages, on one hand, and *ethnè* on the other, can be interpreted as deriving from an evolutionist conception of the history of social formations comparable to that of Morgan or of Engels. *Ethnos* would then be an historical *stage* characteristic of human communities that have not attained the full bloom repre-

sented by the *polis*. But nothing in the text itself indicates categorically whether or not Aristotle thought that, with time, all human communities tended to develop toward the perfect form that is the *polis*." P. Pellegrin, in the commentary to his translation of Aristotle, *La Politique*, 90–91.

24. "Thus, when the Victorian epigoni of Condorcet and Adam Ferguson used the adjectives 'savage' or 'barbarous' or 'uncivilized,' the connotations were no longer what they had been before 1800. Along with 'primitive' and 'lower,' these terms were now applied to 'races' rather than 'nations' and 'peoples' and the imputation of inferiority, although still in the first instance cultural, was now in most cases at least implicitly organic as well. Darwinian evolution, evolutionary ethnology, and polygenist race thus interacted to support a raciocultural hierarchy in terms of which civilized men, the highest products of social evolution, were large-brained white men, the highest products of organic evolution, very fully civilized." G. W. Stocking, Jr., *Race*, 121–122.

25. E. Durkheim, *The Division*; and M. Mauss, *Oeuvres*.

26. Anthropologists of savagery and the philosophers who follow their lead will make this fault into a virtue and find in primitive societies reluctant forms of the state or capitalism. See Amselle, *Le Sauvage*.

27. The study of peculiar societies or cultures supposes the passage from itinerant ethnography to sedentary ethnography. See G. W. Stocking, Jr., *Observers*, 70–120.

28. E. Leach, *Critique*, 14.

29. E. Benveniste, *Le Vocabulaire*, 2: 9.

30. J. Lombard, *Autorités traditionnelles*, 165.

31. C. Ageron, "Du mythe kabyle."

32. H. Deschamps, *Gallieni pacificateur*.

33. H. Spencer, *Principes de sociologie*.

34. H. Deschamps, *Gallieni pacificateur*, 25. According to Deschamps, the diversity of races in Sudan, having been oppressed by the Toucouleurs of Ahmadou and the Malinke of Samory, caused Gallieni to follow this policy, but it was applied in Tonkin for the first time.

35. J. Lombard, *Autorités traditionelles*, 106–9.

36. J.-L. Amselle, "L'ethnicité."

37. Lugard, *Dual Mandate*, 66–79.

38. According to Brévié, the chiefs are the "representatives of ethnic collectivities" and, consequently, they would not remain indifferent to the potential tendencies or reactions of these collectivities.

39. J. Lombard, *Autorités traditionelles*, 131.

40. L. Delafosse, *M. Delafosse*.

41. J. Bazin, "A chacun"; Chauveau and Dozon, "Au coeur des ethnies ivoiriennes"; J.-L. Amselle, "L'ethnicité."

42. *Volkekunde* is the Afrikaans term for *Völkerkunde*, meaning "ethnology." Concerning the source of the politics of segregation, I prefer P. Skalnik's study, "Union soviètique-Afrique du Sud," to S. Dubow's "Race, Civilisation and Culture."

43. Radcliffe-Brown and Forde, *African Systems*, 2.

44. J. Fabian, *Time and the Other*.

45. Fortes and Evans-Pritchard, *African Political Systems*; H. Spencer, *Principes de sociologie*; E. Durkheim, *The Division*; Lugard, *Dual Mandate*.

46. H. Kuklick, "Tribal Exemplars."

47. G. Dieterlen, *Essai*.

48. D. Jonckers, *La Société minyanka*.

49. W. MacGaffey, *Religion and Society in Central Africa*.

50. J. Bazin, "Bambara," in *Encyclopaedia Universalis*.

51. E. Bélime, *Les Irrigations*, 16-17

52. M. Delafosse, *Haut-Sénégal-Niger*.

53. L. Senghor, *Liberté I*.

54. Y. Benot, *Indépendances africaines*.

55. J. Goody, *La Raison graphique*.

56. Clifford and Marcus, *Writing Culture*.

57. Amselle, "L'ethnicité."

58. Amselle, *Le Sauvage*.

59. H. Kuklick, "Tribal Exemplars."

60. M. L. Pratt, "Fieldwork in Common Places."

61. P. Bourdieu, *Choses dites*.

62. Collectif, *Vers des sociétés pluriculturelles*.

63. G. W. Stocking, Jr., *Race*, 200.

64. Ibid., 214.

65. Leibniz, *Principes*.

66. C. Lévi-Strauss, *Les Structures*, 3-48.

67. J. Van Velsen, *Politics of Kinship*; J.-P. Dozon, *Anthropologie et histoire*.

68. Lévi-Strauss, *Race et histoire* and "Race et culture."

69. E. Terray, "Face," 54-55.

70. On this point see N. Dias, "L'eredità." For that matter, Lévi-Strauss explicitly acknowledges Gobineau's influence; see Lévi-Strauss and Eribon, *De près et de loin*, 201-27. By substituting in his writings the term "culture" for "race," one can see Gobineau as the true father of cultural anthropology.

71. M. Augé, "Qui est l'autre?"

72. Even if in France the "Club de l'Horloge" opposes the existence of a multicultural society, it nevertheless professes an identifying antiracism that is distinct from an egalitarian antiracism. In fact, it involves substituting a cultural racism for the no longer acceptable biological one.

73. A. Finkielkraut, *La Défaite*.

74. *Genos* in Greek means family, class, and race. See G. W. H. Lampe, *Lexicon*.

75. Hastings, articles on *ashkenaz* and *sepharad* in *Dictionary of the Bible*. On the differences between Portuguese Jews and German Jews in Holland, on one hand, and the dissimilarities between Portuguese Jews and Avignon Jews in Bordeaux in the eighteenth century, see D. Feuerwerker, *L'Emancipation des Juifs*, 165 and 176, and L. Poliakov, *Histoire de l'antisémitisme*, I: 422-24. On the "Arab" character of the Jews of Djerba, see Udovitch and Valensi, *Juifs en terre d'islam*.

76. J. Abbink, "L'énigme."

77. B. Jewsiewicki, "Formation of the Political Culture of Ethnicity."

78. R. Girard, *La Violence et le sacré*.

79. Dumont, *Essais*.

80. R.-A. Nisbet, *La Tradition sociologique*.

81. E. Durkheim, *The Division*, 121-23.

Chapter 2

1. A. L. Kroeber and C. Kluckhohn, *Culture*, 51-52.

2. Mayer in ibid., 51-52.

3. In the beginning of the twentieth century, the term *völkisch* acquired a distinctly chauvinistic meaning, assigning priority to racial and cultural heritage rather than to political allegiance; on this see J.-P. Faye, *Les Langages totalitaires*. On Rosenberg's rejection of biological racism and the valorization of the German people and language in Heidegger, see V. Farias, *Heidegger et le nazisme*, and J. Derrida, *De l'esprit*.

4. Mayer, in Kroeber and Kluckhohn, *Culture*.

5. Tylor, in Kroeber and Kluckhohn, *Culture*, 81.

6. Kroeber and Kluckhohn, *Culture*, 82.

7. Ibid., 318.

8. For Russia, see W. Berelowitch, "Aux origines de l'ethnographie russe."

9. L. Dumont, *Essais*, 129-30.

10. "What is a nation? A body of associates living under a common law and represented by a single legislature," E. Siéyès, *Qu'est-ce que le Tiers Etat?* 31.

11. J.-G. Herder, *Another Philosophy of History*; and J. G. Fichte, *Addresses*.

12. R. Bastide, *Anthropologie appliquée*, 14.

13. Ibid., 20.

14. Ibid., 21.

15. Amselle, "Le développement."

16. Bastide, *Anthropologie appliquée*, 19.

17. J.-J. Herskovits, *Les Bases*.

18. M. Sahlins, *Stone Age*.

19. Sahlins, *Culture*. Sahlins nuances this culturalist approach in his *Islands of History*.

20. J. Baudrillard, *Le Miroir de la production*.

21. C. Geertz, *Local Knowledge*.

22. C. Geertz, *Works and Lives*.

23. L. Dumont, "La communauté."

24. As stated earlier, anthropological knowledge is universal from the outset, and thus prevents the opposition of cultural rights to the abstract universalism of human rights.

25. J. Clifford, "Power and Dialogue," in G. W. Stocking, Jr., *Observers*.

26. B. Anderson, *Imagined Communities*.

27. See ibid. For a comparison between the nationalist ideology in Finland and in New Caledonia, see A. Bensa, "Vers Kanaky."

28. For Africa among others, see J.-L. Lonsdale, "La pensée"; D. W. Cohen and E. S. Atieno-Odhiambo, "Anany, Malo and Ogot" and *Siaya*; and P. Harries, "Roots of Ethnicity."

29. Removing a practice such as excision from its context permits its classification as a barbarous custom, thus perpetuating colonialist ideology.

30. Mubanza Mwa Bawele, "La dynamique."

31. See Chap 3.

32. J.-J. Herskovits, *Les Bases*.

33. E. Durkheim, *Les Formes élémentaires*, 7–8.

34. Amselle, "Un état."

35. C. Lévi-Strauss, *La Pensée*, 340.

36. D. Jonckers, *La Société minyanka*.

37. R. Merton, *Eléments*.

38. Amselle, "Fonctionnaires."

39. One can easily apply to culture Renan's ideas on the nation: "Oblivion, and I would even say historical error, are an essential factor in the creation of a nation." E. Renan, "Qu'est-ce qu'une nation?" 891.

40. L. Caplan, ed., *Studies*, 6.

41. J. Barr, *Fundamentalism*.

42. Ibid.

43. Tapper and Tapper, "Thank God We're Secular."

44. C. Bollème, *Le Peuple*.

45. Cf. below.

46. Cf. below.

47. In Nazi Germany, "the very fact of not having protested against the presumption of Jewishness was sufficient . . . to justify one's being classed in the category of Jews." R. Hilberg, *La Destruction des Juifs d'Europe*, 70.

48. G. Balandier, *Sens*.

Chapter 3

1. J. Berque, "Qu'est-ce qu'une 'tribu' nord-africaine?"

2. See Chap. 1.

3. J. Gallieni, *Voyage* and *Deux campagnes*; A. Arcin, *La Guinée* and *Histoire*; H. Labouret, *Paysans d'Afrique*; L. Tauxier, *Moeurs et histoire*; M. Richard, *Afrique occidentale*; M. Delafosse, *Haut-Sénégal*; and Lugard, *Dual Mandate*.

4. R. Sarrazin, *Races humaines*; Dr. Lasnet, "Les Races du Sénégal." On *Völkerkunde*, see J. Crozals, *Les Peulhs*.

5. This term is of Arabic origin.

6. M. Dupire, "Réflexions."

7. J. Crozals, *Les Peulhs*.

8. Abbé Boilat, *Esquisses sénégalaises*.

9. A. Texeira da Mota, "Un document nouveau"; Monteil, "Réflexion."

10. It also refers to the long-distance trader; see the *slatees* in M. Park, *Voyage*, 106.

11. M. Dupire, "Réflexions."

12. E.-A. Schultz, "From Pagan to Pullo"; Amselle, "L'ethnicité"; D. Robinson, "Un historien."

13. G. Nicolas, "La Conversion ethnique."

14. Mukarovsky, "Contribution."

15. A. M. Khazanov, *Nomads*.

16. J. Bazin, "Guerre"; J. Schmitz, "L'Etat géomètre"; G. Nicolas, "La Conversion ethnique."

17. B. Barry, *La Sénégambie*, 25, 148-52.

18. *Tarikh Es-Soudan* and *Tarikh El-Fettach*, henceforth abbreviated as *TES* and *TEF*. Written by Arabic historians in Timbuktu, the *Tarikh* chronicle the great Sudanese empires of Ghana, Mali, and Sonrai. They were discovered in the early colonial period.

19. A. Texeira da Mota, "Un document nouveau."

20. Y. Person, "Nyani Mansa"; A.-B. Maliki, *Introduction*.

21. M. Delafosse, *La Langue*, 2; J. Devisse, "Islam."

22. This expression also designates the Moors; see D. Robinson, "Un historien."

23. *TEF*, 83–84.

24. Ibid., 84.

25. Ibid., 87.

26. Compare L. Kouyaté, *Contribution*. According to Moussa Condé de Dandéla (Guinea), cited by Kouyaté, the ancestor of all Foulas, Tinkalan, came from Macina, passing through Fouta Djallon. His seven great-grandsons came to Wasulu: Maliki Diallo, ancestor of the Diallo of Sananfula; Maliki Sangaré; Dian Diallo; Noumoun Sangaré; Yalla Sidibé of Djallon Foula; Seri Moussa; and Samou Sidibe. On Maliki Diallo (Jalo), see pp. 80–86.

27. *TEF*, 72.

28. A.-B. Maliki, *Introduction*.

29. Ibid.

30. Y. Person, "Nyani Mansa." That the claim to a prestigious ancestry, of Sunjata in this case, is groundless does not attest to the Denyanke's being Fulani.

31. For J. Schmitz, "L'Etat géomètre," 353, n. 1, the term *saltigi* in the Mande linguistic sphere is equivalent to the Fulani word *ardo*. But this term, as is the term *tonjon*, is used in the Pular linguistic sphere and therein lies the entire problem of the ethnic group.

32. *TEF*, 74.

33. On the Jakite Saabashi, see Chap. 5. Information on the Jalo of Sananfula was furnished by El Hadj Sekou Diallo of Mandiana (Guinea) on Dec. 29, 1981.

34. J.-L. Amselle, "L'ethnicité."

35. Y. Person, *Samori*.

36. On the different meanings of the term "Bambara," compare J. Bazin, "A chacun"; J.-L. Amselle, "L'ethnicité"; *TES*, 20, n. 7. "The Bambaras are called Bamanas; the term Bambara, used by the French, was borrowed from the Moors." *Monographies du Soudan*, Bamako.

37. The term *senufo* is a generic Bambara term that designates the populations speaking (*fo*) the *senu* or *sena* language or languages, that is, the language of the autochthones or peasants (*senambele*) who distinguish themselves from the *fijambele* (artisan "caste"). On the different meanings of the word *senufo*, compare Richter and Launay. To my knowledge, Binger was the first to use the term *senufo*, with Caillié us-

ing only the term *bambara*. L.-G. Binger, *Du Niger*, 1: 174 ff.; R. Caillié, *Journal d'un voyage*, 1: 466 ff.

38. M. Delafosse, *La Langue*; D. Jonckers, *La Société minyanka*, 5.

39. *TES*, 20, n. 1; J. Devisse, "Islam."

40. R. Caillié, *Journal d'un voyage*, 2: 82-83; J.-L. Amselle, *Les Négociants*, 227.

41. E. Péroz, *Au Soudan*, 383.

42. C. Meillassoux, *Anthropologie*, 75.

43. Dr. Collomb, "Contribution."

44. Ibid., "Les races."

45. H. Labouret, *Les Manding*; L. Tauxier, *Histoire*, 46.

46. M. Samaké, *Pouvoir*, 33.

47. V. Pâques, *L'Arbre*, 176, *Les Bambara*, 9.

48. Information on identity conversions comes from fieldwork we have done, as well as from the thesis by Samaké, which includes information pertaining to the Cendugu: *Pouvoir*, 33.

49. On the Samake lineage, see pp. 96-102.

50. J.-L. Amselle, *Les Négociants*.

51. This is also the case for the Samake Furabala of Jitumu (see Table 1). "Enfranchisement is a secret that, in the Sudano-Sahelien milieu, can be the basis of an alliance between the family of the former master and the freed person," Meillassoux, *Anthropologie*, 122.

52. M. Delafosse, *Haut-Sénégal-Niger*.

53. Monteil, *Les Bambara*; Tauxier, *La Religion* and *Histoire*; Dieterlen, *Essai*; B. N'Diayé, *Groupes ethniques*.

54. H. Bazin, *Dictionnaire*; M. Travélé, *Petit dictionnaire*; Msg. Molin, *Dictionnaire*; C. Bailleul, *Petit dictionnaire*; P. Brasseur, *Bibliographie*.

55. In the Koutiala region, the literacy program has been enacted in Bambara, whereas the peasants speak Minyanka (personal observation).

56. A.-D. Sy, *Le Traditionalisme*.

57. *TEF*, 65, n. 1. For Monteil, the Soninke term "Khassonke" (pl. "Khassonko") designates people from Khasso, who refer to themselves as "Khassongalou" (sing. "Khassonko"), *Les Khassonké*.

58. Ibid.

59. Gallieni, *Voyage*, 599.

60. Mamadi Keita, Narena, Dec. 29, 1980.

61. Fina Saara Camara, Bamako, Apr. 25, 1983.

62. P. Pereira, *Esmeraldo*, 71; R. Jobson, *Golden Trade*, 10; C.-A. Walckenaer, *Collection*.

63. Senegal, Guinea, Guinea-Bissau, Gambia, Sierra Leone, Liberia, Ivory Coast, Mali, Burkina Faso, etc.

64. Are the Gouro, for example, part of the Mandingo civilization?

65. See B. Barry, *La Sénégambie*, 69, regarding the Maane and Saane with the joola praise names who founded the Manding nobility of Kaabu.

66. By calling them "peanut eaters."

Chapter 4

1. Fortes and Evans-Pritchard, *African Political Systems*, henceforth designated as *APS*.

2. R. H. Lowie, *Origin of the State*.

3. Alexandre remarks that *APS* is a "classic work that established once and for all the distinction between segmentary societies and centralized societies." P. Alexandre, "African Political Systems Revisited."

4. E. Terray, "Sociétés segmentaires."

5. J. Bazin and E. Terray, eds., *Guerres de lignages*.

6. P. Clastres, *La Société*.

7. On the French side, Delafosse also adopted the naturalist method in *Haut-Sénégal-Niger*.

8. L. H. Morgan, *Ancient Society*.

9. The eight societies are the Zulu, Ngwato, Bemba, Ankole, Kedi, the Bantu of Kavirondo, Tallensi, and Nuer.

10. One cannot help but think of Montesquieu's *L'Esprit des Lois*.

11. M. Gluckman, *Order and Rebellion*.

12. E. Durkheim, *The Division of Labor*, 175, 176.

13. A. Singer and E. Gellner, eds., *A History of Anthropological Thought by Evans-Pritchard*.

14. J. Middleton and D. Tait, eds., *Tribes Without Rulers*; R. Horton, "Stateless Societies."

15. According to these authors there in fact exists, in Central Africa, decentralized societies without incorporated lineages (cognatic societies). In East Africa, the age sets play an important role, whereas in Nigeria this function is filled by village councils and their associations. Middleton and Tait, *Tribes Without Rulers*.

16. Compare L. Roussel, *Région de Korhogo*; J. Capron, *Communautés villageoises*.

17. In fact, as Khazanov has brilliantly shown, nomadic societies never exist autonomously; rather, they are defined relative to an exterior group (peasant societies, etc.). Consequently, their political systems have dispositional properties.

18. A. Southall, *Alur Society*.

19. Ibid., 251-52.

20. S.-F. Nadel, *Black Byzantium*.

21. H. Claessen and P. Skalnik, eds., *Early State*.

22. R. Cohen, "State Origins," and in Claessen and Skalnik, *Early State*, 31-75; M. Fried, *Evolution of Political Society*.

23. E. Leach, *Political Systems* and *Rethinking*.

24. J. Fabian, *Time and the Other*.

25. G. Leclerc, *L'Observation de l'homme*, 33-40.

26. S. Feuchtwang, "The Discipline."

27. R. Stevenson, *Population*.

28. A. Southall, "Nuer and Dinka."

29. R. Cohen, "State Foundations."

30. M. Fried, *Evolution of Political Society*.

31. Amselle, "Au-delà."

32. R. Cohen, "State Origins: A Reappraisal," 37.

33. See Chap. 6.

34. Compare J.-L. Siran, "Emergence et dissolution"; E. Copet-Rougier, "Du clan à la chefferie."

35. Precolonial situations are not necessarily precapitalist situations, as Wilks has shown regarding the Akan case in "The State."

36. Copet-Rougier, "Du clan à la chefferie."

37. M. Godelier, "Ethnie-tribu-nation."

38. On this, see Gellner's comparison between the segmentarity of the Berbers in the Moroccan Atlas Mountains and the functioning of the United Nations, *Contemporary Thought and Politics*.

39. Here I use Castoriadis's expression in *L'Institution*, 481.

40. It seems to me difficult to talk about purely segmentary societies in Africa because there are always states located more or less nearby. From this point of view, Copet-Rougier's rapprochement of the Amba studied by Winter, in Middleton and Tait, and the Mkako seems to contradict his thesis; the Amba typify the population pushed out to the periphery of a kingdom, for example, the Bunyoro-Toro. The same occurs in North Africa, compare on this Berque, *Structures*, 475 ff. Until it can be disproved, the case of New Guinea seems more relevant to me in that here is an insular group that does not contain a state.

41. Copet-Rougier, "Du clan à la chefferie."

42. Compare E. Weil, *Philosophie politique*, 138.

43. H. Kuklick, "Tribal Exemplars."

44. J. Bazin, "Le bal."

45. E. Terray, "Intervention à la séance."

Chapter 5

1. Amselle et al., "Littérature orale"; "Qu'est-ce qu'un *kafo*?"

2. "Before the arrival of the Europeans, there was anarchy, war. People were always in conflict with one another. Might was right. There was armed robbery and lawlessness. The Europeans brought law. Here, there was no such thing as the enthronement of a king (*mansa*)." Bremajan, Zumana and Cemoko Jakite, Tabako, May 3, 1983. Though told almost a hundred years later, this story corresponds exactly with Gallieni's *Voyage* (1885), 597-99.

3. According to M. Delafosse, *La Langue mandingue*, the word *jamana* comes from the Arabic *diwan*; the Bambara equivalent, *kafo*, signifies "assembly," "reunion."

4. "No Fulani had been able to dominate, no Fulani took booty from another Fulani." Jeli Solomani Dunbiya, Yorobugula, Mar. 10. 1969.

5. See, for Segu, M. Park, *Voyage*, 310; C. Monteil, *Les Bambara*, 90; Bazin, "Etat guerrier et guerres d'Etat," in Bazin and Terray, eds., *Guerres de lignages*, 353.

6. D. Diakité, *Contribution*.

7. See, among others, D. Robinson, *La Guerre sainte.*

8. According to certain informers, the king was called Solon Samake and lived at Solona in Basidibe. Laji Seku Jalo, Manjana, Dec. 7, 1981; Jeli Nfamogo Jabate, Niantanina, Dec. 28, 1981.

9. According to this version, Wasolon means "Get out of Solon." Fina Saaran Kamara, Bamako, Apr. 16, 1983; Sidiki Dunbiya, Kola, Dec. 15, 1979. This is a griot version of the word.

10. Jume Jakite, Kabaya, Dec. 20, 1979.

11. R. Caillié, *Journal d'un voyage*, 1: 427-21.

12. Compare E. Péroz, *Au Soudan*, 375-76.

13. On the Fulani war, see Chap. 7.

14. Amselle, "L'ethnicité."

15. Ibid.

16. Amselle et al., "Littérature orale."

17. Shielen and Gondo are perhaps locatives, because the suffix *kaw* (people) generally follows place names.

18. The last descendant who lived in Tabako was drafted into Samori's army and died during the siege of Sikaso in 1887. Other descendants later lived in Badogo in the present Republic of Guinea.

19. D.-T. Niane, *Sounjata.*

20. According to Meillassoux, the Jara of Murja were also Kolobakari (personal communication).

21. Mininian (python), Namakoro (hyena), Jakuma (cat), etc.

22. M. Samaké, *Pouvoir traditionnel*, 224.

23. Touze, "Territoire du Soudan français," in vol. 5, Archives nationales du Mali, Bamako, 1954.

24. Amselle et al., "Littérature orale."

25. Dec. 8, 1979; Jume Jakite, Kabaya, Dec. 15, 1979.

26. Here, I follow the version of Lamin Jalo, Berele, Dec. 20, 1969.

27. Sister of Serimusa, ancestor of the Sidibe of Basidibe. As we can see, the myth of Jalo attempts to encompass the entirety of Wasolon's history.

28. Yaya Konate, Kuruba, Jan. 8, 1981; Bremajan, Zumana, and Cemolo Jakite, Tabako, May 3, 1983.

29. On the role of human sacrifice in foundation rituals, see also below.

30. Amselle et al., "Littérature orale."

31. Seriba Dunbiya, Kankeri, Dec. 5, 1979; Joman Dunbya, Kola, Dec. 7, 1979; Fina Saaran Kamara, Bamako, Apr. 16, 1983.

32. The village of Faraba no longer exists; J. Gallieni, *Voyage*, 599.

33. E. Terray, "Nature et fonctions de la guerre dans le monde akan," in Bazin and Terray, *Guerres de lignages*, 388–99.

34. G. Laing, *Voyage*, 382–86.

35. J. Bazin, "Etat guerrier," in Bazin and Terray, eds., *Guerres de lignages*, 353.

36. M. Park, *Voyage*, 310.

37. R. Caillié, *Journal*, 1: 430.

38. Bremajan, Zumana, and Cemoko Jakite, Tabako, May 3, 1983.

39. Seriba Dunbiya, Kankeri, Dec. 20, 1979; Fode Amara Sidibe, Gwalala, Dec. 9, 1979.

40. C. Monteil, *Les Bambara*, 99.

41. Y. Person, *Samori*, 1: 157.

42. Y. Sangaré, *Samori*, 27.

43. Barijan Jakite, Yorobugula, Dec. 7, 1979.

44. We saw earlier that the Saabashi and the Malikishe were allied by marriage.

45. Jamana in what is now Guinea.

46. This is what J. Bazin, in Bazin and Terray, *Guerres de lignages*, 341, regarding Segu, defines as "the energizing phase in the process of becoming a state."

47. Kafo in what is now Guinea.

48. "Tribal consciousness usually has a political meaning: in case of military danger or opportunity, it easily provides the basis for joint polit-

ical action on the part of tribal members or *Volksgenossen* who consider one another as blood relatives." M. Weber, *Economy and Society*, 1: 394.

49. On war and the segmentary state, see also Chapter 6.

50. "Since their victory against Kankan Mori, the Wasolon States broke the alliance that had united them in their war of independence and have once again fallen into complete anarchy. Thanks to that anarchy, and by joining with one group and then with the other, Samori was able to take over the entire country all the way to Ba-oule (red river), hardly firing a single shot. Kissi, Sananfoula, Diago, Lenguessoro, and Ganan [Gwanan] already belonged to him, when a close alliance with the Mamby of Kangaba made him the most powerful king of the right bank." E. Péroz, *L'Empire*.

51. Lamin Jalo, Berele, June 20, 1969.

52. In what is now Guinea.

53. Jeli Solomani Dunbya, Yorobugula, Dec. 7, 1979.

54. According to Y. Sangaré, *Samori*, 72, n. 1, at the time of the siege of Sikaso, Farabalay had already been relieved of his position as chief of Gwanan. He then took refuge with Ceba because of his attempted revolt against Samori. After 1882, his brothers served the French as "enlisted drivers," which explains the nomination of the Jakite Saabashi of Madina Jase as *chefs de canton* during the colonial period.

55. Touze, "Territoire du Soudan français."

56. J. Meniaud, *Les Pionniers*, 2: 487-89.

57. Lamin Jalo, Berele, June 20, 1969.

58. Barijan Jakite, Yorobugula, Dec. 25, 1968; Jeli Solomani Dunbya, Yorobugula, Dec. 7, 1979.

59. Jeli Solomani Dunbya, Yorobugula, Dec. 7, 1979.

60. Touze, "Territoire du Soudan français."

61. Amselle et al.

62. Touze, "Territoire du Soudan français."

63. Sekujan Jakite, Madina Jasa, Dec. 7, 1979.

64. "A trip around Gwanan allowed the administration to see in Madina the family of Lae Diakite (Farabalay), a Moslem personage who enjoys a certain prestige, which comes more from his once having been *chef de canton*, a position he left, than from religion. Chief of a large family comprising ten wives as well as eight sons who were raised Moslem, Lae Diakite retains an indisputable and considerable renown in all of Ouiassoulou, which his forebears once commanded." Rapports politiques, 1st trimester, 1923. "The *chef de canton* Noumory Diakite, named in 1916, is a sedentary old man who, from 1919 to 1922, let himself be dominated by the family of Lae Diakite, a religious personage

currently the Madina village chief, who had once ruled Gwanan but sud-denly relinquished his post because of legal trouble with a griot. When I arrived, Noumory Diakite complained of his increasing loss of power at the hands of Lae Diakite, who, Noumory Diakite claimed, was under the protection of the main interpreter." The district leader subse-quently decided to consolidate Noumory Diakite's power by designat-ing his nephews Noumoutie and Lamine Diakite as his assistants or rep-resentatives. Rapport sur la tournée.

65. "In the canton of Gwanan, a rivalry existed between the family of the current chief and that of the former chief of Ouassoulou, Fara-balay. I will not hide the fact that the former chief's family appears to me more intelligent than the family to whom the canton leadership was given, perhaps rather arbitrarily, following a relatively serious incident a few years ago. Upon the death of the current chief, we must closely study the matter of the transference of power." Rapports politiques, Dec. 6, 1925.

66. "Most of the *chefs de canton* are not of 'noble race,' but of hum-ble origin. Only the Keleyadugu, the Gouantiedugu have noble chiefs. Mamadou Ba Diakite, a canton chief who died in 1931, was supposedly a captive." Rapports politiques, 3rd trimester, 1931.

67. The account of the following events comes from the Rapport sur les dissimulations de population relevées au canton de Gouanan by the district officer-deputy, J. Lennon, June 3, 1950. Rapports politiques, 1950.

68. Revue des événements du 3ème trimestre 1953, by Touze, dis-trict officer, Rapports politiques, 1953.

69. Rapports politiques, 1956.

70. Rapports politiques, Oct. 1957.

Chapter 6

1. As we saw in Chap. 5, colonial ethnology merely reproduces this local political theory by taking it literally, thereby assimilating these "mythical charters" to a real historical process. Such a reproduction is what makes this ethnology truly colonial.

2. See for the neighboring Keleyadugu, Amselle, "Un Etat."

3. See D. Traoré, "Sur l'origine," 26; and "Une seconde," 7, Fako Samaké, Ferekoroba, Oct. 24, 1976. According to these sources, the Ni-akhaté-Niaré, upon arriving in the Bamako region, expelled Banba Saganogo, who went toward Siguiri. According to M. Delafosse, Banba Sakho or Sarhanorho, both of whom were certainly of Soninké origin, must have lived in the village of Moribabugu, located between Bamako

and Koulikoro (*Renseignements coloniaux et documents publiés par le Comité de l'Afrique française et le Comité du Maroc*, no. 3, 1910). Unfortunately, in his otherwise remarkable article on the history of Bamako, C. Meillassoux did not elaborate on the people who preceded the Niaré ("Histoire et institutions").

4. These Dunbiya are joking relatives (*senanku*) of the Bagayogo of Keleyadugu and the Jara of Segu. The panther (*warakalan*) is their taboo (*tana*).

5. Hence the name of the *kafo*: Morila.

6. They come from Solon.

7. Riou, "Compte rendu d'une tournée effectuée en mai 1957 dans le canton du Djitoumou," Rapports politiques du cercle de Bamako, 1957.

8. On the idea of "state dissidence," see Amselle, "Ethnies et espaces," in Amselle and E. M'Bokolo, *Au coeur de l'ethnie*, 27-31.

9. Not all the Samake fled Ntinkadugu. Some of them remained in Kola, Sanba Fonba, Nchibabugu, and Bisi Fonba, Ntenkoni, July 5, 1985.

10. The story in fact concerns a Fulani shepherd of Jitumu Musa, ancestor of the Samake Somala lineage. It is common in this type of narrative that dependents become brothers and sons.

11. The same goes for Saaba Jakite of Gwanan.

12. V. Pâques, "Les Samaké," 369-90.

13. Many slaves who left for forced labor, substituting for their masters, never returned.

14. L.-G. Binger, *Du Niger*, 1: 126; Y. Person, *Samori*, 1: 521.

15. For more details, see below.

16. This is a political system with a revolving capital. In other *kafo*, the chief leaves his native village to reside in a fixed capital. See Samaké, "Kafo et pouvoir lignager."

17. Fako Samaké, Ferekoroba, Dec. 1976.

18. On Segu's domination in this region, see Chap. 7.

19. He was instrumental in the spread of geomancy. The joking relationship (*senankuya*) supposedly originated in the relations sealed by Jitumu Musa with Biton. This is a *senankuya nyogonya* that does not prohibit matrimonial relations. *Senankuya* could also have been initiated with the Kulibali of Jakokironin, who claimed to be Bitonshi.

20. C. Monteil, *Les Bambara*, 90.

21. On the relations between Segu and its periphery, see J. Bazin, "Etat guerrier," in Bazin and Terray, eds., *Guerres de lignages*.

22. The colonial term "Toucouleur" is unknown in the region.

23. Y. Person, *Samori*, 1: 393–94.

24. L.-G. Binger, *Du Niger*, 1: 126.

25. Y. Person, *Samori*, 1: 394.

26. If Segu had occupied the region, the result would have perhaps been the same. But, as we have seen, this state ruled from a distance or did not possess enough men and materiel to set up garrisons in the vassal provinces. For this reason, the notion of "warrior state" used by Roberts and Bazin (in Bazin and Terray) regarding Segu does not seem entirely accurate.

27. A thief will have his hand cut off in Wolosebugu, see L.-G. Binger, *Du Niger*, 1: 35–36.

28. It was a smallpox epidemic, see L.-G. Binger, *Du Niger*, 1: 18, 59.

29. Riou, Rapports politiques du cercle de Bamako, 1957.

30. In fact, there was well and truly a chief from Jitumu before this date, since in 1904 the district officer noted that "the village of Dinfara is not one of the three cantons (lineages?) that have the privilege of supplying a province chief." Rapports politiques du cercle de Bamako, Apr. 1904.

31. In colonial terminology, "Dioula" means Kooroko, "marabout" means Moslem, and "griot" means people of caste.

32. Segmentary politics was also instrumental in affiliations with the different parties that appeared in 1946. When the P.S.P. was in the majority in Jitumu, the first villagers who joined the R.D.A. were those led by the Serimana.

33. See Amselle, "La conscience," 339–55.

34. A. Southall, *Alur Society*, 251–52.

35. S.-F. Nadel, *Black Byzantium*, 122–23.

Chapter 7

1. J. Gallieni, *Voyage*, 578, 590, 603–4.

2. L.-G. Binger, *Du Niger*, 1: 152–53. Later, when he was governor of Ivory Coast, Binger relied more on the Moslem "dyulas." Compare C. Harrison, *France and Islam*, 97. Even so, Binger was not immune to racial policies. See also Harrison, 39.

3. A. Le Chatelier, *L'Islam*, 34, 155–56. On this point, I disagree with Harrison, who sees Le Chatelier as a partisan of Islam. See C. Harrison, *France and Islam*, 31.

4. Harrison's book is full of examples: see particularly the chapter on Futa Jalon. The racial policies adopted in West Africa come directly from the Berber policy followed in North Africa.

5. P. Marty, *La Politique indigène*.

6. On Clozel, see C. Harrison, *France and Islam*, 98.

7. J. Brévié, *Islamisme contre naturisme*.

8. Ibid., vii.

9. Ibid.

10. Compare the same ideas in M. F. Clozel in *Haut-Sénégal Niger*, who drew from Renan. C. Harrison, *France and Islam*, 99.

11. Brévié refers here to Renan.

12. See Chapter 1.

13. P. Henry, *L'Ame d'un peuple africain*; L. Tauxier, *La Religion*.

14. L. Tauxier, *La Religion*, xx.

15. P. Henry, *L'Ame d'un peuple africain*, 87.

16. L. Tauxier, *La Religion*, 343.

17. Compare on this G. Balandier, *Sociologie*; M. Augé, *Théorie*.

18. W. MacGaffey, *Religion and Society*, Introduction.

19. Compare on this M. Augé, *Génie*; E. Terray, "Afrique noire," 248–49. Compare also B. Jewsiewicki on the "transfer of knowledge" at our seminar at EHESS 1987–1988.

20. Goody, ed., "Restricted Literacy in Northern Ghana" in *Literacy*, 226; E. Doutté, *Magie et religion*.

21. See C. Harrison, *France and Islam*, on the history of this notion.

22. "Every one who believes he belongs to a religion, belongs to it," M. Chailley, "Aspects de l'islam," 11.

23. R. Caillié, *Journal d'un voyage*, 1: 442.

24. Wilks in J. Goody, ed., *Literacy*, 174; L.-G. Binger, *Du Niger*, 1: 52–59; R. Caillié, *Journal d'un voyage*, 1: 407; J. Goody, ed., *Literacy*.

25. Amselle, "Un Etat."

26. E. Doutté, *Magie et religion*, 377 ff.

27. Amselle et al., "Littérature."

28. Y. Person, *Samori*, 1: 242–45.

29. Amselle et al., "Littérature," 421.

30. Rapports politiques du cercle de Bougouni, 1899, 1902, 1903, 1906, 1907, 1909, 1910, 1912.

31. "The entirely fetishistic native population seems to have been unfortunately influenced by the 'dyulas,' who have come from just about everywhere (Ivory Coast especially), practicing the Moslem religion, and who, though recognizing their inferior origin (castes of blacksmiths, potters, and griots), believe themselves above the others because they are Moslem and wealthy." Rapport de tournée du cercle de Bamako, 1925. "The inhabitants of Ouolossébougou were [1930] as today half agricultural Bambaras and half Dyulas, marabouts, and griots. This last category soon began to flatter the chief, in order to obtain fa-

Mestizo Logics

J. Amselle

His 98/6

£12.95

vors. Believing that nothing was forbidden them, the chiefs became increasingly proud and began to abuse their power. This was the primary reason for the disagreements in Djitoumou." "Compte rendu d'une tournée effectuée en mai 1957 dans le canton de Djitoumou par Marc Riou," Rapport politique du cercle de Bamako, 1957. "Chief of a large family with ten wives and eight sons, who were raised Moslem, Lae (Farabalay) retained an indisputable and considerable renown in all of Ouassoulou, which his ancestors had once ruled. But Lae and his family were happy with this local renown and did not have relations with the outside Moslem world." Rapport politique du cercle de Bougouni, 1923.

32. A. Le Chatelier, *L'Islam*, 299-300.

33. J. Brévié, *Islamisme contre naturisme*, 169-70.

34. Rapport politique du cercle de Bougouni, 1955.

35. M. Augé, *Pouvoirs*, 83.

36. J. Bazin, "Retour," 253-73.

37. See above.

38. This is a *benbe* (*Lannea acida*).

39. The elephant is the taboo, the double (*tana*) of the Samake (literally male elephant).

40. In his research on the history of cults in Minyanka country, Jonckers sometimes went back as far as the Islamized villages, which represented obstacles in his view. Should what is seen as a methodological obstacle not be analyzed as a productive factor? D. Jonckers, *La Société minyanka*, 76.

41. E. Doutté, *Magie et religion*, 184-88.

42. V. Pâques, *L'Arbre cosmique*, 133 ff.

43. G. Dieterlen, "Mythe et organisation," 39-76.

44. G. Dieterlen and Y. Cissé, *Les Fondements*, 287.

45. V. Pâques, "Bouffons sacrés," 65.

46. M. Samaké, "La société d'initiation," 312.

47. J.-P. Colleyn and D. Jonckers, 43-58.

48. V. Pâques, "Les Samaké," 369.

49. G. Dieterlen and Y. Cissé, *Les Fondements*, 21.

50. V. Pâques, "Bouffons sacrés," 73.

51. G. Dieterlen and Y. Cissé, *Les Fondements*, 268-70.

52. On *komo*, see also p. 98.

53. M. Samaké, "La société d'initiation," 313, illustrates clearly that the absence of blood sacrifice in the *kote* makes this institution, in the eyes of its adepts, compatible with Islam.

54. The reference to Hume, *Essays*, comes immediately to mind.

55. Institutions do not have the ability to diffuse all by themselves; for that, they need some kind of agent.

56. G. Dieterlen and Y. Cissé, *Les Fondements*, 37, 306 ff.

57. J.-P. Olivier de Sardan, "Personnalité," 421-45.

58. Y. Cissé, "Signes graphiques," 131-79.

59. J. Berque, "Qu'est-ce qu'une 'tribu' nord-africaine?"

60. M. Mauss adopted this point of view in his study of the Latin *persona*, Mauss, *Sociologie*, 352-53.

61. Tournée de J. Martin in Bolon canton, Rapport politique du cercle de Bougouni, 1948, Archives nationales du Mali, Bamako.

Chapter 8

1. P. Boiral et al., *Peasants*.

2. D. Jonckers, 183; J. Benhamou, H. Raymond, and J. Zaslavsky, *Evaluation*, 25; C. Rondeau, *La Société senufo*; B. Beredogo, *Le Système*.

3. C. Monteil, "Le coton." The word for cotton (*kori*) in the Mande languages comes from the Arabic *qawr*. See M. Delafosse, *La Langue mandingue*, 403.

4. R. Caillié, *Journal d'un voyage*, 1: 442; 2: 82.

5. Ibid., 1: 445.

6. Ibid., 1: 433, 436.

7. Ibid., 1: 388, 391, 446.

8. Ibid., 1: 204, 229, 250, 269.

9. L.-G. Binger, *Du Niger*, 1: 204, 229, 250, 269.

10. R. Caillié, *Journal d'un voyage*, 1: 442.

11. M. Park, *Voyage*, 258, 310.

12. J. Gallieni, *Voyage*, 598; L.-G. Binger, *Du Niger*, 1: 130-31.

13. J. Gallieni, 597. A "dyula" (merchant) told Gallieni: "To show just how close the villages are, the natives say that 'the king, without leaving his capital, can transmit orders by voice all the way to the outer limits of his immense empire.'" J. Gallieni, *Voyage*, 320.

14. "All nobles had slaves. They could be bought or won in war. Everywhere, nobles had slaves who worked in the fields. The nobles and the griots stayed in the shade." Jeli Yoro Kuyate, Yanfolila, Dec. 8, 1979. The chief of Ouassoulou, who lived in Sigala (Janjamana), "is considered very rich in gold and slaves." R. Caillié, *Journal d'un voyage*, 1: 439.

15. "The States on the Niger's right bank are particularly rich in grains and livestock, but the most important trade product is rubber, of which there exist immense forests in the Ouassoulou plains, espe-

cially on the river banks. There are also large quantities of gold and ivory, but they all go to the English factories in Sierra Leone, where, it seems, they are sold at a greater price than in our French firms." J. Gallieni, *Deux campagnes*, 420.

16. Ibid., 320.

17. Ibid., 598.

18. Amselle et al., "Littérature orale," 389.

19. On the Senufo and Minyanka societies of Mali, see D. Jonckers, *La Société minyanka*; C. Rondeau, *La Société senufo*; B. Beredogo, *Le Système de parenté*; C. Fay, *Biens, traces*; Diabaté, *Analyse des mutations*.

20. Amselle, *Les Négociants*, 132 ff.

21. J. Vuillet, "L'Agriculture."

22. In 1910 in Koutiala, the A.C.C. bought 70 tons of cotton, or two-thirds of the total harvest, Rapport agricole et économique trimestriel du Haut-Sénégal-Niger, 1910. D. Jonckers was kind enough to convey this information to me after this chapter had been written.

23. C. Rondeau, *La Société senufo*, 418.

24. Notice générale, Archives nationales du Sénégal.

25. Travel report by the adjunct Roux in Kouroulamini, Nov. 13, 1923, Rapport politique du cercle de Bougouni, 1923; Amselle, *Les Négociants*, 136.

26. The ethnic census of 1936 produced the following figures for population distribution by racial group:

Foula-Bambaras	70,534
Markas	1,664
Senoufos	7,883
Malinkes	4,502
Bambaras	103,018

Rapport politique du cercle de Bougouni, 1936. "The Ouassoulou people are lazy, deceitful, poor traders (though breeders of livestock), waiting for the dyulas to buy their products at low prices, and even worse farmers, each year sowing just enough various seeds to keep from dying, using a lot of nere flour and manioc to hold the grain together." Census report by the administrator Lemasson in Dialonfoula and Gouandiaka (Ouassoulou) cantons, Rapport politique du cercle de Bougouni, 1923.

27. Rapports politiques du cercle de Bougouni, 1924, 1926, 1927, 1928.

28. Rapports économiques du cercle de Bougouni, 1930, 1931, 1933, 1934.

29. T.-J. Bassett, "The Development" and *The Development*.

30. Bélime, *La Production*, 45–46.

31. "The native grows food for his needs and nothing more. His efforts are strictly limited to his subsistence needs. Unaware of the plow and animal traction, he has lived for centuries on fertile land that he has never had the idea or the will to make use of. Unlike the Fellah, the Indian, or the Annamite, who are greedy for land and money, the Sudanese vegetate in a communist ambiance that will never develop a capacity for ambition." Gouvernement général de l'AOF, Missions Bélime (1919–20); E. Bélime, *Les Irrigations*, 148.

32. "We will never progress if we do not make up our minds to break apart the sterile economic cell that is the native village. We need to limit and gradually eliminate the lamentable consequences of Sudanese communism and at the same time institute a regime of free, industrial production." E. Bélime, *Les Irrigations*, 16–17.

33. This quantity was attained during the 1960–61 campaign. E. Shreyger, *L'Office du Niger*, 388.

34. C. Rondeau, *La Société senufo*, 445, 467; B. Beredogo, *Le Système de parenté*, 403. In 1933, in the Doutiala district, out of 1,000 tons of raw cotton produced, 100 tons were bought by the European market, whereas the remaining 900 tons supplied the local artisans. Rapport économique du cercle de Koutiala, 1935, information provided by D. Jonckers.

35. Rapport politique du cercle de Bougouni, 1935.

36. T.-J. Bassett, "The Development" and *The Development*.

37. "Peanuts prevailed over dry cotton because cotton's prices are as low as its yields." E. Bélime, *Les Travaux*, 22. On the competition between cotton and food crops, compare T.-J. Bassett, "The Development" and *The Development*.

38. T.-J. Bassett, "The Development" and *The Development*.

39. J. Benhamou et al., *Evaluation*. To this calendar can be added a period of decline (1980–83).

40. This "package" includes use of the plow, a better use of land, production and use of fertilizer with manure and mineral amendments, use of the Allen variety sown early, proper maintenance (weeding with a hoe, etc.), and, finally, regular pesticide treatments. D. Diabaté, *Analyse des mutations*, 313–15.

41. Compare D. Jonckers, *La Société minyanka*; J. Benhamou et al., *Evaluation*; D. Diabaté, *Analyse des mutations*.

42. On the reluctance of the Wasolon people to cultivate land, compare note 26.

43. The population of the Bougouni district, which did not include more that 10,000 inhabitants after Samori passed in 1893, reached 110,000 in 1906. Rapport politique du cercle de Bougouni, 1906.

44. In 1935, peanuts were the primary speculation project in Bougouni District (5,000 hectares), far ahead of cotton (1,687 hectares). Rapport politique du cercle de Bougouni, 1935. The mining of gold boomed in the 1940s with the exploitation of the Kalana placers. Amselle, *Les négociants*, 142.

45. "During my census taking, I noted a fact that seems to demonstrate how poorly native conscription is accepted: nine out of ten young men eligible for military recruitment, between the ages of eighteen and twenty-four, could not be located. When questioned as to their whereabouts, relatives invariably answered in a way that seemed planned in advance, saying that their children had left with other young men of the same age to find work harvesting peanuts in Gambia." "Rapport de tournée de Collomb au Djitoumou, May 25, 1925," Rapport politique du cercle de Bamako, 1925.

"If, aside from workers sent to the plantations, recruits and voluntary departures are not stopped, the entire region will decline, to the advantage of Guinea." "Rapport de tournée de Bancal dans le Kouroulamini, le Bolon, le Danou, le Ba Sidibe and le Dialon foula, Mar. 21, 1928," Rapport politique du cercle de Bougouni, 1928.

46. Ibid.

47. This anti-Fulani attitude eventually led the Malian administration to encourage migration from Dogon into the Bougouni and Yanfolila districts during periods of drought.

48. I. Coulibaly, *Le Wasulu*.

49. Fulani, Bambara, and Malinke women from southwest Mali worked in agriculture less than did their Sunufo and Minyanka counterparts, see D. Diabaté, *Analyse des mutations*, 396–97.

50. "Natives of Mali, Ghana, Benin, and Guinea settled in rural areas as much as in urban ones. Those from Burkina Faso differed in that few were urbanized . . . ; they made up the largest percentage of the immigrants who settled in rural areas." F. Dureau, *Migration et urbanisation*, 309.

51. C. Rondeau, *La Société senufo*; B. Beredogo, *Le Système de parenté*; D. Diabaté, *Analyse des mutations*; and the personal observation I was able to make during my own evaluations of the "village associations" in the C.M.D.T. area. See Amselle and Benhamou, *Réactualisation*.

52. D. Diabaté, *Analyse des mutations*, 396–97.

53. Compare R. Launay, *Traders Without Trade*.

54. Amselle and M'Bokolo, *Au coeur de l'ethnie*, 38.

55. M. Park and R. Caillié particularly.

56. An excess we too have committed: see Amselle, ed., *Les Migrations*.

Chapter 9

1. See J. Copans, *Anthropologie et impérialisme*.

2. F. Pouillon, "Du savoir malgré tout," 79–83.

3. As, for example, in the kingdom of Dahomey for a demographic census, see C. Polanyi, *Dahomey*.

4. On tribute, see also pp. 106–8.

5. Jumè Jakite, Kabaya, Dec. 20, 1979; Jan Sidibe, Balena, July 4, 1985. The *talikise*, a weight currently used to weigh gold, is a grain of *tali* (*Erythrophelum guineense*). According to Park, 300, six *talikese* equal a *mitkal*. Since one *mitkal* makes 4.5 grams, according to Y. Person, *Samori*, 2: 876, one *talikise* is about .7 grams. The paying of tribute to the sovereign was called "going to drink millet cream (*dege*) at Segu." The same expression was used during Samori's time.

6. Y. Person, *Samori*, 2: 875; Touze, "Territoire du Soudan français," in vol. 5, Archives nationales du Mali, Bamako, 1954.

7. In the 15 villages surveyed, slaves represented only a little more than 10 percent of the total population, Rapport politique du cercle de Bougouni, 1894.

8. Etude sur la captivité, report by Captain Barbecot of the Marine infantry, district commander of Bougouni.

9. B. Maupoil, "L'étude des coutumes juridiques," 1–2.

10. C. Monteil, *Les Khassonké*.

11. M. Delafosse, *Haut-Sénégal-Niger*, 1: 24–25.

12. Delteil, Archives nationales du Sénégal.

13. Compare Roume's instructions (1905), in M. Delafosse, *Haut-Sénégal-Niger*, 1: 18.

14. M. Delafosse, *Haut-Sénégal-Niger*, 1: 18.

15. P. Marty, *La Politique indigène*.

16. "Such is, in sum, the organization that allows about 500 French officers or civil servants and an armed forces of about 4,500 Blacks (enlisted men, militia, and district guards) to keep order and security among 5 million indigenous people spread over a territory that, from Faleme to Chad, covers more than 2,800 kilometers and that, from north to south (including the Saharan zone, which we must control) covers rarely lesss than 1,300," Clozel in M. Delafosse, *Haut-Sénégal-Niger*, 1: 9–10. The native chief's duties are the following: (1) maintain order, (2) take the census, (3) publish orders from the district officer,

(4) collect taxes, (5) serve on the district tribunal. In Delteil, Archives nationales du Sénégal.

17. Letter from Captain Bernardy to Lieutenant Colonel Governor of French Sudan, Bamako, Sept. 27, 1895, Archives nationales du Sénégal, Dakar, 15 G 35.

18. J. Lombard, *Autorités traditionelles*, 127-31; Labouret in B. Maupoil, *Coutumiers juridiques*, 7. In fact, Van Vollenhoven's circular confirms a policy change that originated before World War I; see Chapter 6.

19. H. Labouret, *Les Manding*, chap. 2; E. Leynaud and Y. Cissé, *Paysans malinke*, 157-59; M. Samaké, *Pouvoir traditionnel*.

20. A. Aubert, "Coutume bambara."

21. The disappearance of exchange marriages (Senufo, Minyanka, and Bambara) is thus attributed to the advance of Islam, ibid., 71.

22. Aubert's informers were judges, village chiefs, district chiefs, or their representatives in the administrative center.

23. As in Jitumu, for example.

24. "The village chief is chosen by and from among the village hut chiefs. The canton chief is chosen by the village chiefs and from among them with approval of the chief of the colony." Delteil, Archives nationales du Sénégal.

25. On the notion of "working misunderstanding," see J.-P. Chauveau and J.-P. Dozon, "Au coeur des ethnies," in E. Terray, *L'Etat contemporain*.

26. M. Samaké, *Pouvoir traditionnel*, 313; J. Brévié quoted by B. Maupoil, "L'Etude," 11-12.

27. For a comparison with ancient Greece, see Finley; J. Goody, *La Logique*, 100; and E. Terray, "Le débat politique."

28. On the intrusion of parties in segmentary politics of the cantons, see M. Samaké, *Pouvoir traditionnel*, 349-54, and Chapters 5 and 6 in this volume.

29. Koninba Kone, Wure, Dec. 24, 1979.

30. Report on the hiding of drafted men in the canton of Gwanan by the adjunct district commander, J. Lennon, June 3, 1950, Rapport politique du cercle de Bougouni, 1950.

31. A. H. Bâ, *L'étrange destin de Wangrin*.

32. From this point of view, the travel journal by the administrator Riou in Jitumu is far superior to Pâques's article published in the same period, "Les Samaké," *Bulletin de l'IFAN*.

33. "A real climate of confidence seems to have now been established between the general population and the district authorities. This is due to numerous palavers, an increase in visits to the villages, census tak-

ing, the institution of village monographs–all this plus a few spectacular accomplishments." "Revue des événements du 3ème trimestre 1953 par Touze, commandant de cercle." Rapport politique du cercle de Bougouni, 1953.

34. The one by the late Y. Person is an example among others.

35. Here, too, is a resumption of the policy advocated by Ponty.

36. Y. Person, *Samori*; E. Péroz, *Au Soudan*.

37. For J. Bazin, the structuralist interpretation that can be given to the phenomenon of "women kings" in the Segu region is itself inscribed in the indigenous theory. "Princes désarmés," 111-12.

38. J. Goody, "The Impact of Islamic Writing."

Bibliography

Abbink, J. "L'énigme de l'ethnogenèse des Betä Esra'el: une approche anthropo-historique de leurs mytho-légendes." *Cahiers d'études africaines* 120 (30: 4), 1990: 397-449.

Ageron, C. "Du mythe kabyle aux politiques berbères." In *Le Mal de voir*. Paris: UGE, 10/18, 1976.

Alexandre, P. "African Political Systems Revisited." *Cahiers d'études africaines* 87-88 (22: 3-4), 1982.

Amselle, J.-L. "Au-delà de l'anthropologie marxiste." In *Afrique plurielle, Afrique actuelle*. Paris: Karthala, 1986, pp. 47-59.

———. "Ethnies et espaces: pour une anthropologie topologique." In J.-L. Amselle and E. M'Bokolo, eds., *Au coeur de l'ethnie*. Paris: La découverte, 1985, pp. 11-48.

———. "Fonctionnaires et hommes d'affaires au Mali." *Politique Africaine* 26, 1987: 63-72.

———. "La conscience paysanne: la révolte de Ouolossébougou (Juin 1968, Mali)." *Revue canadienne des études africaines* 12 (3), 1978: 339-55.

———. "Le développement vu du village." *Sociologia Ruralis* 28, 1988.

———. *Les Négociants de la savane*. Paris: Anthropos, 1977.

———. "L'ethnicité comme volonté et comme représentation: à propos des Peul du Wasolon." *Annales ESC* 42 (2), 1987: 465-89.

———. "Un Etat contre l'Etat: le Keleyadugu." *Cahiers d'études africaines* 28, 1988: 463-83.

Amselle, J.-L., ed. *Le Sauvage à la mode*. Paris: Le Sycomore, 1979.

———, ed. *Les Migrations africaines*. Paris: Maspero, 1976.

Amselle, J.-L., et al. "Littérature orale et idéologie, la geste des Jakite Sabashi du Ganan (Wasolon, Mali)." *Cahiers d'études africaines* 19 (1-4), 1979: 73-76, 381-433.

———. "Qu-est-ce qu'un *kafo* ou *jamana*? Le cas du Gwanan ou les faux archaïsmes de l'histoire africaine." *Cahiers ORSTOM, série Sciences humaines* 21 (1), 1985: 43-56.

Amselle, J.-L., and J. Benhamou. *Réactualisation de la filière coton au Mali*. Paris: Ministère des Relations extérieures (Coopération et Développement), 1985.

Amselle, J.-L., and E. M'Bokolo, eds. *Au coeur de l'ethnie*. Paris: La Découverte, 1985.

Anderson, B. *Imagined Communities*. London: Verso, 1983.

Archives nationales du Mali, Bamako.

> Note laissée par M. Correnson sur la situation politique, December 6, 1925, Rapport politique du cercle de Bougouni, 1925.
>
> Rapport politique du cercle de Bamako, April 1904.
>
> Rapport de tournée du cercle de Bamako, 1925.
>
> Rapport de tournée de Collomb au Djitoumou, Rapport politique du cercle de Bamako, 1925.
>
> Rapports politiques du cercle de Bougouni, 1894, 1899, 1902, 1903, 1906, 1907, 1909, 1910, 1912, 1923.
>
> Rapport de tournée de l'adjoint Roux dans le Kouroulamini, November 13, 1923.
>
> Rapport sur la tournée de recensement dans les cantons de Dialonfoula et du Gouandiakha (Ouassoulou), Rapport politique du cercle de Bougouni, 1923.
>
> Rapport sur la tournée de recensement du Gouanan effectuée par l'administrateur de 1ère classe Lemasson, commandant de cercle, November 14-30, 1923.
>
> Rapports politiques du cercle de Bougouni, 1924, 1926, 1927, 1928.
>
> Rapport de tournée de Bancal dans le Kouroulamini, le Bolon, le Danou, le Ba Sidibe et le Dialon foula, March 21, 1928, Rapport politique du cercle de Bougouni, 1928.
>
> Rapports politiques du cercle de Bougouni, 1930, 1931, 1933, 1934, 1935, 1936.
>
> Rapports économiques du cercle du Bougouni, 1930, 1931, 1933, 1934.
>
> Rapport sur les dissimulations de population relevées au canton

de Gouanan par l'adjoint au commandant de cercle J. Lennon, 3 Juin 1950, Rapport politique du cercle de Bougouni, 1950.

Rapports politiques du cercle de Bougouni, 1955, 1956, 1957.

Rapport politique du cercle de Koutiala, 1933.

Revue des événements du 3ème trimestre 1953 par Touze, commandant de cercle, Rapport politique du cercle de Bougouni, 1953.

M. Riou, "Compte-rendu d'une tournée effectuée en mai 1957 dans le canton du Djitoumou," Rapport politique du cercle de Bamako, 1957.

R. L. Touze, Monographie du cercle de Bougouni, vol. 5, Territoire du Soudan français, 1954.

Archives nationales du Sénégal, Dakar.

Etude sur la captivité dans les cercles du Soudan, cercle de Bougouni, 1894, rapport du capitaine Barbecot de l'infanterie de marine, commandant du cercle de Bougouni, Archives nationales du Sénégal, K14.

Lettre du capitaine Bernardy au colonel lieutenant gouverneur du Soudan français, Bamako, September 27, 1895, 15 G 35.

Monographies du Soudan, 1 G 351.

Notice générale sur le cercle de Bougouni par l'adjoint Delteil, 1904, 1 G 303.

Rapport agricole et économique trimestriel du Haut-Sénégal-Niger, 1910, 2 G 10-1.

Arcin, A. La Guinée française. Paris: Challamel, 1907.

———. Histoire de la Guinée française. Paris: Challamel, 1911.

Aristotle. The Politics. Trans. T. A. Sinclair. Rev. Trevor J. Saunders. Penguin Books, 1962: 1261a, 1276a.

Aubert, A. "Coutume bambara" (Bougouni district), 1932. In Coutumiers juridiques, vol. 2, Soudan, series A, no. 9.

Augé, M. Génie du paganisme. Paris: Gallimard, 1982.

———. "Qui est l'autre? Un itinéraire anthropologique." L'Homme 27 (3), 103, 1987: 7-26.

———. Pouvoirs de vie, pouvoirs de mort. Paris: Flammarion, 1977.

———. Théorie des pouvoirs et idéologie. Paris: Hermann, 1975.

Bâ, A. H. L'étrange destin de Wangrin. Paris: UGE, 10/18, 1973.

Bailleul, C. Petit dictionnaire bambara-français, français-bambara. Amersham, Great Britain: Avebury Publishing Company, 1981.

Balandier, G. Sens et puissance. Paris: PUF, 1971.

———. Sociologie actuelle de l'Afrique noire. Paris: PUF, 1955.

Barr, J. Fundamentalism. London: SCM Press, 1977.

Barry, B. *La Sénégambie du XVe au XIXe siècles*. Paris: L'Harmattan, 1988.

Bassett, T.-J. "The Development of Cotton in Northern Ivory Coast, 1910-1965." *Journal of African History* 29, 1988: 267-84.

——. *The Development of Cotton in the Ivory Coast, 1910–1984*, 39 pages, manuscript.

Bastide, R. *Anthropologie appliquée*. Paris: Payot, 1971.

Baudrillard, J. *Le Miroir de la production ou l'illusion critique du matérialisme historique*. Paris: Galilée, 1985.

Bazin, Mgr. H. *Dictionnaire bambara-français*. Paris: Imprimerie nationale, 1906.

Bazin, J. "A chacun son Bambara." In J.-L. Amselle et E. M'Bokolo, eds., *Au coeur de l'ethnie*. Paris: La Découverte, 1985, pp. 87-127.

——. "Le bal des sauvages." In J.-L. Amselle, ed., *Le Sauvage à la mode*. Paris: Le Sycomore, 1979, pp. 177-218.

——. "Guerre et servitude à Segou." In Meillassoux, ed., *L'Esclavage en Afrique occidentale*. Paris: Maspero, 1975, pp. 135-81.

——. "Bambara," in *Encyclopaedia Universalis*. Paris: Encyclopaedia Universalis France, 1985.

——. "Princes désarmés, corps dangereux." *Cahiers d'études africaines*, special issue on "Manding," 111-12, 1988: 375-441.

——. "Retour aux choses-dieux." *Le Temps de la réflexion*. In a special edition on "Le corps des Dieux." Paris: Gallimard, 1986.

Bazin, J., and E. Terray, eds. *Guerres de lignages et guerres d'Etats en Afrique*. Paris: Editions des archives contemporaines, 1982.

Bélime, E. *La Production du coton en Afrique Occidentale Française, le programme Carde*. Paris: Publication du Comité du Niger, 1925.

——. *Les Irrigations du Niger*. Paris, 1921.

——. *Les Travaux du Niger*. Direction générale de l'Office du Niger, Gouvernement général de l'AOF. Publications de l'Office du Niger, 1940.

Benhamou, J., H. Raymond, and J. Zaslavsky. *Evaluation des filières coton et maïs au Mali*. Paris: Ministère des Relations extérieures (Coopération et développement), 1983.

Benot, Y. *Indépendances africaines, idéologies et réalités*. Paris: Maspero, 1975.

Bensa, A. "Vers Kanaky: tradition orale et idéologie nationaliste en Nouvelle-Calédonie." In *Kalevala et traditions orales du monde*. Paris: CNRS, 1987, pp. 423-38.

Benveniste, E. *Le Vocabulaire des institutions indo-européennes*. 2 vols. Paris: Minuit, 1969.

Beredogo, B. *Le Système de parenté et les rapports de production chez les Senoufo Cyigbala du Folona.* Thèse de doctorat de 3ème cycle, Université René Descartes-Paris-V, 1982.

Berelowitch, W. "Aux origines de l'ethnographie russe: la Société de géographie des années 1840–1850." *Les Cahiers du monde russe et soviétique* 31 (2–3), 1990: 265–74.

Berque, J. "Qu'est-ce qu'une 'tribu' nord-africaine?" In Berque, *Maghreb, Histoire et Société.* Gembloux, Duculot. Algiers: SNED, 1974, pp. 22–34.

———. *Structures sociales du Haut Atlas.* Paris: PUF, 1978.

Binger, L.-G. *Du Niger au golfe de Guinée par le pays de Kong et le Mossi.* 2 vols. Paris: Hachette, 1982.

Boilat, Abbé David. *Esquisses sénégalaises.* Paris: Karthala, 1984.

Boiral, P., et al., eds., *Paysans, experts et chercheurs en Afrique noire.* Paris: CIFACE-Karthala, 1985.

Bollème, C. *Le Peuple par écrit.* Paris: Le Seuil, 1986.

Bourdieu, P. *Choses dites.* Paris: Minuit, 1987.

Brasseur, P. *Bibliographie générale du Mali.* Dakar: IFAN, 1964. Also *Bibliographie générale du Mali.* Dakar: Les nouvelles éditions africaines, 1976.

Brévié, J. *Islamisme contre naturisme au Soudan français, Essai de psychologie politique coloniale.* Preface by M. Delafosse. Paris: Ernest Leroux, 1923.

Caillié, R. *Journal d'un voyage à Tombouctou et à Jenné dans l'Afrique centrale.* Paris: Anthropos, 1965, 2 vols.

Caplan, L., ed. *Studies in Religious Fundamentalism.* London: Macmillan, 1987.

Capron, J. *Communautés villageoises bwa, Mali-Haute-Volta.* 1: fasc. 1. Paris: Muséum d'histoire naturelle, 1973. Mémoire de l'Institut d'ethnologie, 9.

Cassirer, E. *La Philosophie des Lumières.* Paris: Fayard, 1986.

Castoriadis, C. *L'Institution imaginaire de la société.* Paris: Seuil, 1975.

Chailley, M. "Aspects de l'islam au Mali." In *Notes sur l'islam en Afrique noire.* Recherches et documents du CHEAM. Paris: J. Peyronnet, 1962, pp. 9–51.

Chauveau, J.-P., and J.-P. Dozon, "Au coeur des ethnies ivoiriennes . . . l'Etat." In E. Terray, ed., *L'Etat contemporain en Afrique.* Paris: L'Harmattan, 1987, pp. 221–96.

Cissé, Y. "Signes graphiques, représentations, concepts et tests relatifs à la personne chez les Malinké et les Bambara du Mali." In *La No-*

tion de personne en Afrique noire. Paris: Editions du CNRS, 1973, pp. 131-79.

Claessen, H. and P. Skalnik, eds. *The Early State*. The Hague: Mouton, 1978.

Clastres, P. *La Société contre l'Etat*. Paris: Editions de Minuit, 1974.

Clifford, J. *The Predicament of Culture*. Cambridge, Mass.: Harvard University Press, 1988.

Clifford, J., and Marcus, G.-E., eds. *Writing Culture*. Berkeley: University of California Press, 1986.

Clozel, M. F. In Delafosse, *Haut-Sénégal-Niger*. Paris: E. Larosa, 1912.

Cohen, D. W., and E. S. Atieno-Odhiambo. "Anany, Malo and Ogot, History in Search of a Luo Nation." *Cahiers d'études africaines* 107-8, 1987: 269-86.

————. *Siaya: The Historical Anthropology of an African Landscape*. London: J. Carrey; Athens: Ohio University Press, 1989.

Cohen, R. "State Foundations: A Controlled Comparison." In R. Cohen and E. Service, eds., *Origins of the State*. Philadelphia: ISHI, 1978, pp. 141-60.

————. "State Origins: A Reappraisal." In H. Claesson and P. Skalnik, eds., *The Early State*. The Hague: Mouton, 1978, pp. 31-75.

Collectif. *Vers des sociétés pluriculturelles: études comparatives et situations en France*. Paris: ORSTOM, 1987.

Colleyn, J.-P., and D. Jonckers. "Ceux qui refusent le maître, la conception du pouvoir chez les Minyanka." *Africa* 53 (4), 1983: 43-58.

Collomb, Dr. "Contribution à l'étude de l'ethnologie et de l'anthropologie des races du Haut-Niger," *Bulletin de la Société d'anthropologie de Lyon*. 1885, vol. 4: 145-70.

————. "Les races du Haut-Niger, ethnographie-anthropométrie." *Bulletin de la Société d'anthropologie de Lyon*. 1885, vol. 4: 207-37.

Copans, J. *Anthropologie et impérialisme*. Paris: Maspero, 1975.

Copet-Rougier, E. "Du clan à la chefferie dans l'est du Cameroun." *Africa* 57 (3), 1987: 345-63.

Coulibaly, I. *Le Wasulu, un milieu aux potentialités économiques énormes, une zone d'exode rural massif: tentatives d'explication du paradoxe*. Mémoire de fin d'études de l'Ecole normale supérieure en histoire et géographie, Bamako, 1986.

Crozals, J. *Les Peulhs, études d'ethnologie africaine*. Paris: Maisonneuve, 1883.

————. "Peulhs et Foulahs, étude d'ethnologie africaine." *Revue de Géographie* 10 (Feb.), 1882: 106-24.

Delafosse, L. *M. Delafosse, le Berrichon conquis par l'Afrique*. Paris: Société française d'outre-mer, 1976.

Delafosse, M. *Haut-Sénégal-Niger*. Paris: Maisonneuve et Larose, 1972.

——. *La Langue mandingue et ses dialectes*, vol. 2. Paris: Imprimerie nationale, P. Geuthner, 1955.

——. *Monographie historique du cercle de Bamako*, Bull. Com. africain français. Rens. col. 1910: 57-67.

Derrida, J. *De l'esprit, Heidegger et la question*. Paris: Galilée, 1987.

Deschamps, H. *Gallieni pacificateur*. Paris: PUF, 1949.

Devisse, J. "Islam et ethnies en Afrique." In J.-P. Chrétien et G. Prunier, eds., *Les Ethnies ont une histoire*. Paris: Harthala-ACCT, 1989, pp. 103-115.

Diabaté, D. *Analyse des mutations socio-économiques au sein des sociétés rurales senoufo du Mali*. Paris: EHESS, 1986.

Diakité, D. *Contribution à la connaissance des Peuls du Wasolon, étude de cas: le Gouanan*. DEA thesis, Bamako, Ecole normale supérieure, 1985.

Dias, N. "L'eredità museologica nell'etnologia francese." In *Dal museo al terreno*. Milan: Franco Angeli, 1987, pp. 33-42.

Dieterlen, G. *Essai sur la religion bambara*. Paris: PUF, 1951.

——. "Mythe et organisation sociale au Soudan français." *Journal de la Société des africanistes* 25, fasc. 1 and 2, 1955: 39-76.

Dieterlen, G., and Y. Cissé. *Les Fondements de la société d'initiation du komo*. Paris: Cahiers de l'Homme, 1972.

Dorward, D. C. "Ethnography and Administration: A Study of Anglo-Tiv 'Working Misunderstanding.'" *Journal of African History* 15 (3), 1974: 457-77.

Doutté, E. *Magie et religion dans l'Afrique du Nord*. Paris: Maisonneuve et Geuthner, 1984.

Dozon, J.-P. *Anthropologie et histoire: un mariage de raison?* Working document of the Centre d'études africaines. Paris: EHESS, 1989.

Dubow, S. "Race, Civilisation and Culture: The Elaboration of Segregationist Discourse in the Inter War Years." In S. Marks and S. Trapido, eds., *The Politics of Race, Class and Nationalism in Twentieth Century South Africa*. London: Longman, 1987, pp. 71-94.

Dumézil, G. *Mythe et épopée*, vol. 1, *L'idéologie des trois fonctions dans les épopées des peuples européens*. Paris: Gallimard, 1968.

Dumont, L. *Essais sur l'individualisme*. Paris: Seuil, 1983.

——. "La communauté anthropologique et l'idéologie." *L'Homme* 18, 1978: 83-110.

Dupire, M. "Réflexions sur l'ethnicité peule." In *Itinérances . . . en pays peul et ailleurs, Mélanges à la mémoire de P.-F. Lacroix*. Paris: Mémoires de la Société des africanistes, vol. 2, 1981: 165-81.

Dureau, F. *Migration et urbanisation, le cas de la Côte d'Ivoire, Etudes et Thèses*. Paris: ORSTOM, 1987.

Durkheim, E. *The Division of Labor in Society*. Trans. George Simpson. Glencoe, Ill.: The Free Press, 1933.

———. *Les Formes élémentaires de la vie religieuse*. Paris: PUF, 1985.

Ehrenberg, V. *L'Etat grec*. Paris: Maspero, 1976.

Fabian, J. *Time and the Other*. New York: Columbia University Press, 1983.

Farias, V. *Heidegger et le nazisme*. Lagrasse: Verdier, 1987.

Fay, C. *Biens, traces, ancêtres. La dynamique des pouvoirs chez les Sénoufo du Folona*. Thèse de doctorat de 3ème cycle, Paris, EHESS, 1983.

Faye, J.-P. *Les Langages totalitaires*. Paris: Hermann, 1972.

Feuchtwang, S. "The Discipline and Its Sponsors." In T. Asad, ed., *Anthropology and the Colonial Encounter*. London: Ithaca Press, 1973, pp. 71–100.

Feuerwerker, D. *L'Emancipation des Juifs en France de l'Ancien Régime à la fin du Second Empire*. Paris: Albin Michel, 1976.

Fichte, J. G. *Addresses to the German Nation* (Eng. trans. 1922).

Finkielkraut, A. *La Défaite de la pensée*. Paris: Gallimard, 1987.

Finley, M. *L'Invention de la politique*. Paris: Flammarion, 1985.

Fortes, M., and E. E. Evans-Pritchard, eds. *African Political Systems*. London: Oxford University Press, 1963.

Freud, Sigmund. *Group Psychology and the Analysis of the Ego*. Trans. and ed. James Strachey. New York: W. W. Norton, 1959.

Fried, M. *The Evolution of Political Society*. New York: Random House, 1967.

Fustel de Coulanges. *Histoire des institutions politiques de l'ancienne France*. Paris: Hachette, 1875.

Gaffiot, Félix, "*ethnicus.*" *Dictionnaire de la langue française*. Paris: Hachette, 1863–72.

Gallieni, J. *Voyage au Soudan français*. Paris: Hachette, 1885.

———. *Deux campagnes au Soudan français*. Paris: Hachette, 1891.

Geertz, Clifford. *Local Knowledge*. New York: 1983.

———. *Works and Lives: The Anthropologist as Author*. Cambridge: Polity Press, 1988.

Gellner, E. *Contemporary Thought and Politics*. London: Routledge and Kegan Paul, 1974.

———. *Nations and Nationalism*. Oxford, Basil Blackwell, 1983.

Girard, René. *La Violence et le sacré*. Paris: Le Livre de Poche, 1981.

Gluckman, M. *Order and Rebellion in Tribal Africa*. London: Cohen and West, 1963.

Gobineau, J.-A. *Essai sur l'inégalité des races humaines*. Paris: Firmin Didot, 1854.

Godelier, M. "Ethnie-tribu-nation chez les Baruya de Nouvelle-Guinée." *Journal de la Société des océanistes* 41 (81), 1985: 159-68.

Goody, J. *La Logique de l'écriture*. Paris: A. Colin, 1986.

———. *La Raison graphique* (*The Savage Mind Domesticated*). Paris: Minuit, 1979.

———. "The Impact of Islamic Writing on the Oral Cultures of West Africa." *Cahiers d'études africaines* 11 (43), 1971: 445-66.

Goody, J., ed. *Literacy in Traditional Societies*. Cambridge: Cambridge University Press, 1968.

Griaule, M. *Conversations with Ogotemmjli*. Oxford: Oxford University Press, 1965 (1948).

———. *Dieu d'eau: Conversations avec Ogotemmjli*. Paris: Chêne, 1948.

Harries, P. "The Roots of Ethnicity: Discourse and the Politics of Language Construction in South-East Africa." *African Affairs* 346, 1988: 25-52.

Harrison, C. *France and Islam in West Africa*, 1860-1960. Cambridge: Cambridge University Press, 1988.

Hartog, F. *Le XIXe siècle et l'histoire, le cas Fustel de Coulanges*. Paris: PUF, 1988.

Hastings, J. *A Dictionary of the Bible*. Edinburgh: T. and T. Clark, 1898.

Henry, P. *L'Ame d'un peuple africain, les Bambara*. Extrait d'Anthropos, 1910.

Herder, J.-G. *Another Philosophy of History*, 1774.

Herskovits, J.-J. *Les Bases de l'anthropologie culturelle*. Paris: Payot, 1967.

Hilberg, R. *La Destruction des Juifs d'Europe*. Paris: Fayard, 1988.

Horton, R. "Stateless Societies in the History of West Africa." In J.-F. Ajayi and M. Crowder, eds., *History of West Africa*. London: Longman, 1971, pp. 78-119.

Hume, David. *Essays and Treatises on Several Subjects*. 4 vols. London: 1753-54.

Itinéraires en pays peul et ailleurs. Mélanges à la mémoire de P. F. Le Croix. 2 vols. Paris: Mémoires de la Société des Africanistes, 1981.

Jewsiewicki, B. "The Formation of the Political Culture of Ethnicity in the Belgian Congo, 1920-1959." In L. Vail, ed., *The Creation of Tribalism in Southern Africa*. London and Berkeley: J. Currey and The University of California Press, 1989: 324-49.

———. "Le primitivisme, le post-colonialisme, les antiquités 'nègres' et la question nationale." *Cahiers d'études africaines* 121-22, 1991: 191-221.

Jobson, R. *The Golden Trade*. Teignmouth: Speight and Walpole, 1904.

Jonckers, D. *La Société minyanka du Mali*. Paris: L'Harmattan, 1987.

Kant, Emmanuel. *Anthropologie in pragmatisch Hinsicht*, 1798.

———. "Observation on the Beautiful and the Sublime" (1764). In *Critique of Judgment*, trans. J. H. Bernard. New York: Hafner, 1968.

Khazanov, A. M. *Nomads and the Outside World*. Cambridge: Cambridge University Press, 1983.

Kopytoff, I., ed. *The African Frontier*. Bloomington: Indiana University Press, 1987.

Kouyaté, Lanceï. *Contribution à l'étude traditionnelle du Wasulu présamorien*, essay. Conakry: IPC, 1977.

Kroeber, A. L., and C. Kluckohn. *Culture, A Critical Review of Concepts and Definitions*. New York: Vintage Books, 1952.

Kuklick, H. "Tribal Exemplars: Images of Political Authority in British Anthropology, 1885-1945." In G. W. Stocking, Jr., ed., *Functionalism Historicized*. Madison: University of Wisconsin Press, 1984: 59-82.

Labouret, H. *Les Manding et leur langue*. Paris: Larose, 1934.

———. *Paysans d'Afrique occidentale*. Paris: Gallimard, 1941.

Lafitau, P. *Moeurs des Sauvages Ameriquains comparées aux moeurs des premiers temps*. Paris, 1724.

Laing, G. *Voyage dans le Timanni, le Kouranko et le Soulimanna*. Paris: Delaforest and Arthus Bertrand, 1826.

Lampe, G. W. H., ed. *A Patristic Greek Lexicon*. Oxford: Clarendon Press, 1961.

Lasnet, Dr. "Les Races du Sénégal. Sénégambie et Casamance." In *Exposition universelle de 1900, Les Colonies françaises, Une mission au Sénégal, Ethnographie, botanique, zoologie, géologie par MM. Dr. Lasnet, Aug. Chevalier, A. Cligny, P. Rambaud*. Paris: Challamel, 1900, pp. 1-190.

Launay, R. *Traders without Trade*. Cambridge: Cambridge University Press, 1982.

Leach, Edmund Ronald. *Critique de l'anthropologie*. Paris: PUF, 1968 (trans. as *Rethinking Anthropology*. London: Athlone Press, 1961).

———. *Political Systems of Highland Burma*. London: The London School of Economics and Political Science, G. Bell and Sons, 1964.

Le Chatelier, A. *L'Islam dans l'Afrique occidentale*. Paris: Steinheil, 1899.

Leclerc, G. *L'Observation de l'homme*. Paris: Seuil, 1979.

Léger, F. "L'Idée de race chez Taine." In P. Guiral and E. Témime, eds., *L'Idée de race dans la pensée politique française*. Paris: CNRS, 1977.

Leibniz, G. W. *Principes de la nature et de la grâce fondés en raison, Principes de la philosophie ou monadologie.* Paris: PUF, 1986.

Lévi-Strauss, C. *Histoire de Lynx.* Paris: Plon, 1991. (Trans. as *The Story of Lynx* by Catherine Tihanyi. Chicago: University of Chicago Press, 1995.)

————. *La Pensée sauvage.* Paris: Plon, 1962.

————. *Les Structures élémentaires de la parenté.* Paris–The Hague: Mouton, 1967.

————. "Race et culture." In *Le Regard éloigné.* Paris: Plon, 1983, pp. 21-48.

————. *Race et histoire.* Paris: Denoël, 1984.

Lévi-Strauss, C., and D. Eribon. *De près et de loin.* Paris: O. Jacob, 1988.

Leynaud, E., and Y. Cissé. *Paysans malinke du Haut-Niger.* Bamako: EDIM, 1978.

Littré, Emile, on "*ethnique.*" *Dictionnaire de la langue française.* Paris: Hachette, 1863-72.

Lombard, J. *Autorités traditionnelles et pouvoirs européens en Afrique noire.* Paris: Armand Colin, 1967.

Lonsdale, J. L. "La pensée politique kikuyu et les idéologies du mouvement mau mau." *Cahiers d'études africaines* 27 (3-4), 1987: 329-57.

Lowie, R. H. *The Origin of the State.* New York: 1927.

Lugard, Lord. *The Dual Mandate in British Tropical Africa.* London: Frank Cass, 1965.

MacGaffey, W. *Religion and Society in Central Africa.* Chicago: University of Chicago Press, 1986.

Maliki, A.-B. *Introduction à l'histoire des Woodabe du Niger.* Rapport préliminaire no. 3, Projet gestion des pâturages et élevage. Niamy: Ministère du Développement rural, USAID Thesis from the Institut d'ethnologie, 9, 1982.

Marcus, G. E., and M. J. Fischer. *Anthropology as a Cultural Critique.* Chicago: University of Chicago Press, 1986.

Marks, S., and R. Rathbone. Introduction to "The History of the Family in Africa." *Journal of African History* 24 (2), 1983.

Marty, P. *La Politique indigène du Gouverneur général Ponty en Afrique occidentale française.* Memoriam, Collection de la Revue du Monde musulman. Paris: Ernest Leroux, 1915.

Maupoil, B. "L'étude des coutumes juridiques de l'Afrique occidentale (étude administrative)." In *Coutumiers juridiques de l'Afrique occidentale*, vol. 1. Senegal: Publications du CEH/AOF, series A, no. 8. Paris: Larose, 1939.

Mauss, Marcel. *Sociologie et Anthropologie.* Paris: PUF, 1960.

————. *Oeuvres. Cohésion sociale et divisions de la sociologie*, vol. 3. Paris: Minuit, 1969.

Meillassoux, C. *Anthropologie de l'esclavage*. Paris: PUF, 1986.

————. "Histoire et institutions du kafo de Bamako d'après la tradition des Niaré." *Cahiers d'études africaines* 4 (2), 14, 1963: 186–227.

Meniaud, J. *Les Pionniers du Soudan*. Paris: Société des publications modernes, 2 vols. Paris: 1931.

Merton, R. *Eléments de théorie et de méthode sociologique*. Paris: Plon, 1965.

Middleton, J., and D. Tait, eds. *Tribes Without Rulers*. London: Routledge and Kegan Paul, 1958.

Molin, P. M., Mgr. *Dictionnaire bambara-français et français-bambara*. Issy les Moulineaux: Les Presses missionaires, 1955.

Monteil, C. "Le coton chez les Noirs." *BCEHSAOF*, 1926: 585–684. The word that designates cotton (*kori*) in the Mande languages comes from the Arabic *qawr*.

————. *Les Bambara du Ségou et du Kaarta*. Paris: Maisonneuve et Larose, 1977.

————. *Les Khassonké*. Paris: E. Leroux, 1915.

————. "Réflexion sur le problème des Peuls." *Journal de la Société des africanistes* 20 (2), 1950: 153–92.

Morgan, L. H. *Ancient Society: Research in the Lines of Human Progress from Savagery through Barbarism to Civilization*. New York: Holt, 1877.

Moulin, A. M. *Le dernier langage de la médecine*. Paris: PUF, 1991.

Mubanza Mwa Bawele. "La dynamique sociale et l'épisode colonial: la formation de la société bangala dans l'entre Zaïre-Ubangui." Typescript.

Mudimbe, V. Y. *The Invention of Africa*. Bloomington: Indiana University Press, 1988.

Mukarovsky, H. "Contribution à l'histoire des langues peul, sérèr et wolof." In *Itinérances* 1, 1981: 123–49.

Nadel, S.-F. *Black Byzantium*. Paris: Maspero, 1971.

N'Diayé, B. *Groupes ethniques au Mali, Bamako*. Editions populaires, 1970.

Niane, D.-T. *Sounjata ou l'épopée mandingue*. Paris: Présence africaine, 1960.

Nicolas, G. "La Conversion ethnique des Peuls du Nigeria." In *Itinérances* 1, 1981: 195–217.

Nisbet, R.-A. *La Tradition sociologique*. Paris: PUF, 1984.

Olender, M. *Les Langues du Paradis*. Paris: Gallimard-Le Seuil, 1989.

Olivier de Sardan, J.-P. "Personnalité et structures sociales." In *La Notion de personne en Afrique noire*. Paris: Editions du CNRS, 1973, pp. 421-45.

Pâques, V. "Bouffons sacrés du cercle de Bougouni." *Journal de la Société des africainistes* 24 (fasc. 2), 1954: 63-110.

———. *L'Arbre cosmique dans la pensée populaire et dans la vie quotidienne du Nord-Ouest africain*. Paris: Institut d'ethnologie, Musée de l'Homme, 1964.

———. *Les Bambara*. Paris: PUF, 1954.

———. "Les Samaké." *Bulletin de l'IFAN, série B. Sciences Humaines* 18 (3-4), 1956: 369-90.

Park, M. *Voyage dans l'intérieur de l'Afrique*. Paris: FM/La Découverte, 1980.

Pellegrin, P., trans. Aristotle's *La Politique*. Livre I, traduction et commentaire de P. Pellegrin. Paris: Nathan, 1983.

Pereira, P. *Esmeraldo de Situ Orbis*. Bissau: 1956.

Péroz, E. *Au Soudan français, Souvenirs de guerre et de mission*. Paris: Calmann-Lévy, 1889.

———. *L'Empire de l'Almamy-Emir Samory ou empire du Ouassoulou*. Mémoires de la société d'émulation du Doubs, conference of December 15, 1887. Paris: Bibliothèque nationale, microfiche.

Person, Y. *Samori, une révolution dyula*, 3 vols. Dakar: IFAN, 1968, 1970, 1975.

———. "Nyani Mansa Mamadu et la fin de l'empire du Mali." In *Le Sol, la parole et l'écrit*. Mélanges en hommage à R. Mauny. Paris: L'Harmattan, 1981, vol. 2, pp. 613-53.

Polanyi, C. *Dahomey and the Slave Trade*. Seattle: University of Washington Press, 1966.

Poliakov, L. *Histoire de l'antisémitisme*. 2 vols. Paris: Calmann-Lévy, 1981.

Pouillon, F. "Du savoir malgré tout: la connaissance coloniale de l'extrême-sud tunisien." In *Connaissances du Maghreb*. Paris: CNRS, 1984: 79-83.

Pratt, M. L. "Fieldwork in Common Places." In Clifford and Marcus, eds., *Writing Culture*. Berkeley: University of California Press, 1986.

Quatremer, J. *Libération*, Jan. 25, 1988.

Radcliffe-Brown, A. R., and D. Forde, ed. *African Systems of Kinship and Marriage*. London: Oxford University Press, 1950.

Renan, E. "Qu'est-ce qu'une nation?" In *Oeuvres complètes*. Paris: Calmann-Lévy, 1947, vol. 1, pp. 887-906.

Richard, Molard. *Afrique occidentale française*. Paris: Berger Levrault, 1949.

Richter, D. "Further Considerations of Caste in West Africa: The Senufo." *Africa* 50 (1), 1980: 37-54.

Ricoeur, P. 1990. *Soi-même comme un autre*. Paris: Seuil (trans. as *Oneself as Another* by Kathleen Blamey (Chicago: The University of Chicago Press, 1992).

Roberts, R. *Warriors, Merchants and Slaves*. Stanford: Stanford University Press, 1987.

Robinson, D. *La Guerre sainte d'al-Hajj Umar*. Paris: Karthala, 1988.

———. "Un historien et anthropologue sénégalais: Shaikh Musa Kamara." *Cahiers d'études africaines* 109, 28 (1), 1988: 89-116.

Rodney, W. *A History of the Upper Guinea Coast from 1545 to 1800*. New York and London: Monthly Review Press, 1970.

Rondeau, C. *La Société senufo du sud Mali (1870–1950), de la tradition à la dépendance*. Thèse de doctorat du 3ème cycle, Université de Paris-VII, 1980.

Roussel, L. *Région de Korhogo, étude de développement socio-économique*. SEDES and Republic of Ivory Coast: 1965.

Sahlins, M. *Culture and Practical Reason*. Chicago: University of Chicago Press, 1976.

———. *Islands of History*. Chicago: University of Chicago Press, 1985.

———. *Stone Age Economics*. Paris: Gallimard, 1976.

Sala-Molins, L. *Le Code noir*. Paris: PUF, 1987.

Samaké, M. "Kafo et pouvoir lignager chez les Manmana, l'hégémonie gonkorobi dans le Cendugu." *Cahiers d'études africaines* 111-12, 1988: 331-54.

———. "La société d'initiation du kotè." In J. Kawada, ed., *Boucle du Niger, approches multidisciplinaires*, vol 1. Tokyo: Institut de recherches sur les langues et les cultures d'Asie et d'Afrique, 1988: 301-24.

———. *Pouvoir traditionnel et conscience politique paysanne: les kafo de la région de Bougouni*. Mali: Doctoral thesis, Paris, EHESS, 1984.

Sangaré, Y. *Samori et le Wassolon malien*. Thesis, Ecole normale supérieure, Bamako, 1987.

Sarrazin, H. *Races humaines du Soudan français*. Chambéry: Imprimerie générale de Savoie, 1902.

Schmitz, J. "L'Etat géomètre, les *leydi* des Peul eu Fuuta Tooro (Sénégal) et du Maasina (Mali)." *Cahiers d'études africaines* 103, 26 (3), 1986: 349-94.

Schultz, E.-A. "From Pagan to Pullo: Ethnic Identity Change in Northern Cameroon." *Africa* 54 (1), 1984: 46-64.

Senghor, Léopold. *Liberté I, Négritude et humanisme*. Paris: Seuil, 1964.

Shreyger, E. *L'Office du Niger au Mali*. Wiesbaden: Steiner, 1984.

Siéyès, E. *Qu'est-ce que le Tiers Etat?* Paris: PUF, 1982.

Singer, A., and E. Gellner, eds. *A History of Anthropological Thought by Evans-Pritchard*. London: Faber and Faber, 1982.

Siran, J.-L. "Emergence et dissolution des principautés guerrières vouté (Cameroun central)." *Journal des africanistes* 50 (1), 1980: 25-57.

Skalnik, P. "Union soviétique-Afrique du Sud: les 'théories' de l'ethnos." *Cahiers d'études africaines* 28 (2), 1988: 157-76.

Southall, Aidan. *Alur Society: A Study in Processes and Types of Domination*. Cambridge: Heffer, 1953.

———. "Nuer and Dinka Are People: Ecology, Ethnicity, and Logical Possibility." *Man* 2, 1976: 463-91.

Spencer, H. *Principes de sociologie*. Paris: Germer Baillière, 1878.

Stalin, J. *Le Marxisme et la question nationale et coloniale*. Paris: Editions sociales, 1913, rpt. 1950.

Stevenson, R. *Population and Political Systems in Tropical Africa*. New York: Columbia University Press, 1968.

Stocking, Jr., G. W., ed. *Observers Observed*. Madison: University of Wisconsin Press, 1983.

———. *Race, Culture and Evolution*. Chicago: University of Chicago Press, 1982.

Sy, A.-D. *Le Traditionalisme bambara: premier niveau d'analyse*. DEA thesis, Paris: EHESS, 1987.

Tapper and Tapper. "Thank God We're Secular: Aspects of Fundamentalism in a Turkish Town." In L. Caplan, ed., *Studies in Religious Fundamentalism*.

Tarikh El-Fettach. Paris: Maisonneuve, 1981.

Tarikh Es-Soudan. Paris: Maisonneuve, 1981.

Tauxier, L. *Histoire des Bambara*. Paris: Larose, 1942.

———. *Moeurs et histoire des Peuls*. Paris: Payot, 1937.

———. *La Religion bambara*. Paris: Paul Geuthner, 1927.

Tempels, P. *La philosophie bantoue*. Paris: Présence africaine, 1949.

Terray, E. "Afrique noire, organisations, règles et pouvoirs." In *Grand atlas des religions. Encyclopaedia Universalis*, 1988.

———. "Face au racisme." In *Magazine littéraire*. Numéro spécial sur Lévi-Strauss, 223, Oct. 1985: 54-55.

———. "Intervention à la séance 'Le politique.'" In *Problèmes et objets de la recherche en sciences sociales*. Paris: EHESS, s.d., multigr., pp. 206-12.

———. "Le débat politique dans les royaumes de l'Afrique de l'Ouest." *Revue française de science politique* 38 (5), Oct. 1988: 720-31.

———. "Sociétés segmentaires, chefferies, Etats acquis et problèmes." In B. Jewsiewicki and J. Letourneau, eds., *Mode of Production: The Challenge of Africa*. Ste Foy: Safi Press, 1985, pp. 106-15.

Texeira da Mota, A. "Un document nouveau pour l'histoire des Peuls au Sénégal pendant les XVe et XIIe siècle." *Boletim cultural da Guiné Portuguesa* 14 (96), 1969: 782-859.

Thierry, Auguste. *Histoire de la conquête de l'Angleterre par les Normands, de ses causes et de ses suites jusqu'à nos jours en Angleterre, en Ecosse, en Irlande et sur le continent*. Paris: Furne, 1851.

Thornton, R. "Culture: A Contemporary Definition." In E. Boonzaier and J. Sharp, eds., *South African Keywords*. Cape Town and Johannesburg: D. Philip, 1988.

Traoré, D. "Sur l'origine de la ville de Bamako." *Notes africaines* 35, 1947.

———. "Une seconde légende relative à l'origine de Bamako." *Notes africaines* 40, 1948.

Travélé, M. *Petit dictionnaire français-bambara et bambara-français*. Paris: Geuthner, 1913.

Udovitch, A.-L., and L. Valensi. *Juifs en terre d'islam, les communautés de Djerba*. Paris: Editions des Archives contemporaines, 1984.

Vacher de Lapouge. *Les Sélections sociales*. Paris: 1896.

Van Beek, W. "Dogon Restudied: A Field Evaluation of the Work of Marcel Griaule." *Current Anthropology* 31 (5), 1991: 139-67.

Van Velsen, J. *The Politics of Kinship*. Manchester: Manchester University Press, 1964.

Vuillet, J. "L'agriculture dans le pays de Segou et les régions voisines." *Renseignements coloniaux*, no. 11, Bulletin du Comité de l'Afrique française, 1930: 169-86.

Walckenaer, C.-A. *Collection des relations de voyages par mer et par terre en différentes parties de l'Afrique depuis 1400 jusqu'à nos jours*. 21 vols. Paris: 1842.

Weber, Max. *Economy and Society*. 2 vols. Berkeley: University of California Press, 1978.

Weil, E. *Philosophie politique*. Paris: Vrin, 1984.

Wilks, I. "The State of the Akan and the Akan States: A Discursion." *Cahiers d'études africaines* 87-88, 1982: 231-49.

———. "The Transmission of Islamic Learning in the Western Sudan." In J. Goody, ed., *Literacy in Traditional Societies*. Cambridge: Cambridge University Press, 1968, pp. 161-97.

Will, Edouard. *Doriens et Ioniens, Essai sur la valeur du critère ethnique appliqué à l'étude de l'histoire et de la civilisation grecques.* Paris: Les Belles Lettres, 1956.

Wilmsen, E. *Land Filled with Flies.* Chicago: University of Chicago Press, 1989.

Wilmsen, E., and J. Denbow. "Paradigmatic History of San-Speaking Peoples and Current Attempts at Revision." *Current Anthropology* 31 (5), 1990: 489–524.

Library of Congress Cataloging-in-Publication Data

Amselle, Jean-Loup.
    [Logiques métisses. English]
    Mestizo logics : anthropology of identity in Africa
and elsewhere / Jean-Loup Amselle : translated
by Claudia Royal.
        p.   cm. – (Mestizo spaces)
    Includes bibliographical references.
    ISBN 0-8047-2429-6 (cl : alk. paper).–
    ISBN 0-8047-2431-8 (pa : alk. paper)
    1. Ethnology–Mali.   2. Ethnology–Guinea.
    3. Ethnology–Philosophy.   4. Ethnicity–
    Philosophy   5. Mali–History.   6. Guinea–
    History.   I. Title.   II. Series.
    GN 652.M25A4713   1998
    305.8'001–dc21   97-26993
                                                                CIP

⊗ This book is printed on acid-free, recycled paper.

Original printing 1998
Last figure below indicates year of this printing:
07 06 05 04 03 02 01 00 99 98